PAUL AS INFANT AND NURSING MOTHER

Society of Biblical Literature

Early Christianity and Its Literature

Gail R. O'Day, Editor

Editorial Board:
Warren Carter
Beverly Roberts Gaventa
David Horrell
Judith M. Lieu
Margaret Y. MacDonald

Number 12

PAUL AS INFANT AND NURSING MOTHER

METAPHOR, RHETORIC, AND IDENTITY IN 1 THESSALONIANS 2:5-8

Jennifer Houston McNeel

SBL Press
Atlanta

Copyright © 2014 by SBL Press

All rights reserved. No part of this work may be reproduced or transmitted in any form or by any means, electronic or mechanical, including photocopying and recording, or by means of any information storage or retrieval system, except as may be expressly permitted by the 1976 Copyright Act or in writing from the publisher. Requests for permission should be addressed in writing to the Rights and Permissions Office, SBL Press, 825 Houston Mill Road, Atlanta, GA 30329 USA.

Library of Congress Cataloging-in-Publication Data

McNeel, Jennifer Houston, author.
 Paul as infant and nursing mother : metaphor, rhetoric, and identity in 1 Thessalonians 2:5-8 / by Jennifer Houston McNeel.
     p. cm. — (Early Christianity and its literature ; number 12)
 Includes bibliographical references and indexes.
 ISBN 978-1-58983-966-3 (paper binding : alk. paper) — ISBN 978-1-58983-967-0 (electronic format) — ISBN 978-1-58983-968-7 (hardcover binding : alk. paper)
  1. Bible. Thessalonians, 1st , II, 5–8—Criticism, interpretation, etc. 2. Paul, the Apostle, Saint. 3. Metaphor in the Bible. I. Title. II. Series: Early Christianity and its literature ; no. 12.
  BS2725.52.M36 2014
  227'.8106—dc23   2014008185

Printed on acid-free, recycled paper conforming to
ANSI/NISO Z39.48-1992 (R1997) and ISO 9706:1994
standards for paper permanence.

Contents

Acknowledgments vii
Abbreviations ix

1. Metaphor as Rhetorical Strategy 1
   1.1. Maternal Imagery in Paul's Letters   2
   1.2. Cognitive Metaphor Theory   8
   1.3. Metaphor and Rhetoric   21

2. Establishing the Text, Grammar, and Translation of
   1 Thessalonians 2 27
   2.1. Issues in 1 Thessalonians   27
   2.2. νήπιοι or ἤπιοι?   35
   2.3. Punctuating 1 Thessalonians 2:5–8   43
   2.4. Understanding and Translating 1 Thessalonians 2:5–8   47
   2.5. Summary   60

3. Historical and Social Backgrounds of the Infant and
   Nurse Metaphors 61
   3.1. Historical and Social Background of the Metaphor   62
   3.2. Historical and Social Background of the Thessalonian
        Community   80
   3.3. Conclusion   97

4. Literary Background of the Infant and Nurse Metaphors 99
   4.1. Infants and Innocence   99
   4.2. Nurses and Nursing Mothers   103
   4.3. The Leader as Nurse   108
   4.4. Conclusion   121

5. Paul as Infant and Nursing Mother among the Thessalonians 123
   5.1. Analysis of the Infant Metaphor   124

        5.2. Analysis of the Nurse Metaphor   132
        5.3. Conclusion   152

6. The Metaphors, the Letters, and Paul the Apostle 155
        6.1. The Metaphors, 1 Thessalonians, and Paul's letters   155
        6.2. Maternal Metaphors and Paul the Apostle   161
        6.3. Conclusion   172

Bibliography 175
Ancient Sources Index 191
Modern Authors Index 197
Subject Index 201

Acknowledgments

I would like to thank ECL General Editor Gail O'Day, the rest of the ECL editorial board, and everyone at SBL Press for making this book happen. In particular I would like to thank Leigh Andersen for shepherding this book—and me—through the process.

Since this book is a revision of my doctoral dissertation, thanks are also due to professors at Union Presbyterian Seminary and beyond who read and commented on my work. I am grateful for the invaluable insights, guidance, and encouragement of Frances Taylor Gench, John T. Carroll, A. Katherine Grieb, and Samuel Adams.

As always, I am grateful to my family, including my parents Dave and Judy Houston and my sister Patty Houston, for offering me love and support in all things. I would also like to express heartfelt love and appreciation to my husband Timothy McNeel, who contributed to this project by supporting our family, encouraging me, and being a proofreader and sounding board. Thank you, Tim.

Abbreviations

Primary Sources

1 Tars.	Dio Chrysostom, *First Tarsic Discourse*
Adul. amic.	Plutarch, *Quomodo adulator ab amico internoscatur (How to Tell a Flatterer from a Friend)*
Ag. Ap.	Josephus, *Against Apion*
Alleg. Interp.	Philo, *Allegorical Interpretation*
BGU	*Aegyptische Urkunden aus den Königlichen Staatlichen Museen zu Berlin, Griechische Urkunden*
Bib. hist.	Diodorus Siculus, *Bibliotheca historica*
CIL	*Corpus Inscriptionum Latinarum*
Cons. ux.	Plutarch, *Consolatio ad uxorem*
Dei cogn.	Dio Chrysostom, *Man's First Conception of God*
Dial.	Tacitus, *Dialogus de oratoribus*
Ep.	Seneca, *Epistulae morales*
Ep. Olymp.	John Chrysostom, *Epistulae ad Olympiadum*
Eth. nic.	Aristotle, *Nicomachean Ethics*
Flaccus	Philo, *Against Flaccus*
Frag.	Musonius Rufus, *Fragments*
Germ.	Tacitus, *Germania*
Inst.	Quintilian, *Institutio Oratoria*
Ira	Seneca, *De ira*
Leg.	Cicero, *De legibus*
LXX	Septuagint
Mor.	Plutarch, *Moralia*
Planting	Philo, *On Planting*
Prov.	Seneca, *De Providentia*
Regn.	Dio Chrysostom, *Kingship*
Sat.	Juvenal, *Satires*
Sobriety	Philo, *On Sobriety*

Spec. Laws	Philo, *On the Special Laws*
Virtues	Philo, *On the Virtues*
Worse	Philo, *That the Worse Attacks the Better*

Secondary Sources

AB	Anchor Bible
ANTC	Abingdon New Testament Commentaries
BDAG	Bauer, Walter, F. W. Danker, W. F. Arndt, and F. W. Gingrich. *A Greek-English Lexicon of the New Testament and Other Early Christian Literature*. 3d ed. Chicago: University of Chicago Press, 2000.
BDB	Brown, Francis, S. R. Driver, and Charles A. Briggs. *The Brown-Driver-Briggs Hebrew and English Lexicon*. Peabody, Mass.: Hendrickson, 1996.
BDF	Blass, Friedrich, Albert Debrunner, and Robert W. Funk. *A Greek Grammar of the New Testament and Other Early Christian Literature*. Chicago: University of Chicago Press, 1961.
BETL	Bibliotheca Ephemeridum Theologicarum Lovaniensium
Bib	*Biblica*
BJS	Brown Judaic Studies
BRLJ	Brill Reference Library of Judaism
BSac	*Bibliotheca Sacra*
BZNW	Beihefte zur Zeitschrift für die neutestamentliche Wissenschaft
CAM	*Civilization of the Ancient Mediterranean,* edited by Michael Grant and Rachel Kitzinger, 3 vols., New York: Scribner's, 1988
CBQ	*Catholic Biblical Quarterly*
ConBNT	Coniectanea biblica: New Testament Series
CTJ	*Calvin Theological Journal*
DJD	Discoveries in the Judean Desert
DSD	*Dead Sea Discoveries*
FF	Foundations and Facets
FN	*Filologia Neotestamentaria*
HNTC	Harper's New Testament Commentaries
HTR	*Harvard Theological Review*

IBC	Interpretation: A Bible Commentary for Teaching and Preaching
Int	*Interpretation*
JBL	*Journal of Biblical Literature*
JSNT	*Journal for the Study of the New Testament*
JSNTSup	Journal for the Study of the New Testament Supplement Series
JSOTSup	Journal for the Study of the Old Testament Supplement Series
LCBI	Literary Currents in Biblical Interpretation
LCL	Loeb Classical Library
LNTS	Library of New Testament Studies
LS	*Louvain Studies*
NCB	New Century Bible Commentary
NIB	*The New Interpreter's Bible*, edited by Leander E. Keck. 12 vols. Nashville: Abingdon, 1996–2004.
NICNT	New International Commentary on the New Testament
NICOT	New International Commentary on the Old Testament
NIGTC	New International Greek Testament Commentary
NIV	New International Version
NovT	*Novum Testamentum*
NRSV	New Revised Standard Version
NTL	New Testament Library
NTOA	Novum Testamentum et Orbis Antiquus
NTS	*New Testament Studies*
OTL	Old Testament Library
RevQ	*Revue de Qumran*
RSV	Revised Standard Version
SBLSP	Society of Biblical Literature Seminar Papers
SemeiaSt	Semeia Studies
SHBC	Smyth & Helwys Bible Commentary
SJC	Studies in Christianity and Judaism
SP	Sacra Pagina
STDJ	Studies on the Texts of the Desert of Judah
TynBul	*Tyndale Bulletin*
UBS	United Bible Societies
WBC	Word Biblical Commentary
WUNT	Wissenschaftliche Untersuchungen zum Neuen Testament

1
Metaphor as Rhetorical Strategy

At their core, Paul's letters are attempts to persuade. Each time he wrote, Paul hoped to convert his audience to his way of thinking regarding one or more topics. He had a variety of means by which to accomplish his purpose, such as emotional appeals, logic, and references to the Scriptures. In addition to these, Paul's use of metaphor also ought to be considered, for it is one of the most important literary tools that he used to persuade his audience to adopt his point of view. His metaphors do not simply decorate the text, but are designed to affect the reader at a cognitive or emotional level, and thus are an integral part of Paul's rhetorical strategy.

Paul employed a variety of metaphors, drawn from many different aspects of human life and experience, such as kinship, athletics, agriculture, nature, and the temple cult.[1] A number of the metaphors Paul employed fall into the category of maternal imagery. He used this imagery surprisingly often; metaphors of childbirth or breastfeeding appear in four out of the seven undisputed epistles.[2] Why did Paul employ such metaphors? What associations would they have evoked for Paul's audience? How did they function as means by which Paul achieved his rhetorical goals? Using the tools of cognitive metaphor theory and social identity analysis, this book will focus on the infant and nursing metaphors found in 1 Thess 2:5–8 and investigate their meaning and function as part of Paul's identity-shaping rhetorical strategy in 1 Thessalonians.

---

1. Analysis of the great variety of Paul's metaphors can be found in Raymond F. Collins, *The Power of Images in Paul* (Collegeville, Minn.: Liturgical Press, 2008).

2. Rom 8:22; 1 Cor 3:2; 15:8; Gal 4:19; and 1 Thess 2:7; 5:3. Except where otherwise noted, New Testament quotations in this book are my own translation, Old Testament quotations are from the NRSV, and Dead Sea Scrolls quotations are from Florentino García Martínez and Eibert J. C. Tigchelaar, *The Dead Sea Scrolls Study Edition* (Leiden: Brill, 1997).

1.1. Maternal Imagery in Paul's Letters

Feminist scholars have often criticized Paul for his androcentric perspective. Androcentrism can, indeed, be identified in many places in Paul's letters, yet the reader is periodically startled by his application of distinctly feminine images to himself and his coworkers. Contending for the church in Galatia, Paul likens his struggle to being in labor, trying to give birth to the community (Gal 4:19). In a decidedly different tone, Paul tells the Thessalonians that he and his partners in ministry have cared for them like a wet nurse tenderly caring for her own children (1 Thess 2:7). And in another allusion to breastfeeding, Paul admonishes the Corinthians, saying that he has had to feed them with milk because they are not yet ready for solid food (1 Cor 3:2). In an even more startling manner, in 1 Cor 15:8 Paul refers to himself as an ἔκτρωμα: a miscarriage, abortion, or premature birth. In addition to these self-references, Paul also uses birth metaphors in two other passages. Romans 8:22 employs the metaphor on a cosmic scale, where all creation is groaning in labor pains as it waits eagerly for the dawning of God's new age. The metaphor is employed in a more conventional sense in 1 Thess 5:3, where reference to the labor pains of a pregnant woman echoes several Old Testament passages.[3]

1.1.1. The Work of Previous Scholars

What is the significance of the appearance of such metaphors in the writings of a first century male missionary and theologian, and how do they function as part of Paul's rhetorical strategy? New Testament scholars have given surprisingly little attention to such questions. Major commentaries on Paul's letters generally comment only briefly on the unusual nature of the imagery, discussing the meaning of vocabulary words and sometimes identifying literary parallels, but they do not engage in significant analysis of the meaning, context, or potential impact of such metaphors on the audience.[4] While many books and articles have been written on women in

---

3. E.g., Isa 13:8 and Mic 4:9–10.
4. Such commentaries on 1 Thess 2:7 include Victor Paul Furnish, *1 Thessalonians, 2 Thessalonians* (ANTC; Nashville: Abingdon, 2007); Abraham J. Malherbe, *The Letters to the Thessalonians: A New Translation with Introduction and Commentary* (AB 32B; New York: Doubleday, 2000); Earl Richard, *First and Second Thessalonians* (SP 11; Collegeville, Minn.: Liturgical Press, 1995); F. F. Bruce, *1 and 2 Thessalonians*

Paul's time and what Paul says about women, very few have considered the significance of Paul's use of maternal metaphors.

In recent years, however, several scholars have begun to investigate these metaphors and their significance. The work of Beverly Roberts Gaventa is of primary importance. Gaventa has written a number of articles on Paul's use of maternal imagery over the course of the last twenty years,[5] which are now collected in the book *Our Mother Saint Paul*.[6] Other scholars have also begun to contribute insights. Sandra Hack Polaski, in *A Feminist Introduction to Paul*, comments on Paul's use of feminine imagery as part of her feminist analysis.[7] Susan Eastman has made a significant contribution to our understanding of how Gal 4:19 functions within Gal 4:12–5:1 and the letter as a whole.[8] Several other scholars have offered brief commentary on one or more of the images.[9] Several important insights

---

(WBC; Waco, Tex.: Word, 1982); Ben Witherington III, *1 and 2 Thessalonians: A Socio-rhetorical Commentary* (Grand Rapids: Eerdmans, 2006).

5. Beverly Roberts Gaventa, "Apostles as Babes and Nurses in 1 Thessalonians 2:7," in *Faith and History: Essays in Honor of Paul W. Meyer* (ed. John T. Carroll, Charles H. Cosgrove, and E. Elizabeth Johnson; Atlanta: Scholars Press, 1990), 193–207; Beverly Roberts Gaventa, "The Maternity of Paul: An Exegetical Study of Galatians 4:19," in *The Conversation Continues: Studies in Paul and John in Honor of J. Louis Martyn* (ed. Robert Tomson Fortna and Beverly Roberts Gaventa; Nashville: Abingdon, 1990), 189–201; Beverly Roberts Gaventa, "Mother's Milk and Ministry in 1 Corinthians 3," in *Theology and Ethics in Paul and His Interpreters: Essays in Honor of Victor Paul Furnish* (ed. Eugene H. Lovering Jr. and Jerry L. Sumney; Nashville: Abingdon, 1996), 101–13; Beverly Roberts Gaventa, "Our Mother St. Paul: Toward the Recovery of a Neglected Theme," in *A Feminist Companion to Paul* (ed. Amy-Jill Levine and Marianne Blickenstaff; London: T&T Clark, 2004), 85–97.

6. Beverly Roberts Gaventa, *Our Mother Saint Paul* (Louisville: Westminster John Knox, 2007).

7. Sandra Hack Polaski, *A Feminist Introduction to Paul* (St. Louis: Chalice, 2005).

8. Susan G. Eastman, *Recovering Paul's Mother Tongue: Language and Theology in Galatians* (Grand Rapids: Eerdmans, 2007).

9. These include J. Louis Martyn, *Galatians: A New Translation with Introduction and Commentary* (AB 33A; New York: Doubleday, 1997); Luzia Sutter Rehmann, "To Turn the Groaning into Labor: Romans 8:22–23," in *A Feminist Companion to Paul* (ed. Amy-Jill Levine and Marianne Blickenstaff; London: T&T Clark, 2004), 74–84; Calvin J. Roetzel, *Paul: A Jew on the Margins* (Louisville: Westminster John Knox, 2003); Margaret Aymer, "'Mother Knows Best': The Story of Mother Paul Revisited," in *Mother Goose, Mother Jones, Mommie Dearest: Biblical Mothers and Their Children* (ed. Cheryl A. Kirk-Duggan and Tina Pippin; SemeiaSt 61; Atlanta: Society of Biblical Literature, 2009), 187–98.

about Paul's use of maternal imagery have emerged from this collective work, three of which are particularly relevant for this project, and will be considered in turn: (1) the images are integral to Paul's proclamation of the gospel; (2) the images are connected to Paul's broader theology; and (3) the images are relevant for feminist interpretation of Paul's letters.

1.1.1.1. Maternal Metaphors and Paul's Proclamation

Several scholars have argued persuasively, some using cognitive metaphor theory, that Paul's use of maternal imagery is not mere ornamentation but rather an integral part of his proclamation of the gospel. Gaventa takes particular note of how these images are connected not to Paul's life in general but specifically to his vocation as an apostle. Indeed, they are "a vital part of communicating what the apostolic task involves."[10] Eastman argues in a similar vein, noting that, with Paul, "the medium and the message are inseparable."[11] The type of discourse (metaphor, allegory, emotional appeal, etc.) that Paul chooses to convey the gospel message is itself part of the gospel's expression. Themes of nurture, teaching, nourishment, and life-giving struggle are conveyed by Paul's nursing and birth metaphors in ways that simpler and more direct language could not express.

1.1.1.2. Maternal Metaphors and Paul's Theology

A second important insight that has emerged from recent scholarly discussion is the connection between Paul's maternal metaphors and his broader theology. In introducing her study of the metaphors, Gaventa rightly points out that we cannot confine an exploration of Paul's theology only to certain "discrete portions" of Paul's letters because "Paul's urgent need to announce and interpret what God has done in Jesus Christ pervades everything he writes."[12] Everything Paul writes is intended to communicate some aspect of the gospel to his audience. In particular, Gaventa seeks to tie Paul's maternal metaphors to the apocalyptic nature of his theology. This connection is easy to make for the birth/birth pangs metaphors in Rom 8:22 and Gal 4:19, since the images of birth and birth pangs were already associated with the tribulations and renewal of God's people in

---

10. Gaventa, *Our Mother Saint Paul*, 7.
11. Eastman, *Recovering Paul's Mother Tongue*, 6.
12. Gaventa, *Our Mother Saint Paul*, ix–x.

the Old Testament.¹³ Along the same lines, but with more specificity than Gaventa, J. Louis Martyn ties the metaphor of Gal 4:19 to Isa 45:7–11. Noting several similarities between the two passages, Martyn argues that Paul, either consciously or unconsciously, had the Isaiah passage in mind as he wrote Gal 4:19, thus tying the formation of Christ in the Galatian community to the creation of God's corporate people.¹⁴

Eastman also links Gal 4:19 to Paul's apocalyptic theology, arguing that the metaphor expresses Paul's sense that his gospel ministry represents his participation in God's apocalyptic labor, in terms of both God's anguish and God's creative power.¹⁵ Such an argument is strengthened by the use of birth pangs in Rom 8:22; Paul saw all creation groaning in labor, longing for the coming redemption of God. And all those who are in Christ participate in that painful longing for God's promised future (8:23). Thus it comes as no surprise that in his struggle to keep the Galatians on the right track in their collective life in Christ, Paul would turn to an image of childbirth, picturing his gospel ministry as part of the labor of all creation and, indeed, as part of God's labor to bring about a new age.

Paul's metaphors of nursing in 1 Cor 3:2 and 1 Thess 2:7 may be less apocalyptic in nature than his birthing metaphors, but nonetheless provide a theological understanding of Paul's ministry and God's work in the world. Focusing on 1 Thessalonians, Gaventa argues that, in this earliest of New Testament documents, Paul uses the metaphors of infant and nurse to explain the meaning of "apostle."¹⁶ Apostles of Christ do not seek their own glory or gain but are as innocent as infants and care as tenderly as a nurse for those to whom they preach. Such behavior distinguishes those preaching the true gospel of what God has done in Christ from those peddling poor substitutes. In addition, the kinship aspects of this language serve as a reminder and an exhortation to the Thessalonians to persist in family-like relationships with one another.¹⁷ This social function of the metaphors will be explored in detail in this study. Paul also uses the image of nursing (feeding with milk) in 1 Cor 3:2 to reflect on the nature of the apostolic task and to build community. Apostles are not only like farmers

---

13. See Isa 13:8; 26:17–19; 66:6–9; Hos 13:12–13; and Mic 4:9–10.
14. Martyn, *Galatians*, 427–30.
15. Eastman, *Recovering Paul's Mother Tongue*, 120–21.
16. Gaventa, *Our Mother Saint Paul*, 26.
17. Ibid., 27.

and builders (3:6–15) but are also like mothers giving milk to their children, then urging them on to solid food when the time is right.

1.1.1.3. Maternal Metaphors and Feminist Interpretation

A third important insight emerging from discussion of maternal imagery in Paul's letters is that these metaphors are relevant to feminist interpretation of Paul's writings. Feminist work on Paul has typically focused on passages such as Rom 16:1–16; 1 Cor 11:1–16; and Gal 3:28, where women and gender concerns are explicitly mentioned or discussed. Scholars have also analyzed broader theological themes in Paul's letters from a feminist perspective, some lauding them as compatible with feminism and others critiquing them as hierarchical and androcentric.[18] Few scholars, however, have applied feminist analysis to Paul's use of female images and metaphors. But surely the use of images of birthing and nursing by one often described as androcentric and even misogynistic needs to be considered. As Polaski puts it, a first century male "representing himself metaphorically 'in drag'" may not conform to his culture's standards of proper gender roles as closely as is often thought.[19]

Gaventa's observations on this topic are particularly helpful. In the introduction to part one of *Our Mother Saint Paul*, Gaventa argues that dividing Paul's letters into "hierarchical" and "egalitarian" sections that create a "bad" Paul and a "good" Paul is not helpful to the feminist task, nor does it provide an accurate picture of the man.[20] Moreover, even if one attempts such a distinction, Paul's maternal metaphors do not fit neatly into either category. They cannot be termed "egalitarian," because the mother has authority over her children and Paul uses them to enhance his apostolic authority in the communities. But neither can they be termed "hierarchical," because in employing them Paul takes on the "weaker" role of mother and nurse as compared to the more powerful image of the *pater familias* in Roman society. Moreover, according to Gaventa, Paul brings

---

18. An example of the former is Kathy Ehrensperger, *That We May Be Mutually Encouraged: Feminism and the New Perspective in Pauline Studies* (New York: T&T Clark, 2004). An example of the latter is Elizabeth A. Castelli, *Imitating Paul: A Discourse of Power* (LCBI; Louisville: Westminster John Knox, 1991).

19. Polaski, *A Feminist Introduction to Paul*, 24–25.

20. Gaventa, *Our Mother Saint Paul*, 13.

on himself the shame of presenting himself as a "female-identified male."[21] These metaphors, then, reveal the futility of attempting to categorize Paul's thinking as conventionally "egalitarian" or "hierarchical." Indeed, Paul confounds such categories by presenting himself as "the authority who does not conform to standard norms of authority."[22] Like everything else, Paul sees apostolic authority through the lens of the cross of Christ, which turns the wisdom of the world upside down. In expressing his experience of what it means to live a cruciform life as an apostle among the churches,[23] Paul turns repeatedly to language of birthing and nursing, a fact that should be of considerable interest to scholars with feminist commitments.

1.1.2. Unexplored Avenues

Though Paul's maternal metaphors have begun to receive attention in recent years, much work is left to do. Gaventa has provided a helpful foundation for study of these images, but because she has focused broadly on all the images she has not fully drawn out the implications of each one. More sustained attention to each individual image in its own context is needed. Gaventa persuasively argues that these images can be grouped together as a category due to their complexity, their distinct features in comparison to paternal imagery in the letters, their connection to Paul's vocation, and their connection to apocalyptic themes.[24] However, it is also important that each metaphor be studied independently, since Paul's goals and rhetorical strategies in employing them are different in each letter.

The birth metaphors in Rom 8:22 and Gal 4:19 have received a fair amount of attention in recent years, generating interest due to their connection to apocalyptic thought.[25] Paul's nursing metaphors, however, have been neglected. This study will focus on the infant and nurse metaphors in 1 Thess 2:7 and how each functions within Paul's rhetorical strategy in the letter as a whole. Cognitive metaphor theory and social identity analysis

---

21. Ibid., 14.
22. Ibid.
23. See Michael J. Gorman, *Cruciformity: Paul's Narrative Spirituality of the Cross* (Grand Rapids: Eerdmans, 2001).
24. Gaventa, *Our Mother Saint Paul*, 4–8.
25. Important works on these passages include Eastman, *Recovering Paul's Mother Tongue*, 89–126; Rehmann, "To Turn the Groaning into Labor: Romans 8:22–23," 74–84; Martyn, *Galatians*, 426–31.

will be the tools that uncover the way Paul[26] uses these metaphors in his attempt to strengthen and uplift a congregation struggling with theological questions and issues of social identity.

1.2. Cognitive Metaphor Theory

Cognitive linguistics is an umbrella term encompassing a variety of approaches to linguistics, all of which share the view that language is a means for understanding and processing information about the world around us. Language mediates our experience of the world, giving us "a structured collection of meaningful categories that help us deal with new experiences and store information about old ones."[27] Language does not merely reflect back what we see and experience in the world, but actually affects how we understand the world. It "imposes a structure on the world" and is "a way of organizing knowledge that reflects the needs, interests, and experiences of individuals and cultures."[28] Our knowledge of the world is mediated through language. Such an understanding attributes tremendous power to the words we use.

Within the field of cognitive linguistics researchers have studied metaphor and the ways it mediates our understanding of the world. For the purposes of this study, a metaphor is understood as a figure of speech in which a word or phrase that literally designates one thing is applied to something else, such as in the sentence "God is a rock." A metaphor has two main parts, a "target domain" and a "source domain." That which is

---

26. While the letter includes cosenders, evaluation of Paul's letters in general reveals little connection between the listing of cosenders and the intensely personal "I" perspective often found in the letters. Thus it is assumed in this book that Paul's singular voice is the driving rhetorical voice behind the letter. Where Paul employs "we" language, he may at times be referring to his coworkers, but this does not automatically imply that those coworkers were true coauthors of the letter. Additionally, Paul may at times be using the "authorial" or "epistolary" plural to refer only to himself (e.g., 3:1). For arguments related to sole authorship and the authorial plural, see Malherbe, *The Letters to the Thessalonians*, 86–89; Furnish, *1 Thessalonians, 2 Thessalonians*, 30–31; Charles A. Wanamaker, *The Epistles to the Thessalonians: A Commentary on the Greek Text* (NIGTC; Grand Rapids: Eerdmans, 1990), 126–27.

27. Dirk Geeraerts and Hubert Cuyckens, "Introducing Cognitive Linguistics," in *The Oxford Handbook of Cognitive Linguistics* (ed. Dirk Geeraerts and Hubert Cuyckens; Oxford: Oxford University Press, 2007), 5.

28. Ibid.

being described by the metaphor, such as "God" in the above example, is called the "target domain." The idea or object from which the metaphorical image is drawn ("rock") is called the "source domain."

1.2.1. Max Black

Though a philosopher rather than a cognitive linguist by profession, several of Max Black's observations in a 1954 essay on metaphor are relevant to this project.[29] Drawing in part on the earlier work of literary critic I. A. Richards, Black challenged traditional "substitution" and "comparison" understandings of metaphor. According to the substitution view, a metaphor is a figurative word or phrase used in place of a literal expression. In other words, a literal expression could easily be substituted for the metaphor without any loss in meaning.[30] For example, according to this view the sentence "Richard is a lion" has the same meaning as the sentence "Richard is brave."[31] The reader simply has to solve the puzzle by figuring out what literal expression is equivalent to the meaning intended by the author of the metaphor. In this case the metaphor does not communicate any particular meaning to the hearer, but is simply a way for an author to "decorate" a text in order to give pleasure to the reader.[32]

Another traditional view of metaphor discussed by Black is the "comparison" view. This view asserts that the creator of a metaphor is simply making a comparison between two similar things, or two things that have similar attributes. To continue the previous example, the comparison view of metaphor would suggest that the sentence "Richard is a lion" means the same thing as the sentence "Richard is *like* a lion (in being brave)."[33] In reality, the comparison view is a type of the substitution view, holding that a metaphorical word or phrase can be replaced by a statement of literal comparison without any loss in meaning.

While Black acknowledges that the substitution and comparison views of metaphor may be accurate for very simple metaphors, both understandings of metaphor are inadequate for more complex metaphors.

---

29. Reprinted as a chapter in Max Black, *Models and Metaphors: Studies in Language and Philosophy* (Ithaca, NY: Cornell University Press, 1962).
30. Ibid., 31–32.
31. Ibid., 33.
32. Ibid., 34.
33. Ibid., 36.

Black's main example for illustrating his own view is the metaphor "man[34] is a wolf." Can we substitute a simple literal comparison for this metaphor without any loss of meaning? For example, we could say "man harms others for his own benefit." Does such a sentence communicate the full meaning and impact of "man is a wolf"? Even if we extend the sentence and add more literal expressions denoting ways that men and wolves are similar, we would not be able to encompass the full meaning and impact of the metaphorical phrase. To try to translate a complex metaphor into literal language fails, not because the literal language is boring and prosaic, but because cognitive content is lost: "it fails to be a translation because it fails to give the insight that the metaphor did."[35]

A more helpful understanding of metaphor, according to Black, is what he calls the "interaction view." According to this understanding metaphors function by holding up two things or ideas that are "active together" and produce new meaning out of their interaction.[36] In the example "man is a wolf," the idea of "man" interacts with the idea of "wolf" in order to communicate new meaning about "man."[37] This occurs through the source domain's "system of associated commonplaces," which acts as a filter for the target domain. The "system of associated commonplaces" refers to those things that are commonly held to be true about the source domain, in this case about wolves. Such "commonplaces" will vary from culture to culture and may not even be true in a scientific sense, but need only be commonly held as true in a given culture in order for the metaphor to be effective in that culture.[38]

Black suggests the word "wolf" evokes the following commonplaces: wolves are fierce, hungry, carnivorous, and treacherous.[39] When we hear the phrase "man is a wolf," such commonplaces act as a filter on our view of man. Any attributes of man that can be seen as compatible with these commonplaces will be brought to the forefront, and any attributes of man that are inconsistent with these commonplaces will be temporarily filtered

---

34. For clarity I will maintain Black's use of masculine terminology for humankind in this section.
35. Black, *Models and Metaphors*, 46.
36. Ibid., 38.
37. It is also important to note that the idea of "wolf" will be altered in the interaction process as well because of its association with "man."
38. Black, *Models and Metaphors*, 40.
39. Ibid., 40–41.

out and pushed to the background. Through this system of emphasis and suppression, the metaphor "*organizes* our view of man. ... we can say that the principal subject is 'seen through' the metaphorical expression."[40]

One of the most important aspects of Black's work for this project is his assertion of a metaphor's power to cause shifts in attitude. Because a metaphor highlights some things about a subject and filters out others, it can change how we see the subject and our attitudes towards it. To use another of Black's examples, if we talk about war in terms of a chess game, certain aspects of war will be highlighted, such as strategy and movement, while other aspects, such as death and emotional trauma, will be filtered out.[41] Extensive use of metaphors like this can change social attitude toward a particular military action and even change the foreign policy of a nation.

1.2.2. Lakoff and Johnson

Within the field of cognitive linguistics, the most influential work on metaphor has been that of George Lakoff and Mark Johnson, particularly their 1980 book *Metaphors We Live By*.[42] Lakoff and Johnson define metaphor as "understanding and experiencing one kind of thing in terms of another."[43] According to Lakoff and Johnson, the conceptual structures that organize our understanding of the world are largely metaphorical. In particular, we often draw upon knowledge of objects and actions in the physical domain to think about other types of realities that involve emotions, relationships, and ideas.[44] This type of metaphorical thought is pervasive in the conceptual system of all human beings, making metaphor central to how we understand the world.

1.2.2.1. The Pervasiveness of Metaphorical Thought

Conventional metaphors are those that are "automatic, effortless, and generally established as a mode of thought among members of a linguistic

---

40. Ibid., 41 (emphasis original).
41. Ibid., 41–42.
42. This work was reprinted in 2003 with a new afterword: George Lakoff and Mark Johnson, *Metaphors We Live By* (2nd ed.; Chicago: University of Chicago Press, 2003).
43. Ibid., 5.
44. Ibid., 244.

community."[45] Examples illustrate the central role that metaphors of this kind play in the daily thought processes of human beings. Lakoff and Johnson begin by exploring how we conceive of arguments in terms of war. We devise strategies, attack and defend positions, demolish an opponent, and win the argument. Lakoff and Johnson point out that this is not just a fancy way of *talking* about arguments, but it is actually how we *conceive* of arguments, and therefore this metaphor influences not only our words, but also our behavior, our actions, and our emotions in an argument. If we had a different metaphor for argument, such as "argument is a dance," then our actions and attitudes would be dramatically different.[46] But such a change in metaphor would seem extremely strange, because we do not only talk about arguments in terms of war, but we actually conceive of them that way and act accordingly.[47]

Several more examples will illustrate how pervasive metaphor is in human thought processes. Lakoff and Johnson speak of metaphorical concepts that govern our thinking, which can then be expressed in a variety of ways in particular instances of speech or writing. The following are examples of metaphorical concepts along with a few of their common particular expressions:

Time is money.[48]
You are *wasting* my time.
How do you *spend* your time?
Invest your time in something *worthwhile*.
I am *running out of* time.

Theories are buildings.[49]
What is this theory's *foundation*?
Support your arguments with *solid* facts.
The theory will *stand* or *fall* on the *strength* of that argument.

---

45. George Lakoff and Mark Turner, *More Than Cool Reason: A Field Guide to Poetic Metaphor* (Chicago: University of Chicago Press, 1989), 55.
46. Lakoff and Johnson, *Metaphors We Live By*, 4–5.
47. Ibid., 5.
48. Ibid., 7–8.
49. Ibid., 46.

Understanding is seeing.[50]
I *see* what you mean.
Look at it from my *point of view*.
He *pointed out* to me that ...

Good/status/power is up.[51]
He is at the *height* of his power.
He is *under* my control.
She'll *rise* to the *top*.
We are at an all-time *low*.

Using such metaphors feels second nature to us because these metaphorical concepts have become engrained in the conceptual structures of our minds.[52] The above expressions are not flowery or fanciful language but rather conventional ways of speaking about money, theories, understanding, and goodness. The metaphors guide how we think about those realities. In fact, it is difficult to reflect on these concepts without thinking metaphorically, though in the normal course of the day we are not conscious of the fact that we are thinking metaphorically.

1.2.2.2. Highlighting, Hiding, and Entailments

Max Black wrote of metaphors as filters that emphasize and suppress various aspects of the target domain. In a similar fashion, Lakoff and Johnson argue that metaphors work by means of highlighting and hiding; that is, metaphors highlight certain aspects of the target domain and hide others. For example, to understand argument as war highlights certain aspects, such as being in opposition to another person and trying to "win," and hides others, such as the cooperative nature of interacting with another person who gives of his or her time to achieve greater mutual understanding.[53] The aspects of the source domain that are applied to the target domain, and therefore highlighted, are called entailments. For example, the entailments of the "time is money" metaphor include that time is a limited resource, has value, can be given to someone else, and should be

---

50. Ibid., 48.
51. Ibid., 15–16.
52. For a discussion of metaphor as a "neural phenomenon" in our brains, see Lakoff and Johnson, *Metaphors We Live By*, 254–59.
53. Ibid., 10.

budgeted carefully. Lakoff and Johnson's "entailments" are very similar to Black's idea of the "system of associated commonplaces."

1.2.2.3. Metaphor and the Construction of Reality

By arguing that metaphors are central to the conceptual system, to the way our brains work and understand the world, Lakoff and Johnson maintain that metaphor is a central part of the way that human beings construct reality. According to Lakoff and Johnson, the traditional view that metaphor is merely ornamental description implies that reality external to human beings can be observed objectively. But this understanding "leaves out human aspects of reality, in particular the real perceptions, conceptualizations, motivations, and actions that constitute most of what we experience."[54] The way we see and understand the world—what is "real" for us—is always filtered through the conceptual system that our brains use to process information, and this conceptual system is grounded in metaphor.

While Lakoff and Johnson claim that metaphor is central to the construction of all types of reality, this is especially true of the construction of social reality. Cultures define for their members a social reality in which members can function and make sense of the world. An individual's interaction with his or her physical environment is defined by the social reality of culture, a social reality shaped by metaphorical concepts.[55] In this way metaphorical concepts shape our understanding of both human society and the physical world that societies inhabit. Metaphors, in part, determine what is real in a given culture.

1.2.2.4. Metaphor and Behavior

Metaphors define what is real for people, and people act according to their understanding of reality. Therefore, like Black, Lakoff and Johnson argue that metaphors have the power to shape attitudes and affect behavior. In considering whether or not a metaphor is "true," Lakoff and Johnson suggest that often the more appropriate question addresses perceptions and

---

54. Ibid., 146.
55. Ibid.

perspectives that derive from it and, by extension, the actions that are "sanctioned" by it:

> In all aspects of life, not just in politics or in love, we define reality in terms of metaphors and then proceed to act on the basis of the metaphors. We draw inferences, set goals, make commitments, and execute plans, all on the basis of how we in part structure our experience, consciously and unconsciously, by means of metaphor.[56]

Consider the prominence of the "time is money" metaphor in American culture. We not only talk about time as if it is a monetary resource, but we conceive of it that way and therefore act as if it is. For example, compensation for most work in our culture is paid per hour. Interest paid on loans is based on time. We make decisions about courses of action based on how we think our time should be *spent* or *invested*. We do specific things in order to *save* time. We urge people to do certain things so that they will not be *wasting* or *squandering* their time. Lakoff and Johnson suggest that such actions derive from the conceptual metaphor "time is money" shared by those in American and some other cultures. However, this is not the only way to conceive of time, and not all cultures use this metaphor. Members of cultures who conceive of time differently would not have the same set of behaviors in relation to time.[57]

Metaphors for love can also influence an individual's behavior. How a person understands love will affect not only how he or she views a relationship, but also how he or she behaves in the relationship. English-speaking culture has several conceptual metaphors for love:

Love is a journey.
We are at a *crossroads*.
This relationship is not *going anywhere*.
Look *how far we've come*.
Our marriage is *on the rocks*.

Love is a physical force.
There were *sparks* between us.
I was *drawn/attracted* to her.

---

56. Ibid., 158.
57. Ibid., 8–9.

They *gravitated* to each other.
His whole life *revolves* around her.

Love is a medical patient.
They have a *healthy* marriage.
Can their relationship be *revived*?
Our marriage is *on the mend*.
Their relationship is *in really good shape*.

Love is madness.
I'm *crazy* about her.
He constantly *raves* about her.
I'm *mad* about you.
She's *wild* about him.

Love is magic.
She *cast a spell* over him.
The *magic* is gone.
He was *spellbound/entranced/charmed*.
She is *bewitching*.

Love is war.
His *advances* eventually *overpowered* her.
He is known for his many *conquests*.
She *pursued* him and *fought* for him.
He is slowing *gaining ground* with her.[58]

While all of these metaphors are active in American culture because they all highlight different aspects of a complex concept, an individual may give more weight to one or more of the metaphors, thus allowing those particular metaphors to shape his or her conception of love. And a person's conception of love will shape his or her behavior within a relationship. For example, what is the appropriate action to take when a romantic relationship is troubled? For the person who understands love as a journey it may be time for a heart-to-heart talk with the beloved about how they can work together to get the relationship back on the right track. For the person who understands love as a patient perhaps a gift of flowers and some quiet time together to seek healing will be required. For people who view love as

---

58. Ibid., 44–45, 49.

magic a trip to a romantic place from their past may be called for in order to try to recapture the feeling of enchantment once shared. For the person who views love as a physical force, it might be time to let the relationship go and find someone else who exerts greater attraction. Of course, most of us operate with more than one love metaphor at a time for any given relationship, but these examples reveal how a particular conceptual metaphor can affect behavior by providing a particular perspective on reality.

1.2.2.5. The Experiential Basis of Metaphor

An important caveat to keep in mind is that, while conceptual metaphors affect a person's understanding of reality, external reality also affects the creation of conceptual metaphors. Particularly in the 2003 afterword to their book, Lakoff and Johnson stress that primary conceptual metaphors are grounded in the experience of reality, which means some conceptual metaphors are found in almost all cultures, because they are grounded in physical reality and the way human beings' brains process and experience physical reality. For example, in many cultures affection or friendliness is metaphorically understood as warmth, such as when those in English-speaking cultures say "he is finally warming up to her" or "she is cold as ice." Lakoff and Johnson suggest that this metaphor is built on the primary human experience of infants and small children being held close to their parents' bodies.[59] From the beginning of our lives affection is connected in our brains to physical warmth.

Basic metaphors such as "affection is warmth" are seen across cultures. More complex metaphors are often built on basic metaphors, extending them in various ways using more complex ideas from more "grown-up" experiences. Because such complex metaphors make use of cultural information, they can be radically different across cultures, even if they are built on common primary metaphors derived from basic human experience.[60] For example, in the 2003 afterword, Lakoff and Johnson suggest that their example "argument is war" is built on the more basic metaphor "argument is struggle." This metaphor is grounded in the childhood experience of struggling against the physical "manipulations" of parents. Through this experience the child's brain links angry words with physical struggle. Later

---

59. Ibid., 255–57.
60. Ibid.

the metaphor is elaborated as the child learns about war and begins internalizing his culture's understanding of war.[61]

1.2.2.6. The Creation and Effect of New Metaphors

While much of Lakoff and Johnson's work is focused on conventional conceptual metaphors of everyday language that have long been part of the conceptual system of a given culture or even across cultures, they also discuss what they call new metaphors. These are creative or poetic metaphors that differ from conventional metaphors. They may be brand-new metaphors created by an author or speaker, or they may be creative extensions of existing conceptual metaphors. Either way, Lakoff and Johnson argue that new metaphors work in the same way that conventional metaphors do. They highlight and hide, giving structure to a new perspective on the target domain.[62] And if they are effective, they can become part of the conceptual system of an individual, community, or culture, and thus have the power to change the way that individual or group understands the world and to affect behavior. In this way, "new metaphors have the power to create new reality."[63]

As noted above, English-speaking cultures have numerous conceptual metaphors for love, such as "love is a journey" and "love is madness." Lakoff and Johnson discuss what would happen if a member of such a culture were to encounter a new metaphor for love, such as "love is a collaborative work of art." This metaphor has various possible entailments, such as "love is work," "love requires cooperation and compromise," "love requires patience," "love regularly brings frustration," "love is unique in each instance," and "love involves creativity."[64] These are some of the aspects of love that are highlighted by this metaphor. Other aspects of love are downplayed or hidden by the metaphor, such as those highlighted by the "love is a physical force" and the "love is war" metaphors.[65]

If the person encountering the metaphor "love is a collaborative work of art" agrees that the entailments implied by the metaphor are important aspects of love, then the metaphor can "acquire the status of a truth" for

---

61. Ibid., 265.
62. Ibid., 139.
63. Ibid., 145.
64. Ibid., 140.
65. Ibid., 149.

that person.[66] Once this happens, the metaphor begins to guide the person's thinking, causing his focus to shift to those aspects of love entailed by the metaphor and affecting future behavior in love relationships. Lakoff and Johnson call this a "feedback effect."[67] On the other hand, if the person encountering this metaphor has a very different idea of love than what is implied by the metaphor's entailments, the metaphor will not make sense to her and she may reject the metaphor out of hand.[68] New meaning and new reality are created only when the hearers of a metaphor accept it as true based on their personal and cultural experiences. But once a metaphor does achieve truth status it can have a powerful effect on behavior. Someone who operates with the understanding that love is madness does not expend much effort to maintain his love relationship because he believes love is irrational and does not come about as a result of his own initiative, but even against his will. However, if this person comes to accept that love is a collaborative work of art, his attitudes and behaviors will change because he now believes that love requires a special kind of effort and is an ongoing process.

1.2.3. Lakoff and Turner

Lakoff and Johnson's *Metaphors We Live By* focused largely on conventional use of cognitive metaphors in everyday language. Nearly a decade later, Lakoff, along with cognitive linguist Mark Turner, published a book on the poetic use of metaphor.[69] While the book focuses largely on interpreting metaphors in poetry, much of their work is also applicable to the type of creative prose that Paul employs in 1 Thess 2. While this work is not as foundational to my argument as Lakoff and Johnson's earlier work, several of their observations are pertinent.

One of the central observations of the book is that the metaphors of poets (and other creative authors) are often grounded in the basic conceptual metaphors already shared by a culture, rather than being wholly new. Poets, however, use these conventional metaphors in creative and, in the case of good poetry, skillful ways. Lakoff and Turner identify three ways in which poets work with conventional metaphors: (1) they can simply

---

66. Ibid., 142.
67. Ibid.
68. Ibid., 143.
69. Lakoff and Turner, *More Than Cool Reason*.

"versify" them without adding anything new, which results in "lame, feeble, and trite verse"; (2) they can skillfully employ them by combining, extending, or using them to create vivid imagery; or (3) they can step outside of them and employ them in unusual ways to "destabilize" the picture of reality provided.[70] The second way Lakoff and Turner observe authors working with conventional metaphors is particularly relevant for a study of Paul's use of metaphor in 1 Thess 2:7, and thus requires some elaboration here.

Creative authors often extend or elaborate on conventional metaphors. For example, sleep is a common metaphor for death, but Shakespeare creatively takes this a step further when he writes, "To sleep? Perchance to dream! Ay, there's the rub; / For in that sleep of death what dreams may come?" Dreams, though associated with sleep, are not usually a part of our "death is sleep" metaphor, and thus this verse is a creative extension of an already existing metaphor.[71] Authors may also combine conventional metaphors in creative ways. Shakespeare writes of life and death in sonnet 73, "black night doth take away [the twilight]." Lakoff and Turner identify several metaphors at work here, including "light is a substance" that can be taken away, "a lifetime is a day," "life is light," and "life is a precious possession" that we do not want taken away.[72] This phrase and the passage in which it is found combine numerous conceptual metaphors to speak creatively about life and death, thereby providing new ways to think about these subjects.

1.2.4. Summary

The following aspects of cognitive metaphor theory are the most pertinent for interpretation of Paul's metaphors in 1 Thess 2:7:

(1) Metaphors are not simply decorative but carry cognitive content.
(2) Metaphors are conceptual in nature. That is, they are part of the way we think and are central to the ways in which we process information about the world.

---

70. Ibid., 51.
71. Ibid., 67.
72. Ibid., 70–71.

(3) Due to their conceptual nature, metaphors play an important role in the construction of individual and social reality.
(4) Metaphors give structure to our understanding of the target domain because the entailments of the source domain highlight certain aspects of the target domain and hide others.
(5) Primary metaphors are grounded in human experience of the world, and therefore are often shared across cultures. More complex metaphors are often grounded in primary metaphors, but also make use of cultural information and therefore will differ across cultures.
(6) Because metaphors give structure to our understanding of the target domain, they have the power to influence attitudes toward the target domain and behaviors in relation to the target domain.
(7) When a "new" metaphor is accepted as true, it is accepted at the conceptual level, and thus begins to influence thinking and behavior.
(8) New metaphors often extend or combine conventional metaphors in creative ways, giving them the power to provide a new understanding of the target domain.

1.3. Metaphor and Rhetoric

In biblical studies today "rhetorical criticism" has come to mean many different things, such as identifying the patterns of formal ancient rhetoric within New Testament texts, analyzing the composition and literary artistry of texts, and exploring the use of texts by those with power as means of social persuasion and control over those with less power.[73] While my approach may overlap with a variety of rhetorical approaches, for the purposes of this project a simpler definition of "rhetoric" is the most helpful. In differentiating the term "rhetoric" as used in biblical studies from its more negative connotation in popular discourse, C. Clifton Black provides a definition of rhetoric that is both straightforward and consistent with how the term will be applied in this book:

---

73. See summaries of these and other rhetorical approaches in C. Clifton Black, "Rhetorical Criticism," in *Hearing the New Testament: Strategies for Interpretation* (ed. Joel B. Green; Grand Rapids: Eerdmans, 1995), 256–77.

> For wherever someone attempts, in speech or in writing, to persuade others—whether from the pulpit or the Op-Ed page, in a term paper or around the kitchen table—there you will find rhetoric employed. As we will be using the term here, therefore, rhetoric generally bears on those distinctive properties of human discourse, especially its artistry and argument, by which the authors of biblical literature have endeavored to convince others of the truth of their beliefs.[74]

Paul used many tools and strategies in his letters to attempt to persuade his hearers of the truth of his message. This book focuses on metaphor as one of the key "properties of human discourse" by which Paul sought to convince his hearers to change their understanding of the world.

1.3.1. The Persuasive Power of Metaphor

Metaphors have the power to persuade. Lakoff and Turner discuss the persuasive power of conventional metaphors. Conventional metaphors have become a part of the way we think. They have power over us precisely because we are usually unaware of them.[75] Because we have already accepted their validity and engage them as part of the way we think, when someone else makes use of a conventional metaphor in speech or writing we are "predisposed to accept its validity."[76] For example, the "ideas are fashions" conventional metaphor predisposes one to view newer ideas as better than older ones. Therefore, if a speaker labels an idea as "old-fashioned," the hearer is likely to view the idea negatively even before knowing much about it. On the other hand, the label "up-to-date" will predispose the hearer to view the idea positively.

Along with predisposing us to accept or reject certain ideas, metaphors also have a tremendous power over the way we reason and evaluate situations. For example, conventional metaphors can trap us in conventional ways of thinking, causing us to miss opportunities for insight, growth, and creativity. As an example, imagine someone being told that she has come to a dead end in life. Because the "life is a journey" metaphor has been conventionalized in our culture, she will likely be predisposed to accept this metaphor's point of view. Thus she may see her life as "going

---

74. Ibid., 256.
75. Lakoff and Turner, *More Than Cool Reason*, 63.
76. Ibid.

nowhere." This is a negative evaluation, because if she accepts that life is a journey, she thinks that life ought to be "going somewhere." Thus lack of progress is a problem. Thinking in terms of this metaphor may prove helpful if it provides motivation in life, but it could also result in a missed opportunity to see her life in different terms; for example, to view life "in terms of the security and stability that could result from stasis."[77]

But the persuasive power of metaphor is not only negative. Metaphors also have the power to give us flashes of new insight, enabling us to see the world in a new way. When we encounter a new metaphor, for example, we encounter an opportunity to expand our thinking. By highlighting and hiding certain aspects of the target domain, the new metaphor gives us an opportunity to see the target domain in a new light. New perspective can lead to new insight, and new insight to new behavior. The new metaphor, "love is a collaborative work of art," discussed in the previous section, is an example. An author or speaker who wishes to change an audience's perspective on love might employ such a new metaphor as part of a rhetorical strategy in presenting his or her point of view on love.

These examples are not meant to suggest that conventional metaphors are bad and new metaphors are good. Conventional metaphors are crucial to our daily functioning in the world, giving us tools that help us evaluate situations, communicate with others, and decide on courses of action. Additionally, new metaphors can be used not only to provide new insight and wisdom, but also to obscure and control. By simultaneously highlighting and hiding, metaphors draw attention only to certain aspects of the target domain—namely, those that the author or speaker wants to highlight—while suppressing others. Thus metaphors can be instruments of power over others. Politicians, for example, wield metaphors not only as a means of uniting and inspiring people, but also as a means of promoting agendas and justifying controversial courses of action. An effective metaphor will draw attention to precisely the aspects of the subject that the speaker wants to highlight and obscure those upon which the speaker does not want the audience to focus. The more powerful the speaker, the more potentially dangerous his or her metaphors.[78]

The task before us, then, is not to determine which categories of metaphors are "good" and "bad" but rather to analyze and evaluate individual

---

77. Ibid., 65.
78. Lakoff and Johnson, *Metaphors We Live By*, 157.

metaphors as we encounter them. In this process we become conscious of the metaphors that we use so that we can explore how they work and what our response to them ought to be. What is the metaphor highlighting? What is it hiding? Are the entailments of the metaphor consistent with our broader understanding of truth? What behaviors or courses of action does the metaphor imply if we accept it as "true"? Questions such as these are crucial in helping readers and hearers uncover and evaluate the rhetorical impact of a particular metaphor.

1.3.2. Metaphor, Rhetoric, and Identity

Thus far we have seen that metaphors are part of the way human beings think; metaphors shared within a culture are central in the construction of social reality, and metaphors have the power to persuade us to adopt certain points-of-view—both when we are aware of their persuasive power and even when we are not. It follows from this that metaphor also plays an important role in the construction of social identity. If metaphors are part of how human beings think and understand reality, then they are part of how human beings understand themselves and who they are in relation to others. When a person or group is the target domain of a metaphor, the metaphor, whether conventional or new, exerts influence on self-understanding.

A common example of such a metaphor in the Bible is the presentation of the people of God as sheep. The source domain "sheep" provides many entailments that illumine the identity of the people of God and inspire certain kinds of behavior. Often, the metaphor conveys a need for leadership, as when the people are described as "sheep without a shepherd" (1 Kgs 22:17; Mark 6:34; Matt 9:36). If people understand themselves as sheep they will try to think as a flock, which involves sticking together and looking to the leadership of the shepherd. Sheep that go astray from the fold are in danger of getting lost and in danger from predators. This theme is used in numerous ways: "sheep" confess their wandering (Ps 119:176; Isa 53:6); bad "shepherds" who have not done their job to protect the people are reprimanded (Jer 23:1–4; Ezek 34:1–31); and a hopeful longing that God will gather the lost sheep from all the places to which they have been scattered is expressed (Isa 40:11; Jer 50:6, 17). The metaphor of people as sheep is often used to inspire people to look to their leaders for guidance and protection, whether the shepherd is a human leader (Ps 78:71), God (Pss 95:7; 100:3) or Jesus (John 10:1–18; Heb 13:20; 1 Pet 2:25). The sheep metaphor shapes the identity, attitudes, and behaviors of the people of God.

In recent years, biblical scholars,[79] as well as social scientists,[80] have increasingly given attention to the topic of identity formation. Of particular interest for Pauline scholars has been the question of whether Christian identity in Pauline communities obliterated previous ethnic and cultural identity in favor of new identity in Christ, or whether difference and diversity continued to be recognized and upheld by those "in Christ."[81] Much of this debate centers on Jew/Gentile identity, an issue that is not central to this project. However, the larger issue of the construction of early Christian identity and Paul's role in shaping it are relevant to a study of his use of infant and nursing metaphors. For this project "identity" concerns the way in which people, both individually and as members of groups, understand themselves in relation to one another, to the society in which they live, and to those perceived as outsiders.[82]

In my analysis of Paul's metaphors, group identity will be of particular interest because Paul sought to shape the social identities not only of individuals, but also of entire Christian communities.[83] Metaphors shared

---

79. For explorations of identity formation in the New Testament and early Christian communities, see William S. Campbell, *Paul and the Creation of Christian Identity* (LNTS 322; London: T&T Clark, 2006); Philip Francis Esler, "'Keeping It in the Family': Culture, Kinship and Identity in 1 Thessalonians and Galatians," in *Families and Family Relations as Represented in Early Judaisms and Early Christianities: Texts and Fictions; papers read at a NOSTER Colloqium in Amsterdam, June 9-11, 1998* (ed. Jan Willem van Henten and Athalya Brenner; Leiden: Deo, 2000), 145–84; Philip Francis Esler, *Conflict and Identity in Romans: The Social Setting of Paul's Letter* (Minneapolis: Fortress, 2003); Bengt Holmberg, ed., *Exploring Early Christian Identity* (WUNT 1/226; Tübingen: Mohr Siebeck, 2008); Bengt Holmberg and Mikael Winninge, eds., *Identity Formation in the New Testament* (WUNT 1/227; Tübingen: Mohr Siebeck, 2008); V. Henry T. Nguyen, *Christian Identity in Corinth: A Comparative Study of 2 Corinthians, Epictetus and Valerius Maximus* (WUNT 2/243; Tübingen: Mohr Siebeck, 2008).

80. For more on the work of social scientists, see Richard Jenkins, *Social Identity* (3rd ed.; London: Routledge, 2008); W. Peter Robinson, ed., *Social Groups and Identities: Developing the Legacy of Henri Tajfel* (Oxford: Butterworth-Heinemann, 1996); Henri Tajfel, *Differentiation Between Social Groups: Studies in the Social Psychology of Intergroup Relations* (European Monographs in Social Psychology 14; London: Academic Press, 1978); Henri Tajfel, *Human Groups and Social Categories: Studies in Social Psychology* (Cambridge: Cambridge University Press, 1981).

81. Campbell, *Paul and the Creation of Christian Identity*, 1–2.

82. See the discussion of "social identity" in Nguyen, *Christian Identity in Corinth*, 1–9.

83. Aspects of group identity in ancient Mediterranean cultures will be explored further in §3.2, below.

within a culture or subculture are crucial for strengthening the ways in which people understand themselves as part of a group and behave in relationship to insiders and outsiders. In 1 Thess 2, metaphor, rhetoric, and social identity intersect. Paul uses *metaphor* to *persuade* the Thessalonians to view *their relationships* with each other, with him, and with society in accordance with their relationship with Christ. Through metaphor Paul presents a particular view of reality and invites the Thessalonians to share that view. We cannot determine whether or not they accepted his view, but analysis of his invitation to them will enable us to observe the potential power of language to wield influence, create community, and inspire change in attitude and behavior.

2
Establishing the Text, Grammar, and Translation of 1 Thessalonians 2

The second chapter of 1 Thessalonians contains several thorny textual and grammatical issues. Before proceeding to an evaluation of the infant and nurse metaphors found in 2:7 it is necessary to establish the text and context of this verse. Of central concern is the text critical matter of whether Paul described himself and his coworkers as νήπιοι ("infants") or ἤπιοι ("gentle") in 2:7. Clearly, an analysis of Paul's presentation of himself as an infant will depend greatly on the conviction that this should be considered the original reading of the text, as will be demonstrated. Interpretation of the nurse metaphor also depends on this text critical matter, because it must be determined whether or not Paul is using the adjective "gentle" to describe the way in which he is like a nurse. Several other textual and grammatical issues are also important for this work, such as the proper punctuation of the passage and the meaning of key words. Consideration of several introductory matters related to 1 Thessalonians will set the stage for these analyses.

2.1. Issues in 1 Thessalonians

Individual words, phrases, and verses in Paul's letters must always be interpreted in context, and a study that is rhetorical in nature must consider Paul's goals and strategies in the surrounding verses, chapters, and in the letter as a whole. Thus, consideration of the purpose of 1 Thessalonians and the function of 2:1–12 within the letter is crucial for understanding Paul's aims in employing the infant and nurse metaphors in 2:7. In addition to these matters, the authenticity of 2:13–16 will be discussed in this section, in order to determine if that passage is part of the literary context that informs evaluation of 2:7.

2.1.1. The Occasion and Purpose of 1 Thessalonians

What can be known of the historical situation of the Thessalonian church and Paul's relationship with them will be discussed in §3.2.3-4, below. Here it is necessary only to give a brief introduction to scholarly discussion of the occasion and purpose of Paul's letter to this church. Most New Testament scholars consider 1 Thessalonians the earliest of Paul's extant letters. While there is not perfect agreement on the details, they generally think that Paul's ministry in Thessalonica occurred in 49 CE, after which he traveled to Athens, sent Timothy back to Thessalonica, traveled to Corinth, and then wrote 1 Thessalonians from Corinth in 50 CE, after receiving Timothy's report on the congregation.[1] This timeline means that the letter was written only a few months after Paul's original ministry in Thessalonica, to a congregation that was still young in faith.

While Paul's discussion of the return of Christ and the resurrection of the dead in chapters 4 and 5 has traditionally received the most attention in studies of 1 Thessalonians, analysis of the letter as a whole reveals Paul's broader concerns for the situation of the Thessalonian church. Proper eschatological understanding is only one of these concerns. Careful reading of the letter reveals that one of Paul's central aims in the letter is to encourage the formation of Christ-centered group identity in these new believers. While chapters 4 and 5 have traditionally been viewed as parenetic in nature, Malherbe argues that the entire letter is characterized by a parenetic style.[2] That is, the very form of the letter as a whole is designed to shape the behavior of recent converts.[3] Alternatively, Victor Paul Furnish identifies the letter as pastoral. He calls the letter, and 2:1-12 in particular, not parenetic but *paracletic,* "a term that comes from the vocabulary of the letter itself, and embraces the ideas of encouragement, assurance, consolation, and exhortation."[4] Donfried articulates sharper disagreement with Malherbe, claiming that the letter should not be characterized as parenetic,

---

1. For a more extensive discussion of dating and the movements of Paul and his coworkers, see Abraham A. Malherbe, *The Letters to the Thessalonians: A New Translation with Introduction and Commentary* (AB 32B; New York: Doubleday, 2000), 67-78.
2. Ibid., 81.
3. Ibid., 85.
4. Victor P. Furnish, *1 Thessalonians, 2 Thessalonians* (ANTC; Nashville: Abingdon, 2007), 52.

but as a *consolatio*.[5] Donfried concedes that there are parenetic elements within the letter, but argues that, overall, Paul writes not to exhort but to comfort and give hope to a congregation feeling discouraged.[6] Donfried emphasizes the strong associations the letter has with epideictic rhetoric, with the Thessalonians themselves as the object of Paul's praise.[7]

Malherbe and Donfried both point to important aspects of Paul's aims in 1 Thessalonians. A sharp distinction should not be drawn between understanding the letter as parenetic and understanding it as *consolatio*. Clearly, Paul is seeking to give comfort and hope to the Thessalonian church. But that consolation always includes the exhortation to view themselves, their faith, and Christ in certain ways—ways that Paul believes will bring them the comfort they need and secure their future in Christ. In 1 Thessalonians Paul seeks both to strengthen and to shape the young Thessalonian congregation.

Paul's intent to console, encourage, and exhort the Thessalonians by strengthening their identity in Christ is clear from the very beginning of the letter. The thanksgiving section (1:2-10) is packed with encouraging language that reminds the Thessalonians of who they are as a community in Christ. Paul expresses his pride in the community, reminding them that they are chosen by God (1:4), that the gospel first came to them not only in word but in power (1:5), that their imitation of Paul made them an example to believers far and wide (1:6-8), and that, because of their service to the true God, they have hope of a secure future—of a savior who will come from heaven (1:9-10). Here in the letter's thanksgiving one already senses that Paul's reminders about the past and his praise of the Thessalonians's current life of faith are designed to strengthen those who may have doubted themselves or their faith, and thus their Christian identity, in some way. As Malherbe writes, "The letter is adapted to the emotional condition of converts who are anxious and distressed. This is evident in his language, which is redolent with positive feeling designed to strengthen."[8]

---

5. Karl P. Donfried, *Paul, Thessalonica, and Early Christianity* (Grand Rapids: Eerdmans, 2002), 120.

6. Ibid., 138.

7. Ibid., 172-73.

8. Malherbe, *The Letters to the Thessalonians*, 85.

2.1.2. The Function of 1 Thessalonians 2:1-12

The infant and nurse metaphors of 2:7 are found within 2:1-12, which is usually considered a unit in the study of 1 Thessalonians. Often called an "apology," this section contains Paul's retrospective on his previous ministry in Thessalonica. Coming immediately after the traditional Pauline thanksgiving in 1:2-10, the passage can be considered the opening of the letter's body. In this section Paul looks back on his original missionary visit to Thessalonica and emphasizes the sincerity and integrity of his motives and conduct, along with that of his coworkers. He engages in a defense of his ministry among the Thessalonians. The central debate about this passage is whether or not it truly is a defense. In other words, is Paul defending himself against an actual attack on his authority in Thessalonica, whether from within the Christian community or outside of it? Or is this language parenetic in nature, designed not to ward off a real attack but to present his conduct to the Thessalonians as an example of proper behavior for a follower of Christ?[9]

Once again, Malherbe and Donfried take opposite sides in the debate. Malherbe compares Paul's language to that of contemporaneous philosophers, especially Dio Chrysostom, and concludes that the language Paul employs in 2:1-12 does not necessarily reflect an actual threat to the author's authority.[10] Malherbe notes that these philosophers defend their behavior against that of other philosophers, of whom they disapprove, in order "to establish themselves as trustworthy before they turned to advise their listeners or readers on practical matters."[11] In other words, this section prepares the Thessalonians to receive Paul's forthcoming advice in a favorable manner, because it reestablishes Paul's right to speak with authority in the congregation by reminding them of the integrity of his original preaching. In Malherbe's view, however, such a strategy does not imply that Paul was facing actual attacks against his authority in Thessalonica. It is, rather, a literary strategy.

---

9. For the details of this debate, see part 1 of Karl P. Donfried and Johannes Beutler, eds., *The Thessalonians Debate: Methodological Discord or Methodological Synthesis?* (Grand Rapids: Eerdmans, 2000).

10. Abraham J. Malherbe, "Gentle as a Nurse: The Cynic Background to 1 Thess 2," *NovT* 12 (1970): 203-17.

11. Malherbe, *The Letters to the Thessalonians*, 80.

Donfried, on the other hand, argues that the letter provides evidence that Paul faced real challenges to his authority in Thessalonica that required him to defend himself and his gospel to the Thessalonians. Donfried acknowledges that there are similar phrases in Dio Chrysostom, but emphasizes the difference in Paul and Dio's contexts and self-understandings, placing Paul within an Old Testament prophetic context rather than among Greco-Roman philosophers.[12] Donfried also emphasizes the very real persecution that the Thessalonian church faced in their social environment as a result of their acceptance of Paul's gospel.[13] Therefore, in order to console and give hope to the Thessalonians, Paul must defend the gospel that he had preached to them. A defense of his gospel necessitates also a defense of himself, because "the power and effectiveness of the word is ultimately linked with the credibility of the messenger; the truth of the divine logos is demonstrated by his ethos, that is, by Paul's embodiment of the gospel, and by his divine authorization."[14] If the Thessalonians doubt the messenger then they will doubt the message. If they doubt the message then they will lose the hope that came with their new faith in Christ. For this reason Paul defends the manner in which he preached the gospel to them during his first visit.

It may not be possible to know historically who was saying what about Paul and his gospel in Thessalonica, but Donfried is right to point out the context of persecution that the Thessalonians were facing and the very real need for Paul to defend his message in order to offer the Thessalonians comfort and hope.[15] Thus, the rhetorical function of 2:1–12 in the letter is to strengthen the relationship between Paul and the Thessalonians, and thus to strengthen their relationship to the gospel. To a community struggling with suffering and drastically changed social realities, a reminder of the trustworthiness of their original calling would serve as motivation to persevere. Lest any of them forget the reason why they are suffering, Paul reminds them of their initial encounter with the gospel, which he and his coworkers facilitated. Paul's defense of his motives and behavior in 2:1–12 serves to strengthen the Thessalonians's Christ-centered identity through

---

12. Donfried, *Paul, Thessalonica, and Early Christianity*, 135–36.
13. Ibid., 120–34.
14. Ibid., 177.
15. The social situation of the Thessalonian church and the evidence for persecution will be discussed further in §3.2, below.

a reminder of their connection to the gospel that he preached and continued to defend.

2.1.3. The Problem of 2:13–16

In order to interpret the infant and nurse metaphors in 2:7, one must analyze Paul's aims in the larger section of 2:1–12 and in the letter as a whole. One important aspect of analyzing Paul's purpose and aims in writing to the Thessalonians involves determining the historical situation of the Thessalonian church and what kind of suffering and persecution, if any, they were enduring. The suffering and persecution of the Thessalonian congregation is addressed in 2:13–16. A number of scholars, both past and contemporary, have questioned the authenticity of this passage, suggesting that part or all of it was a later interpolation. Historical clues in 2:13–16 serve as background for my analysis of the metaphors found in 2:7; therefore, an argument for the authenticity of 2:13–16 is needed before proceeding further.

There are no extant manuscripts in which any portion of 2:13–16 is missing, nor are there any other external reasons to suppose that this passage is a later interpolation. However, three major difficulties in the interpretation of this passage have led some scholars to doubt its authenticity. The first difficulty is the very harsh language that Paul uses against the Jews:

> For you, brothers and sisters, became imitators of the churches of God in Christ Jesus that are in Judea, for you suffered the same things from your own compatriots as they did from the Jews, who killed both the Lord Jesus and the prophets, and drove us out; they displease God and oppose everyone by hindering us from speaking to the Gentiles so that they may be saved. Thus they have constantly been filling up the measure of their sins; but God's wrath has overtaken them at last. (1 Thess 2:14–16, NRSV)

Many scholars find it difficult to reconcile such language to Paul's more positive reflections on the current state and future fate of the Jews in Rom 9–11, leading them to question the passage. The second major difficulty involves interpretation and translation of the final phrase of the passage (ἔφθασεν δὲ ἐπ' αὐτοὺς ἡ ὀργὴ εἰς τέλος) and the determination of what it refers to. In the NRSV translation, the phrase seems to refer to a specific event in the past, and many interpreters have understood it this way. Some have suggested that the destruction of Jerusalem in 70 CE is the most logical referent, which would obviously make the passage a post-Pauline interpolation. The third difficulty is that some have argued that severe persecution in Judea did not take place during Paul's lifetime, which would not recommend the churches of Judea as models for endurance of suffering.[16]

The arguments for interpolation have not gone unchallenged. Many have pointed out that the final phrase of the passage need not refer to a concrete and dramatic historical event of the past, such as 70 CE. There are a variety of ways to understand the precise meaning of εἰς τέλος and its relationship to the aorist ἔφθασεν.[17] Various literary and linguistic arguments for interpolation have also been challenged.[18] Perhaps most importantly, several scholars have addressed the problem of the seemingly anti-Jewish tone of the passage by arguing that Paul could not have been speaking of all Jews.[19] Jonas Holmstrand, for example, draws attention to the parallels between what the Thessalonians are facing and what the churches in Judea had faced; each had to deal with persecution from the hands of their own

---

16. For arguments against the authenticity of the passage, see Birger A. Pearson, "1 Thessalonians 2:13–16: A Deutero-Pauline Interpolation," *HTR* 64 (1971): 79–94; Daryl Schmidt, "1 Thess 2:13–16: Linguistic Evidence for an Interpolation," *JBL* 102, (1983): 269–79; Earl Richard, *First and Second Thessalonians* (SP 11; Collegeville, Minn.: Liturgical Press, 1995), 123–27.

17. For a variety of options, see Carol J. Schlueter, *Filling up the Measure: Polemical Hyperbole in 1 Thessalonians 2:14–16* (JSNTSup 98; Sheffield: JSOT Press, 1994), 30. Donfried's approach is among the most helpful. He argues that "at last" or "finally" are inappropriate translations for εἰς τέλος. Instead, he translates the phrase, "And now God's wrath has come upon them until the end." In this interpretation, the coming of God's wrath was a past event; at the death and resurrection of Jesus it came upon all human beings who did not confess faith in Christ. But the last two words, εἰς τέλος, refer to the future, to the time of Jesus' return and the ultimate triumph of God. God's wrath upon Jews who do not have faith in Christ is only "until the end," a theology that is compatible with Rom 9–11. See Donfried, *Paul, Thessalonica, and Early Christianity*, 205–7.

18. See Jon A. Weatherly, "The Authenticity of 1 Thessalonians 2.13–16: Additional Evidence," *JSNT* 41 (1991): 79–98; John C. Hurd, "Paul Ahead of His Time: 1 Thess. 2:13–16," in *Anti-Judaism in Early Christianity* (ed. Peter Richardson and David Granskou; vol. 1; SJC 2; Waterloo, Ont.: Wilfrid Laurier University Press, 1986), 27–30.

19. E.g., Jeffrey S. Lamp, "Is Paul Anti-Jewish? Testament of Levi 6 in the Interpretation of 1 Thessalonians 2:13–16," *CBQ* 65 (2003): 410.

kinsmen.[20] Thus, only some in the city of Thessalonica and only some in Judea cause problems, not the entirety of any race or religion.[21]

For solid arguments against interpolation and an explanation of why Paul would have chosen such harsh language for the Jewish persecutors, Carol Schlueter's extensive study of the passage proves helpful.[22] Schlueter rejects theories of interpolation, as well as attempts to harmonize the passage with Rom 9–11. Instead, she argues that 2:14–16 consists of polemical hyperbole, and calls attention to the rhetorical and historical context of 1 Thessalonians.[23] According to Schlueter, Paul exaggerates the suffering of both the Judean churches and the Thessalonians for rhetorical purposes, in order to achieve his goal of strengthening the Thessalonian congregation.[24] By exaggerating the sins of the Jews and then comparing them to those who are troubling the Thessalonians, Paul sought to inspire the Thessalonians to stand firm in their situation and view themselves as aligned with the side of truth.[25] This is consistent with the "us" versus "them" dynamic present in 1 Thessalonians. Paul urges the Thessalonians to imitate the righteous, who are also always the persecuted ones.[26] Exaggeration of the evils of those considered "outsiders" is a strategy for strengthening the group identity of those considered "insiders." "Inflated praise" of insiders serves the same purpose, and Paul employs this strategy with the Thessalonians as well.[27] These aspects of group identity will be explored further in the next chapter.

---

20. Jonas Holmstrand, *Markers and Meaning in Paul: An Analysis of 1 Thessalonians, Philippians, and Galatians* (Stockholm: Almqvist & Wiksell International, 1997), 43.

21. See also the grammatical argument made by Frank Gilliard, who notes that the trouble interpreters have with the passage is occasioned by the comma that modern translators place between v. 14 and v. 15. This comma implies that Paul's remarks reference all Jews. Once the comma is removed, Paul's remarks clearly apply only to those particular Jews who did the killing and the driving out. Frank Gilliard, "The Problem of the Antisemitic Comma between 1 Thessalonians 2:14 and 15," *NTS* 35 (1989): 481–502.

22. Schlueter, *Filling up the Measure*.

23. Ibid., 11–12.

24. Ibid., 53.

25. Ibid., 124.

26. Ibid., 121. See also Elizabeth A. Castelli, *Imitating Paul: A Discourse of Power* (LCBI; Louisville: Westminster John Knox, 1991), 94.

27. Schlueter, *Filling up the Measure*, 65.

2.2. νήπιοι or ἤπιοι?

In 1 Thess 2:7, did Paul write that he and his coworkers had been "gentle" (ἤπιοι) among the Thessalonians or that they had been "infants" (νήπιοι) among them? These two textual variants have been much debated. The previous word (ἐγενήθημεν) ends in ν, which means that both variants could have arisen from a common transcriptional error: either νήπιοι in the case of dittography or ἤπιοι in the case of haplography. Even without a ν preceding, these two words are so similar to one another that scribes confused them elsewhere in the New Testament as well. In 2 Tim 2:24 the author writes that "a servant of the Lord must not quarrel, but must be gentle [ἤπιον] to all." Most manuscripts support this reading; however, one sixth-century manuscript (D^p), two ninth-century manuscripts (F^p and G^p), and the Ethiopic version all contain the variant νήπιον. In Eph 4:14, manuscripts are nearly universal in supporting νήπιοι, but Codex Alexandrinus contains ἤπιοι. Similarly, in Heb 5:13, νήπιος is quite clearly the correct reading, but one minuscule manuscript (33) contains ἤπιος. These three examples are not as difficult to adjudicate as the variants in 1 Thess 2:7, but they serve to illustrate how easily these two words could be mistaken for each other by New Testament scribes. It is also important to note that the mistake happens in both directions. Scribes sometimes write νήπιοι for ἤπιοι, and sometimes ἤπιοι for νήπιοι. Therefore, these other examples are of little assistance in determining the direction of the mistake in 1 Thess 2:7. In order to decide which was most likely the original reading, both internal and external evidence needs to be considered.

2.2.1. Manuscript Evidence

Manuscript evidence clearly supports the reading νήπιοι. "Infants" is found in early witnesses in both the Alexandrian and Western text traditions (e.g., P^65, Sinaiticus, Vaticanus, Ephraemi, Bezae, and Old Latin). "Gentle" is found in Alexandrinus and stands as a correction in several uncial manuscripts. Νήπιοι is the stronger reading whether the manuscripts are evaluated on the basis of date, geographical distribution, or genealogical relationship.[28] Based largely on the strength of manuscript evidence, the

---

28. Timothy B. Sailors, "Wedding Textual and Rhetorical Criticism to Understand the Text of 1 Thessalonians 2.7," *JSNT* 80 (2000): 84; Jeffrey A. D. Weima, "'But We

26th edition of the Nestle-Aland *Novum Testamentum Graece* adopted the UBS reading of νήπιοι, though previous editions had printed ἤπιοι.

However, despite the manuscript support for νήπιοι, the vast majority of English Bible translations and 1 Thessalonians commentaries have adopted the reading "gentle."[29] The manuscript evidence is not in dispute. Even those who argue for ἤπιοι concede that the external evidence for νήπιοι is stronger. For these translators and commentators the arguments based on internal evidence bear greater weight than those based on external evidence.[30] But as Jeffrey Weima points out, given the strong manuscript evidence, the "burden of proof" lies with those who argue for ἤπιοι.[31] Arguments in favor of ἤπιοι would have to be very compelling to justify rejection of such strong manuscript evidence. While several arguments for ἤπιοι are worthy of consideration, each can be refuted, leaving no compelling reason to reject the manuscript evidence. The most significant of these arguments include the following: that reading νήπιοι creates an incomprehensible mixed metaphor, that Paul would never refer to himself as an infant, and that ἤπιοι is the rarer of the two words, making it more likely that copyists would have replaced it with the more familiar νήπιοι. Each of these arguments will be considered in turn.

Became Infants among You': The Case for NHΠIOI in 1 Thess 2.7," *NTS* 46 (2000): 548.

29. Commentary authors adopting ἤπιοι include Bruce (F. F. Bruce; *1 and 2 Thessalonians* [WBC; Waco, Tex.: Word, 1982]), Richard, Felder (Cain Hope Felder, "1 Thessalonians," in *True to Our Native Land: An African American New Testament Commentary* [ed. Brian K. Blount et al.; Minneapolis: Fortress, 2007]), Malherbe, Wanamaker (Charles A. Wanamaker, *The Epistles to the Thessalonians: A Commentary on the Greek Text* [NIGTC; Grand Rapids: Eerdmans, 1990]), Witherington (Ben Witherington III, *1 and 2 Thessalonians: A Socio-Rhetorical Commentary* [Grand Rapids: Eerdmans, 2006]), and many others. Fee (Gordon D. Fee, "On Text and Commentary on 1 and 2 Thessalonians," in *Society of Biblical Literature 1992 Seminar Papers* [SBLSP 31; Atlanta: Scholars Press, 1992]), Furnish, and Gaventa (Beverly Roberts Gaventa, *First and Second Thessalonians* [IBC; Louisville: Westminster John Knox, 1998]) depart from the mainstream by adopting νήπιοι in their commentaries.

30. For an argument that internal considerations should be given greater weight than external considerations in this case, see Bruce Manning Metzger and Bart D. Ehrman, *The Text of the New Testament: Its Transmission, Corruption, and Restoration* (4th ed.; New York: Oxford University Press, 2005), 330.

31. Weima, "But We Became Infants among You," 549.

2. ESTABLISHING THE TEXT

2.2.2. The Problem of a Mixed Metaphor

The primary reason many commentators and translators reject "infants" is that they think "gentle" fits the context better.[32] The specific context to which they refer is the image of the nurse, which immediately follows. With the traditional punctuation, the adoption of νήπιοι results in the following or similar translation: "But we were infants among you, like a nurse tenderly caring for her own children." Not only do many scholars feel that "gentle" is more appropriate to this context, but some also react very strongly against the idea that Paul could possibly have compared himself to an infant and a nurse in the same sentence. Malherbe, for example, calls the abrupt change from infants to nurse "incomprehensible."[33] Helmut Koester writes "there cannot be the slightest doubt that νήπιοι is wrong."[34] Bruce Metzger and Bart Ehrman write that the "violence" done to the meaning of the text by choosing νήπιοι is "intolerable," and that such a reading is "little short of absurdity."[35] While I acknowledge the challenge of reading "infants," the more difficult reading is usually preferred by text critics.[36] One ought not to dismiss the more difficult reading out of hand, therefore, without attempting to make sense of it. As Kurt and Barbara Aland observe, "here as elsewhere the exegetes confuse their own interpretation with what Paul should have said."[37]

Gaventa rightly points out that it is by no means unusual for Paul to employ mixed metaphors (e.g., Gal. 4:19) and engage in abrupt changes in

---

32. While *A Textual Commentary on the Greek New Testament* adopts the reading νήπιοι, note the dissenting opinion in brackets by Bruce Metzger and Allen Wikgren, which argues that context should be the most crucial factor in making this decision. See Bruce M. Metzger, *A Textual Commentary on the Greek New Testament* (2nd ed.; New York: UBS, 1994), 562.

33. Malherbe, *The Letters to the Thessalonians*, 145.

34. Helmut Koester, "The Text of 1 Thessalonians," in *The Living Text: Essays in Honor of Ernest W. Saunders* (ed. Dennis E. Groh and Robert Jewett; Lanham, Md.: University Press of America, 1985), 225.

35. Metzger and Ehrman, *The Text of the New Testament*, 329–30.

36. Beverly Roberts Gaventa, *Our Mother Saint Paul* (Louisville: Westminster John Knox, 2007), 20.

37. Kurt Aland and Barbara Aland, *The Text of the New Testament: An Introduction to the Critical Editions and to the Theory and Practice of Modern Textual Criticism* (trans. Erroll F. Rhodes; Grand Rapids: Eerdmans, 1989), 284–85.

thought and image.³⁸ In fact, Paul describes himself as a father and then as an orphan later in this very chapter, albeit not in the same sentence. Gaventa's argument that Paul is quite capable of such an abrupt change within one sentence has merit, but punctuation considerations provide an even stronger refutation of the argument based on context. If one alters the traditional punctuation of the passage, the two images no longer appear in the same sentence at all. This possibility will be discussed in detail later in §2.3, below.³⁹

2.2.3. Paul as Infant?

While some scholars argue that Paul would not use "infant" and "nurse" to describe himself in the same sentence, many also insist that Paul would not have referred to himself as an infant in any context. Charles Wanamaker, for example, points out that Paul nowhere else refers to himself as a νήπιος, and therefore he rejects this reading.⁴⁰ This is a weak argument, however, since Paul also nowhere else refers to himself as a nurse (τροφός), and yet no one argues that this must be a corruption of the text. Only in 1 Cor 3:10 does Paul refer to himself as an ἀρχιτέκτων, a "master builder," and only in 1 Cor 15:8 does Paul compare himself to an ἔκτρωμα, a "mis-

---

38. Gaventa, *Our Mother Saint Paul*, 19–20. See also the committee's argument in Metzger, *A Textual Commentary on the Greek New Testament*, 562.

39. A third solution to this difficulty has been presented by Charles Crawford, who supports the suggestion of seventeenth century scholar Daniel Whitby that νήπιοι should be understood as a vocative. See Charles Crawford, "The 'Tiny' Problem of 1 Thessalonians 2,7: The Case of the Curious Vocative," *Bib* 54 (1973): 69–72. Crawford argues that the word fits Paul's usage of the vocative and that this interpretation allows one to accept the better attested variant while avoiding all the major problems associated with that reading, including a mixed metaphor and the perceived impossibility of Paul referring to himself as an infant. Interpreted thus, the passage would be translated roughly as follows: "But, Infants, we were among you like a nurse cherishing her own children." This argument has not found support from other scholars. Nowhere else does Paul use νήπιοι as a vocative; ἀδελφοί is his common practice in similar constructions. But more importantly, such a reading is difficult grammatically. It is much more natural to take νήπιοι as the object of ἐγενήθημεν ("became infants") rather than to take it as a vocative and leave ἐγενήθημεν without an object ("became/ were"). See the convincing argument against Crawford in Stefano Cotrozzi, "1 Thes 2:7—a Review," *FN* 12 (1999): 159.

40. Wanamaker, *The Epistles to the Thessalonians*, 100.

carriage" or "abortion." We cannot limit Pauline authenticity only to things that he writes more than once.

Taking the argument further, some scholars argue not only that Paul nowhere else refers to himself as a νήπιος, but also that he would never do so. Cain Hope Felder, for example, rejects νήπιοι because "this awkward rendering flies in the face of Paul's more common parental self-designations," and therefore "gentle" is "the better and more sensible rendering."[41] Felder and others claim that Paul uses the term "infants" elsewhere always in reference to converts, not leaders, and it carries the negative connotation of immaturity. Therefore, they conclude, it makes no sense for Paul to attribute immaturity to himself.

However, it is by no means clear that Paul's use of νήπιοι elsewhere *always* has a negative connotation of immaturity as these scholars claim. It does have a negative connotation in 1 Cor 3:1–2, where Paul notes that, as infants in Christ, the Corinthians are not mature enough for spiritual food. Likewise, in Gal 4:1–3 Paul describes the pre-Christ state of being enslaved to elemental spirits as one of infancy. But the term is less clearly negative in Rom 2:20 and 1 Cor 13:11, where it simply describes a stage of life that one naturally experiences and then grows out of. Certainly in these verses there is still a sense of immaturity—no one expects an infant to be mature—but there is no sense of judgment or negativity associated with the term. More importantly, when Paul uses the verbal form, νηπιάζω, in 1 Cor 14:20, the connotation is quite positive. While one should not be childish in thinking, with respect to evil one should be an infant. This sense of innocence associated with infants in 1 Cor 14:20 is precisely the connotation that I would argue is at work when Paul employs νήπιοι in 1 Thess 2:7. Though the verbal form rather than the noun is employed in 1 Cor 14:20, it clearly shows that Paul was capable of expressing the idea of infancy with a positive connotation.

In addition, a later passage in the very same chapter of 1 Thessalonians demonstrates that Paul does not restrict himself to the parental role. In 1 Thess 2:17, Paul takes on the role of the child when expressing his past distress at being separated from the Thessalonian church, using the verb ἀπορφανίζω, a word found only here in the New Testament. While most English Bible translators interpret this verb in the figurative sense of being separated from something, the literal meaning of this verb is to

---

41. Felder, "1 Thessalonians," 393.

"make an orphan of someone."[42] If we assume this literal meaning for the moment, the aorist passive participle form used here (ἀπορφανισθέντες) means roughly "having been made orphans." The first person plural indicates that Paul and his coworkers are the ones who had been orphaned. The addition of ἀφ' ὑμῶν reveals that they were orphaned by their separation from the Thessalonian church.

This literal meaning, however, is not the only option for translation and interpretation. While the literal meaning remained the most common usage in Greek literature, two other uses can be identified. First, as indicated above, the word could be used in the figurative sense of being separated from someone or something. Second, in a small number of cases the verb has been generalized to apply not only to the child but also to the parent—a parent bereft of children.[43] Translators and commentators are divided as to which of these three options is the most appropriate in 1 Thess 2:17. Most English Bible translations opt for the figurative sense; for example, the NIV "we were torn away from you for a short time" and the RSV "we were bereft of you" exhibit this interpretation. Some commentators also translate the verb in this general fashion, though most also discuss the more specific possibilities of "orphan" or "parent bereft of children" in their commentary analysis.[44] Though it is less common to apply ἀπορφανίζω to the parent, many commentators argue that this is how one ought to take it in 1 Thess 2:17 because it makes more sense for Paul to refer to himself as the parent rather than the child, due to his authority in the community.[45]

To argue that Paul could not have meant that he was the orphan because he had the authority of a parent in the community is somewhat beside the point. Certainly Paul viewed himself as having authority in the community, but his authority or lack thereof are not directly under consideration in this verse. Rather, Paul is striving to express an emotion and

---

42. BDAG, 119.

43. For an explanation of all three interpretive options, see Richard, *First and Second Thessalonians*, 128.

44. Bruce, *1 and 2 Thessalonians*, 53; Leon Morris, *The First and Second Epistles to the Thessalonians: The English Text with Introduction, Exposition, and Notes* (NICNT; Grand Rapids: Eerdmans, 1959), 93.

45. Bruce, *1 and 2 Thessalonians*, 54; Richard, *First and Second Thessalonians*, 129; Witherington, *1 and 2 Thessalonians*, 90; Wanamaker, *The Epistles to the Thessalonians*, 120; I. Howard Marshall, *1 and 2 Thessalonians* (NCB; Grand Rapids: Eerdmans, 1983), 85.

lands on a metaphor that gets his point across effectively and dramatically: without the Thessalonians Paul feels as lost as a child bereft of his parents. There is no compelling reason to reject this straightforward way of understanding the text. Indeed, many commentators do accept this reading. Malherbe offers the translation "having been orphaned by being separated from you for a short time."[46] Best translates similarly, and argues that Paul's ability to switch metaphors rapidly ought to lead the interpreter to accept "the more vivid conception" that the image of an orphan brings to the text.[47] Weima argues from an analysis of Greek literature that ἀπορφανίζω is consistently used in reference to children orphaned from their parents and not the other way around. He also points out that the vivid nature of this conception communicates Paul's "deep pain and anguish" more effectively than the alternative interpretations.[48] Several scholars[49] who translate ἀπορφανισθέντες as "orphaned" quote John Chrysostom in support of their argument:

> He [Paul] did not say, 'separated from you,' nor 'torn from you,' nor 'set apart from you,' nor 'left behind,' but 'orphaned from you.' He sought for a word that might sufficiently show the pain of his soul. Though standing in the relation of a father to them all, he yet uses that language of orphan children who have prematurely lost their parent.[50]

Chrysostom, who would have been familiar with ἀπορφανίζω as one natively fluent in Greek, does not hesitate to accept this meaning in Paul's text, and notes it as a powerful metaphor for expressing Paul's emotional pain at being separated from the Thessalonians.

The ἀπορφανίζω metaphor is relevant to the current study in that it casts Paul and his coworkers in the role of children and the Thessalonians in the role of the parents. To Paul, being separated from the Thessalonians made him feel like an orphaned child. This interesting use of metaphor shows that Paul was capable of picturing himself in the role of an infant or

---

46. Malherbe, *The Letters to the Thessalonians*, 182.
47. Ernest Best, *A Commentary on the First and Second Epistles to the Thessalonians* (HNTC; New York: Harper & Row, 1972), 123–24.
48. Weima, "But We Became Infants among You," 558.
49. Gaventa, *First and Second Thessalonians*, 41; Morris, *The First and Second Epistles to the Thessalonians*, 93; Weima, "But We Became Infants among You," 558.
50. John Chrysostom, *Ep. Olymp.* 8.12.37–41, as quoted in Weima, "But We Became Infants among You," 558.

child in relation to his churches. Therefore, reading "infants" in 2:7 is not so far-fetched.

2.2.4. The Supposed Rarity of ἤπιοι

One final objection to the reading "infants" is that νήπιοι is the more common of the two terms, thus making it more likely that copyists replaced the rare ἤπιοι with the familiar νήπιοι rather than vice versa. According to this theory, scribes who had never heard of or read the word ἤπιοι would have replaced it with the similar word that was familiar from its use elsewhere in Paul's letters and the New Testament as a whole. Weima effectively refutes this argument. First of all, he points out that νήπιοι is not as common a word in the New Testament as some would argue, in light of the fact that five of its ten uses in Paul's letters are found in a single verse (1 Cor 13:11); the word is used only four times in the rest of the New Testament. Also, while it is true that ἤπιοι is a very rare word in the New Testament (used elsewhere only in 2 Tim 2:24), it is not so rare in other ancient Greek literature. To assume that scribes would have been confused by this word and felt the need to change it to νήπιοι supposes that the New Testament was the only Greek literature scribes had exposure to. According to Weima, the scribes would have been familiar with both words.[51]

2.2.5. Accepting the More Difficult Reading

It is quite possible that νήπιοι was changed to ἤπιοι accidentally through haplography. However, if the change was intentional, the supposed rarity of ἤπιοι is a much less compelling argument than the possible discomfort scribes may have felt upon encountering the original νήπιοι in the text. Modern commentators exhibit discomfort with the idea that Paul wrote νήπιοι, and this discomfort is likely very similar to what the ancient scribes experienced as well. How could Paul refer to himself as an infant, as one who is immature? Such a designation does not fit the great apostle who was a dignified father to his converts in the gospel!

Something similar happens in Col 1:23. The author, assuming Paul's persona, calls himself a servant (διάκονος) of the gospel. A few manuscripts

---

51. Weima, "But We Became Infants among You," 551. See also Sailors, "Wedding Textual and Rhetorical Criticism," 86–87.

contain alternate readings, including "servant and apostle" (διάκονος καὶ ἀπόστολος), "preacher and apostle" (κῆρυξ καὶ ἀπόστολος), and "preacher and apostle and servant" (κῆρυξ καὶ ἀπόστολος καὶ διάκονος).[52] In the Colossians passage scribes added entire words to increase Paul's honor in the text. In the case of 1 Thess 2:7, the dropping of one tiny letter is all it would have taken to "fix" a difficult text and ensure that Paul's honor was not tainted by association with the immaturity of infancy.

2.3. Punctuating 1 Thessalonians 2:5–8

With manuscript evidence clearly in favor of νήπιοι, and arguments for ἤπιοι based on internal evidence refuted, νήπιοι ought to be considered the original reading. The task, then, is to make sense of reading "infants" in context. A close look at the grammar of the verses surrounding the word suggests that a change in the traditional punctuation of the passage is called for.[53] Indeed, this change in punctuation relieves many of the difficulties that scholars have with making sense of the reading "infants." The major question is where the full stop should be located in verse 7— after ἀπόστολοι or after ὑμῶν? The NRSV adopts what can be considered the traditional punctuation of this passage, based on placing the full stop after ἀπόστολοι:

> As you know and as God is our witness, we never came with words of flattery or with a pretext for greed; nor did we seek praise from mortals, whether from you or from others, though we might have made demands as apostles of Christ. But we were gentle among you, like a nurse tenderly caring for her own children. So deeply do we care for you that we are determined to share with you not only the gospel of God but also our own selves, because you have become very dear to us. (1 Thess 2:5–8 NRSV)

---

52. Metzger and Ehrman, *The Text of the New Testament*, 263. See also Weima, "But We Became Infants among You," 554.

53. Note the difference in the punctuation of this passage in the Nestle-Aland and UBS editions of the Greek New Testament. In this section I will be arguing for a punctuation similar to the UBS 4th revised edition. The Nestle-Aland punctuation is consistent with what I refer to as the traditional punctuation of the passage.

Many scholars who argue for the reading "infants" also argue for changing this punctuation so that a full stop comes after ὑμῶν in verse 7.[54] With this revised punctuation, "infants" is connected to what precedes it and "nurse" is connected to what follows; thus, the words are not part of the same sentence. Gaventa does not feel such a change is warranted, and argues for the traditional punctuation on the grounds that Paul is quite capable of mixing metaphors.[55] I agree with several other scholars, however, who argue for a change in punctuation, not because I think Paul incapable of creating the kind of mixed metaphor the NRSV presents, but because analysis of the Greek syntax demonstrates the need for a change in punctuation.

This change is called for by two parallel structures within the passage. The first is the word pair οὔτε ... ἀλλά. The οὔτε is repeated several times in verses 5–6 and the ἀλλά comes in the middle of verse 7. This results in the structure "*neither* this *nor* this, *but* this." Most translators treat the ἀλλά as the beginning of the next sentence, but this contradicts Paul's usual pattern of a negative followed by ἀλλά.[56] The οὔτε ... ἀλλά structure ought to be left in place. There is no valid reason for breaking it up with a full stop. Laying the Greek out in the following manner, with some phrases left out for the moment, illumines this structure:

<u>Οὔτε</u> γάρ ποτε ἐν λόγῳ κολακείας ἐγενήθημεν ...
   <u>οὔτε</u> ἐν προφάσει πλεονεξίας ...
      <u>οὔτε</u> ζητοῦντες ἐξ ἀνθρώπων δόξαν ...
<u>ἀλλά</u> ἐγενήθημεν νήπιοι ἐν μέσῳ ὑμῶν.[57]

For we never came with flattering words ...
   nor with a motive of greed ...

---

54. Sailors, "Wedding Textual and Rhetorical Criticism," 92–97; Fika Van Rensburg, "An Argument for Reading νήπιοι in 1 Thessalonians 2:7," in *A South African Perspective on the New Testament: Essays by South African New Testament Scholars Presented to Bruce Manning Metzger during His Visit to South Africa in 1985* (ed. J. H. Petzer and P. J. Hartin; Leiden: Brill, 1986), 252–59; Weima, "'But We Became Infants among You'"; Stephen E. Fowl, "A Metaphor in Distress: A Reading of ΝΗΠΙΟΙ in 1 Thessalonians 2:7," *NTS* 36 (1990): 470; Fee, "On Text and Commentary, 178; Furnish, *1 Thessalonians, 2 Thessalonians*, 54–59.

55. Gaventa, *Our Mother Saint Paul*, 20.

56. Fee, "On Text and Commentary," 178.

57. This visual layout of the text is similar to that in articles by Sailors and Weima: Sailors, "Wedding Textual and Rhetorical Criticism," 95; Weima, "But We Became Infants among You," 560.

nor seeking honor from human beings …
but we were infants in your midst.[58]

Complicating this structure slightly is the fact that the third οὔτε phrase contains its own οὔτε … οὔτε phrase:

<u>Οὔτε</u> γάρ ποτε ἐν λόγῳ κολακείας ἐγενήθημεν …
　<u>οὔτε</u> ἐν προφάσει πλεονεξίας …
　　<u>οὔτε</u> ζητοῦντες ἐξ ἀνθρώπων δόξαν, <u>οὔτε</u> ἀφ' ὑμῶν <u>οὔτε</u> ἀπ' ἄλλων …
<u>ἀλλὰ</u> ἐγενήθημεν νήπιοι ἐν μέσῳ ὑμῶν.

For we never came with flattering words …
　nor with a motive of greed …
　　nor seeking honor from human beings, whether from you or from others …
but we were infants in your midst.

Recognizing the οὔτε … ἀλλά structure leads to the placement of a full stop at the end of the ἀλλά phrase, that is, after ὑμῶν, since the ἀλλά phrase serves as a contrasting conclusion to what precedes it. At first, verse 7a (δυνάμενοι … ἀπόστολοι) seems to disrupt this theory, which is why many scholars understand this phrase as the conclusion of the sentence. This traditional punctuation places a full stop after ἀπόστολοι and a comma after ὑμῶν, thus linking the ἀλλα phrase, which contains the infant metaphor, to the description of the nurse that follows. However, several scholars have correctly recognized that verse 7a is one of three parenthetical phrases that Paul inserts, one after each main οὔτε phrase.[59] When understood in this way, verse 7a does not interrupt the flow of the οὔτε … ἀλλά construction; it simply results in a much more complex sentence structure, and therefore the full stop after ὑμῶν can be maintained:

<u>Οὔτε</u> γάρ ποτε ἐν λόγῳ κολακείας ἐγενήθημεν,
　καθὼς οἴδατε,
<u>οὔτε</u> ἐν προφάσει πλεονεξίας,

---

58. Explanation for the translations found in this section will be given in §2.4, below.

59. Weima, "But We Became Infants among You," 560. See also Sailors, "Wedding Textual and Rhetorical Criticism," 93–94.

θεὸς μάρτυς,
<u>οὔτε</u> ζητοῦντες ἐξ ἀνθρώπων δόξαν, <u>οὔτε</u> ἀφ' ὑμῶν <u>οὔτε</u> ἀπ' ἄλλων,
δυνάμενοι ἐν βάρει εἶναι ὡς Χριστοῦ ἀπόστολοι,
<u>ἀλλὰ</u> ἐγενήθημεν νήπιοι ἐν μέσῳ ὑμῶν.

> For we never came with flattering words,
>   just as you know,
>   nor with a motive of greed,
>   as God is witness,
>   nor seeking honor from human beings, whether from you or
>   from others,
>   though we could have insisted on our own importance as
>   apostles of Christ,
> but we were infants in your midst.

This complicated sentence structure is easy to see and understand when laid out as above but is difficult to manage when written in regular prose form. The use of parentheses in the English translation is helpful:

> For we never came with flattering words (just as you know), nor with a motive of greed (as God is witness), nor seeking honor from human beings, whether from you or from others (though we could have insisted on our own importance as apostles of Christ), but we were infants in your midst.

Once a full stop is placed after ἐν μέσῳ ὑμῶν, it becomes clear that the verses that follow (7c–8) are governed by a second word pair, ὡς ... οὕτως: "*as/like* this, *so/in the same way* this."

<u>ὡς</u> ἐὰν τροφὸς θάλπῃ τὰ ἑαυτῆς τέκνα,
<u>οὕτως</u> ὁμειρόμενοι ὑμῶν εὐδοκοῦμεν μεταδοῦναι ὑμῖν οὐ μόνον τὸ εὐαγγέλιον τοῦ θεοῦ ἀλλὰ καὶ τὰς ἑαυτῶν ψυχάς, διότι ἀγαπητοὶ ἡμῖν ἐγενήθητε.

> Like a nurse taking tender care of her own children,
>   in the same way, longing for you, we were pleased to share with you
>   not only the gospel of God, but also our very selves, because you had
>   become beloved to us.

Those who break up this natural structure by putting a full stop in the middle (after τέκνα), as in the NRSV, are forced to translate οὕτως as "so much" or "so deeply," interpreting it as an adverb indicating degree rather than as a correlative with ὡς.⁶⁰ This is not a good solution. As both Fee and Weima point out, use of οὕτως in this manner has no parallel elsewhere in Paul's letters and "conflicts with ordinary Greek usage."⁶¹ Keeping the ὡς ... οὕτως structure in place and translating "like ... in the same way" makes much more sense and is more faithful to Greek grammar.

Punctuating the text in this manner results in two distinct sections within 2:5–8. In the first (2:5–7b), what Paul and his coworkers were *not* like in their mission work in Thessalonica is contrasted with a metaphor of what they were in fact like: "infants." In the second part (2:7c–8), the apostles' sharing of the gospel and of their very selves with the Thessalonians is compared to the behavior of a nurse toward her own children. This structure relieves many of the difficulties commentators and translators have with accepting the reading νήπιοι, because νήπιοι and τροφός are now separated from one another. Paul does not write "we were infants among you like a nurse caring for her own children." Rather, νήπιοι, with its connotation of innocence, serves as a concluding contrast to the behaviors described in preceding verses. Accepting this structure also changes the meaning implied by the nurse metaphor. It is not gentleness that Paul highlights through the nurse image, but rather the way in which he longed for the Thessalonians and shared his very self with them as he shared the gospel. Paul likens these emotions and attitudes to those of a nurse with her own children.

2.4. Understanding and Translating 1 Thessalonians 2:5–8

The key text critical matter in 2:7 as well as the grammatical structures in 2:5–8 and their effect on punctuation have been discussed. What remains to be discussed is the meaning of the words themselves and how best to render them in an English translation. Such an analysis is critical before engaging in an exploration of the metaphors found in this section. The following step-by-step walk through the text presents an exploration of its words and my understanding of how best to translate them in this particular context.

---

60. Fee, "On Text and Commentary," 178.
61. Weima, "But We Became Infants among You," 556. See also Fee, "On Text and Commentary," 178.

Οὔτε γάρ ποτε ἐν λόγῳ κολακείας ἐγενήθημεν / For we never came with flattering words

In the first verse of chapter 2, Paul introduces the topic of his initial visit to Thessalonica and his founding of the Thessalonian church. He then refers to the past difficulties he and his coworkers faced at Philippi and to their boldness in proclaiming the gospel at Thessalonica (2:2). He defends the purity of their motives in preaching the gospel, insisting that they do so to please God rather than human beings (2:3-4). Paul begins verse 5 with οὔτε, the first of the three οὔτε clauses that are correlated with the ἀλλά in the middle of verse 7. In this first οὔτε clause Paul refers again to his original visit to Thessalonica using the verb ἐγενήθημεν. Richard calls this verb "amorphous" and points out that its precise meaning in this context is difficult to pin down.[62] In combination with οὔτε ... ποτε, some translate "we never used," while others translate "we never came with." A similar use of γίνομαι in 1:5 strengthens the impression that Paul uses ἐγενήθημεν here to refer to his original visit, and it is therefore best translated as "came."[63]

Referencing the original visit, Paul states that he and he coworkers did not come among the Thessalonians with λόγῳ κολακείας, which may be translated literally as "a word of flattery," or more smoothly in English as "flattering words."[64] Κολακείας is a *hapax legomenon* in the New Testament, but flattery was a common topic among Greco-Roman writers. Bruce calls the flatterer a "stock character" in Greco-Roman ethical literature, commented upon by Aristotle, Dio Chrysostom, Plutarch, and many others.[65] Such authors generally criticized the flatterer for empty speech designed not for the benefit of the ones addressed but for the flatterer's own benefit.[66] Plutarch, in *Adul. amic.*, contrasts flattery with the "boldness of speech" (παρρησία) that characterizes true friendship.[67] With these words Paul denies engaging in this commonly criticized vice. His words to the Thessalonians did not convey excessive praise designed to benefit himself. According to Paul, as he has just stated in verse 4, his preaching of the gospel was designed to please God, not human beings.

---

62. Richard, *First and Second Thessalonians*, 81.
63. Ibid.
64. BDAG, 555.
65. Bruce, *1 and 2 Thessalonians*, 29.
66. Furnish, *1 Thessalonians, 2 Thessalonians*, 55.
67. *Mor.* 48E-74E. See Wanamaker, *The Epistles to the Thessalonians*, 97.

καθὼς οἴδατε / (just as you know)

These words, "just as you know," form the first parenthetical phrase correlated with the first οὔτε clause. According to Paul, the fact that he and his coworkers did not operate like flatterers among the Thessalonians is something that they should be able to recall from their own experience of Paul's visit. This exact phrase appears four times in 1 Thessalonians (1:5; 2:2, 5; and 3:4), but not in any other Pauline letter. Paul has a special concern in 1 Thessalonians to remind the congregation of what he has already told them and what they already know. Such language serves Paul's objectives in the letter of encouraging and giving hope to the Thessalonians. Paul reminds them of what they already know about the gospel and of the nature of their reception of it, in order to strengthen them in their faithfulness to his message in the midst of social hostility and theological questioning.

οὔτε ἐν προφάσει πλεονεξίας / nor with a motive of greed

In the second οὔτε clause Paul's refers to his motive in preaching the gospel to the Thessalonians and insists that he did not do so with a motive of greed (πλεονεξίας). The word indicates not just a desire to have more than one has, but a desire to have more than one has a right to have, particularly that which belongs to another.[68] Paul condemns greed several times in his letters, and πλεονεξία was also commonly found in the vice lists of Greco-Roman writers.[69] Here Paul employs the term to indicate that he did not preach the gospel to the Thessalonians for the purpose of his own financial gain; his motive was not to take from them what was theirs.

Προφάσει proves a bit more difficult to translate than πλεονεξίας. The word can mean either an actual motive for doing something, or a false motive, often translated "pretext" in the latter case.[70] Many translate as "pretext" in this case, assuming that the phrase indicates that Paul did not have greed as his hidden motive. This would make his use of the word here very similar in meaning to its use in Phil 1:18. But others point out

---

68. Bruce, *1 and 2 Thessalonians*, 30; BDAG, 824.
69. Malherbe, *The Letters to the Thessalonians*, 142. For other references to greed in the Pauline corpus, see Rom 1:29; 1 Cor 5:10–11; 6:10; 2 Cor 9:5; Eph 4:19; 5:3; and Col 3:5.
70. BDAG, 889.

rightly that when πρόφασις means "pretext" it refers to the false, outer motive, not the true, hidden motive. Therefore, "pretext of greed" does not make sense, because that would indicate that greed was Paul's outward, ostensible motive among the Thessalonians, while his true hidden motive was something else.[71] Προφάσει is more naturally understood, then, as indicating Paul's actual motive. Paul did not come among the Thessalonians with a "motive of greed."

θεὸς μάρτυς / (as God is witness)

In the first half of verse 5, when Paul insists that he did not come with flattering words, he calls on the Thessalonians to witness to the truth of his claim. They themselves can remember that Paul did not win their favor through flattery. In the second half of the verse, however, Paul is talking about motive. Since a person's motives are much more difficult to ascertain than their spoken words, Paul does not call on the Thessalonians as his witness, but on God, who would know Paul's heart and his intentions. Paul also calls on God as a witness to his words in Rom 1:9; 2 Cor 1:23; Phil 1:8; and only a few verses later in 1 Thess 2:10. The rhetorical impact of Paul's words is strengthened by calling on God as a witness, because it serves to emphasize the truth of what he is writing.

οὔτε ζητοῦντες ἐξ ἀνθρώπων δόξαν / nor seeking honor from human beings

Having stated that his words and actions were not financially motivated, in the third οὔτε clause Paul addresses rewards of a more social nature. Ζητοῦντες can have a range of meanings, including to seek or look for something, to strive for or desire something, and to request or demand something.[72] Wanamaker argues that to translate ζητοῦντες as "demanding" or "requiring" fits the context of the second half of this verse, in which Paul mentions his right to wield authority.[73] While Wanamaker's perspective has some merit, it is not clear that this more dramatic translation is necessary. "Seeking" seems sufficient to capture the sense of what Paul was or was not looking to receive from the Thessalonians during his ministry.

---

71. Furnish, *1 Thessalonians, 2 Thessalonians*, 55; Wanamaker, *The Epistles to the Thessalonians*, 97.

72. BDAG, 428.

73. Wanamaker, *The Epistles to the Thessalonians*, 98.

Paul writes that he was not seeking δόξαν. This word is often translated as "glory" and applied to God, Christ, transcendent beings, or human beings' participation in the life to come.[74] Since Paul applies the word to himself in this verse, and the immediate context is a discussion of past behavior rather than the eschatological future, another common meaning of δόξα, that of "honor" or "recognition," seems more appropriate.[75] Within an honor-shame society, Paul understood his ministry in a countercultural fashion. While a philosopher or preacher might be expected to seek honor, the one whose life has truly been transformed by the cross will be in constant disrepute, no longer judged by the world's standards.[76] Paul was not looking for honor or trying to bolster his reputation by preaching the gospel to the Thessalonians.

Paul adds an important qualification with the words ἐξ ἀνθρώπων. It was not from *human beings* that Paul sought honor. This qualification reinforces his words in verse 4: Paul did not speak to please people, but to please God. Similarly we may presume that verse 6 implies that Paul did seek δόξα from God as a result of his ministry, even though he did not seek it from human beings. Interestingly, Paul uses δόξα later in this chapter to refer to the Thessalonians: "For what is our hope or joy or crown of boasting before our Lord Jesus at his coming? Is it not you? Yes, you are our glory and joy!" (2:19–20 NRSV). Though Paul did not seek δόξα from the Thessalonians, the Thessalonians are the source of Paul's δόξα before the Lord. Paul expresses a similar idea in 2 Cor 3:1–4, where he describes the Corinthian believers as his metaphorical letter of recommendation.

οὔτε ἀφ' ὑμῶν οὔτε ἀπ' ἄλλων / whether from you or from others

This οὔτε ... οὔτε phrase is part of the third οὔτε clause in 2:5–7. Some commentators have speculated that Paul may have had a particular group of "others" in mind when he says he did not seek honor "from you or from others." This need not be the case, and even if it is we cannot know with certainty what group he had in mind. Nonetheless, the basic meaning of the phrase is clear. Paul did not seek honor from the Thessalonians or from anyone else.

---

74. BDAG, 256–58.
75. Malherbe, *The Letters to the Thessalonians*, 143.
76. See 2 Cor 6:3–10; 11:21–33; Gal 6:14; Phil 3:8.

δυνάμενοι ἐν βάρει εἶναι ὡς Χριστοῦ ἀπόστολοι / (though we could have insisted on our own importance as apostles of Christ)

This phrase forms the third parenthetical phrase in 2:5-7, and it is correlated to Paul's insistence that he did not seek honor from the Thessalonians or anyone else. The first task is to interpret δυνάμενοι, the present participle of δύναμαι, which means to be able or capable of doing something. In relation to the οὔτε clause with which it is correlated, interpreting δυνάμενοι as a concessive circumstantial participle makes the most sense. This leads to the translation "though being able" or, more smoothly in English, "though we could have."

The precise meaning of ἐν βάρει εἶναι in this context is debated. The literal meaning of βάρος is "weight" or "burden," indicating something heavy. Scholars understand Paul's metaphorical use of this phrase in three different ways. Malherbe argues that the meaning is "to make harsh demands," citing the literary context and similar descriptions of philosophers in Paul's era.[77] The key for Malherbe is that ἐν βάρει εἶναι stands in contrast to ἤπιοι in the next phrase; Paul and his coworkers could have made harsh demands, but instead were gentle. However, as argued above, ἤπιοι is not likely the original reading. This makes "harsh demands" a less likely meaning for ἐν βάρει εἶναι.

Another option is that the phrase has a financial connotation.[78] This idea has some merit. Tapping into the "burden" sense of βάρος, there are several texts in which Paul uses a related word to indicate the imposition of a financial burden. In 2 Cor 12:16 Paul employs καταβαρέω in his discussion of why he did not accept financial support from the Corinthian church. Paul indicates that he did not want to be a burden to them. Similarly, in 1 Thess 2:9, a verse that soon follows, Paul uses ἐπιβαρέω to indicate that he worked day and night so that he would not burden the Thessalonians as he preached the gospel to them. The close proximity of this verse to the use of ἐν βάρει εἶναι in 2:7 leads many to conclude that ἐν βάρει εἶναι also has a financial connotation. The association of the phase with the term ἀπόστολοι strengthens this argument. The right of apostles and others who preach the gospel to be financially supported is a common theme in

---

77. Malherbe, *The Letters to the Thessalonians*, 144.

78. Scholars arguing for this meaning include Bruce, *1 and 2 Thessalonians*, 30-31; Gaventa, *First and Second Thessalonians*, 26; Witherington, *1 and 2 Thessalonians*, 80.

the New Testament, a right that Paul claims to voluntarily forgo.[79] This could be another case in which Paul makes this argument.

While the financial connotation has merit, it is ultimately not convincing because it does not relate well to its immediate context as the parenthetical phrase for the third οὔτε clause of 2:5–7. Once again, proper punctuation of 2:5–8 is helpful in determining meaning. The immediate context for ἐν βάρει εἶναι is Paul's insistence that he did not seek honor (δόξα) from the Thessalonians. Beginning the parenthetical phrase with the concessive participle places it in contrast with the δόξα clause. If ἐν βάρει εἶναι is interpreted financially, then the text would read, "nor seeking honor from human beings, whether from you or from others (though we could have imposed a financial burden on you as apostles of Christ)." This does not make very much sense; there is not a strong enough connection between the seeking of honor and the imposing of financial burdens for Paul to place them in such a relationship.

The most convincing possibility is that the phrase refers to the "weight" of a person's importance.[80] This connotation for βάρος is also found in other Greek writings and is similar to the English expression "to throw one's weight around."[81] By using the phrase, Paul was calling attention to the "dignity, authority, or influence" that would naturally be accorded to those considered apostles.[82] While they *could* have insisted on being treated with such dignity and importance, in fact they did not seek honor from the Thessalonians or any other human beings. This meaning fits perfectly within the structure of Paul's grammar and rhetoric in 2:5–7.

Scholars have made much of the use of ἀπόστολοι in this phrase, because this is its earliest appearance in a New Testament document and the only occurrence in 1 Thessalonians. In particular, scholars have debated who, precisely, Paul means to include with this term. Only himself? Himself and the letter's cosenders, Silvanus and Timothy? Everyone who assisted his preaching during his original visit to Thessalonica? If Paul means to include Silvanus, Timothy and/or others in the term, then its

---

79. See Mark 6:7–13; Matt 10:5–15; Luke 10:1–12; 1 Cor 9:1–19; 2 Cor 11:7–9; 12:14–16.

80. Scholars arguing for this meaning include Best, *A Commentary on the First and Second Epistles to the Thessalonians*, 100; Richard, *First and Second Thessalonians*, 82; Wanamaker, *The Epistles to the Thessalonians*, 99.

81. BDAG, 167.

82. Wanamaker, *The Epistles to the Thessalonians*, 99.

meaning here is very general, referring to a variety of emissaries commissioned by God to preach the gospel, as opposed to the more technical definitions of apostles found elsewhere in the New Testament.[83] On the other hand, if Paul's "plural" really only refers to himself, then a more narrow definition can be maintained.[84] Both understandings are possible. When Paul says "we" in 1 Thessalonians, he sometimes seems to truly mean only himself (e.g., 3:1), and so he may have a stricter definition of apostles in mind. However, resolving this matter is not crucial for an understanding of the basic intent of Paul's rhetoric in this passage. As an apostle, Paul (and perhaps those working with him) could have considered himself a "weighty" presence in Thessalonica, but chose to seek honor only from God, not human beings.

ἀλλὰ ἐγενήθημεν νήπιοι ἐν μέσῳ ὑμῶν / but we were infants in your midst

The ἀλλά that begins the next clause signals a major shift in the grammar and rhetoric of the passage. The repetition of ἐγενήθημεν, which appeared

---

83. "Apostle" has a variety of definitions in the New Testament. For the most part the Gospels use the term to refer to the twelve men selected for special leadership by Jesus during his ministry (Mark 3:14; Matt 10:2; Luke 6:13). The book of Acts continues this strict definition, exhibited by the need to replace Judas and maintain a distinct group of twelve known as "the apostles" (Acts 1:15-26). On the other hand, by applying the term to Barnabas in 14:14, Acts also hints that a broader definition may have been in use during the early church. Paul clearly does not restrict the term to Jesus' twelve selected followers, as evidenced by his application of the term to himself (e.g., Rom 1:1; 1 Cor 1:1; Gal 1:1), to Andronicus and Junia (Rom 16:7), and to James, the Lord's brother (Gal 1:19); 1 Cor 9:1 seems to imply that Paul understood apostles to be those who had seen the risen Lord. If Paul means to include the letter's cosenders and his coworkers in Thessalonica when he employs the term in 1 Thess 2:7, the term may have an even broader definition for Paul, at least at this stage of his career. Those who argue for a very general use of the term "apostle" in this verse include Bruce, *1 and 2 Thessalonians*, 31; and Gaventa, *First and Second Thessalonians*, 26. In whatever manner the boundaries were drawn in Paul's mind, to him the lives of true apostles were filled with hardship, weakness, disrepute, humility, material want, etc. (1 Cor 4:9-13; 2 Cor 11:5-33). True apostles also performed signs and wonders among those to whom they preached (2 Cor 12:12).

84. See the argument for ἀπόστολοι as an "epistolary plural" in Malherbe, *The Letters to the Thessalonians*, 144. For general arguments related to Paul's use of the epistolary or authorial plural in 1 Thessalonians, see ibid., 86-89; Furnish, *1 Thessalonians, 2 Thessalonians*, 30-31; Wanamaker, *The Epistles to the Thessalonians*, 126-27.

in the first clause of verse 5, strengthens this shift. Verses 5–7a describe what Paul and his coworkers were *not* like when they came among the Thessalonians, and verse 7b begins the description of what they *were* like. In particular, this brief phrase (ἀλλά ... ὑμῶν) forms a contrast to the entirety of verses 5–7a; the ἀλλά phrase concludes the series of three οὔτε clauses.

In contrast to those who use flattery, those who are motivated by greed, and those who seek honor and deferential treatment, Paul states that he and his coworkers were νήπιοι among the Thessalonians. Νήπιος is a common word in Greek literature, appearing fifteen times in the New Testament, and refers to an infant or very young child.[85] The word can have a negative connotation of immaturity, but it can also be a simple reference to a particular life stage, or have a positive sense of purity and innocence.[86] The significance of Paul's choice of this image, the particular manner in which it serves as a contrast to verses 5–7a, and its impact within Paul's rhetoric in 1 Thessalonians will be discussed at length in the coming chapters.

ὡς ἐὰν τροφὸς θάλπῃ τὰ ἑαυτῆς τέκνα / Like a nurse tenderly caring for her own children

This clause begins a new sentence and also introduces a new image into the text: the nurse. The words ὡς ἐὰν signal a comparison; Paul introduces another metaphor for the reader to ponder, closely on the heels of the infant metaphor. The word τροφός is a *hapax legomenon* in the New Testament, but common enough in Greek literature that its basic meaning is not disputed. While there is some evidence that the word could be used of nursing mothers, by far the most common use was to refer to a woman who breastfed and cared for the child of another.[87] Indeed, this is the meaning each time the word appears in the LXX.[88] In the Greco-Roman world,

---

85. BDAG, 671.

86. For specific references, see my discussion of the text critical matter in §2.2, above.

87. BDAG, 1017.

88. See Gen 35:8; 2 Kgs 11:2; 2 Chr 22:11; and Isa 49:23. In all four of these cases τροφός indicates a woman who cares for the child of another. Also in each case τροφός translates the *hiphil* substantive participle of ינק. The root means "to suck," and the *hiphil* substantive participle indicates a nurse. See BDB, 413.

sometimes the τροφός was a wet nurse employed only during infancy, and sometimes she was a slave who had an ongoing role in raising the children she had nursed into adulthood. As with the infant metaphor, the social role of the τροφός and the rhetorical impact and meaning of Paul's choice of this image will be discussed in detail later in this book.

The verb in this clause, θάλπῃ, indicates the particular activity of the nurse that Paul wishes to highlight. The literal meaning of this word is to "make warm." It had developed the figurative meaning to "cherish" or "comfort" or "take care of."[89] The figurative meaning is also employed in Eph 5:29, which urges a husband to care for his wife as he cares for his own body. Attention to the use of the word in the LXX proves enlightening. In Deut 22:6 the word describes the actions of a mother bird with her chicks or eggs in the nest. Presumably both the literal and figurative meanings are in play here, as the mother bird keeps her brood warm, fed, and safe.[90] Similarly, the literal and figurative meanings seem to be mixed in 1 Kgs 1:1–4, where the participial form of the verb refers to the young virgin brought in to tend to David and keep him warm in his old age. The original connotation of warmth is not lost from the word, but it is employed to indicate the tender, affectionate care that one gives to the very young or the very ill. This understanding is consistent with the word's use in other Greek literature as well.[91]

For whom does the nurse in 2:7 so tenderly care? In this case it is τὰ ἑαυτῆς τέκνα, "her own children." The τροφός who usually cares for the children of another is now lovingly tending to her own children, and so is also a mother. There is some debate on this point, however. Some scholars point out that ἑαυτῆς does not always retain its reflexive force in this period of the language's development, but could be used as a simple possessive pronoun.[92] If this were the case in this verse the text would be translated "her children" and could be interpreted to mean "her charges," that is, the children of another woman. Most commentators, however, feel that the reflexive force is retained in this verse, basing their conclusions both on the context of this verse and on parallel constructions elsewhere in Paul's

---

89. BDAG, 442.

90. See also the similar, but in many ways opposite, image in Job 39:14, which employs θάλπω in its description of the ostrich who leaves her eggs on the ground with no one but the earth to warm them, care for them, and protect them from danger.

91. Malherbe, *The Letters to the Thessalonians*, 146.

92. BDF, 147–48.

writings. Malherbe summarizes the arguments well, which include the very similar uses of ἑαυτοῦ in 1 Thess 2:8 and 4:4 and the placement of ἑαυτοῦ in parallel structure with ἴδιον in 1 Cor 7:2.[93] Comparison with its use in 2:8 in particular highlights the reflexive nature of ἑαυτοῦ in 2:7; like a nurse with her own children, so Paul and his coworkers shared their own selves with the Thessalonians. From these and other arguments Malherbe concludes that Paul "intensifies" the tenderness of the image by indicating a woman already known for tenderness in her work, but this time with her own children.[94] It is also interesting to note that τέκνα and ἑαυτοῦ are used together again in verse 11, where Paul continues to employ family metaphors, stating that he was also like a father with his own children.

οὕτως ὁμειρόμενοι ὑμῶν εὐδοκοῦμεν / in the same way, longing for you, we were pleased"

The οὕτως that begins this clause correlates with the ὡς from the previous clause, and thus describes the manner in which Paul was like a nurse to the Thessalonians. What follows is the present participle of ὁμείρομαι, a *hapax legomenon* in the New Testament. The meaning of this rare word is difficult to determine. The meaning suggested by its limited use in extra-biblical Greek literature is "to yearn for" or "to long for."[95] Some scholars, however, object to this meaning here because Paul is describing a time when he was present with the Thessalonians, and so they suggest that a translation such as "having tender affection for" makes more sense than "longing for" in this context.[96] However, evidence for the meaning "long for," while not overwhelming, is strong enough that it ought not be rejected. In addition to the few extra-biblical uses of ὁμείρομαι, the meaning "long for" is confirmed by the following: its appearance in the LXX in Job 3:21 and Ps 62:2 Symmachus; textual variants that substitute ἱμείρομαι, meaning "to long for"; and the evidence of early interpreters, such as the Vulgate's translation as *desidero*.[97] While it is unclear in what way Paul might have longed for the Thessalonians while still present with them, this meaning remains

---

93. Malherbe, *The Letters to the Thessalonians*, 146.
94. Ibid.
95. BDAG, 705.
96. Malherbe, *The Letters to the Thessalonians*, 147; Furnish, *1 Thessalonians, 2 Thessalonians*, 60. See also the NRSV's translation of this verse.
97. Richard, *First and Second Thessalonians*, 83.

the strongest possibility for this verb. A strength of affection such as Paul is claiming to have for the Thessalonians can reasonably be described as "longing" or "yearning" even when he was still present with them. Perhaps Paul meant to imply that he longed for them to know Christ and desired to share in the fellowship of the Spirit with them more deeply.

A wish to share the gospel with them because of this deep longing is precisely what Paul expresses in the remainder of the οὕτως clause. Εὐδοκοῦμεν is best understood as an unaugmented imperfect, expressing the continuing nature of Paul's desire to share both the gospel and himself with the Thessalonians.[98] The word can have a range of connotations, including "pleased" and "determined." It is likely that both of these meanings are present here, captured in Malherbe's translation: "gladly determined."[99] The translation "were pleased" is also appropriate because it emphasizes the voluntary nature of Paul's work among the Thessalonians and ties in well with the image of the nurse, who is no doubt pleased to engage in the care of her own children.

μεταδοῦναι ὑμῖν οὐ μόνον τὸ εὐαγγέλιον τοῦ θεοῦ ἀλλὰ καὶ τὰς ἑαυτῶν ψυχάς / to share with you not only the gospel of God, but also our very selves

What Paul was pleased to do is expressed by the infinitive μεταδοῦναι: to share something with the Thessalonians. The words οὐ μόνον ... ἀλλὰ καὶ indicate that there were two things Paul was pleased to share with them. First, the εὐαγγέλιον τοῦ θεοῦ, a construction that can be understood as a plenary genitive.[100] Aspects of the objective genitive are clear in that Paul preached a message about God to the Thessalonians. This gospel, however, also originated with God, who is ultimately both the subject and object of its proclamation. While the reader might expect the gospel to be the main thing that Paul shared with them, in fact the οὐ μόνον ... ἀλλὰ καὶ structure gives more emphasis to the second thing that Paul indicates he shared: not only the gospel, but also τὰς ἑαυτῶν ψυχάς. The use of the reflexive pronoun here creates a connection to the nurse image in the previous verse.

---

98. Malherbe, *The Letters to the Thessalonians*, 146–47. For description of unaugmented imperfects in the New Testament period, see BDF, 37.

99. Ibid., 146–47.

100. Daniel B. Wallace, *Greek Grammar beyond the Basics* (Grand Rapids: Zondervan, 1996), 119–21.

Like a nurse with her own children, Paul shared his very self with the Thessalonians.

The word ψυχή is multivalent, referring at various times to the "life-principle" that animates animals and humans, the center or "soul" of human inner life that experiences desires and emotions, and the aspect of human life that "transcends the earthly" and receives salvation.[101] Commentators generally see Paul's use of the word in this verse as laden with emotion. Identifying the ψυχή as "the seat of affection and will," Bruce writes that the meaning in this verse goes beyond Paul's willingness to lay down his life for the Thessalonians to a willingness to put himself at the Thessalonians's disposal "without reservation."[102] Wanamaker sees the word tapping into "the inner emotional life of Paul" as he "committed himself totally to the Thessalonians rather than remaining aloof and uninvolved in their struggles to come to terms with the new faith that had been declared to them."[103] Taking note of the context of the verse, Malherbe writes that "Paul's preaching was more than oral communication; it was a giving of himself ... which is the emphatic point of comparison with the nurse."[104] As the nurse or nursing mother, through her milk, shares her very self for the life of the infant, so Paul claims to have given of himself for the life of the Thessalonian community. A translation of "our very selves" captures this sense of a commitment to share the self completely.

διότι ἀγαπητοὶ ἡμῖν ἐγενήθητε / because you had become beloved to us

The use of διότι at the beginning of the final clause of this section indicates that Paul is expressing the reason why he was determined to share his very self with the Thessalonians: they had become beloved to him. Among the wide range of meanings γίνομαι can encompass, Paul's use of the word here emphasizes the transition from one state to another. Previously unknown to him, the Thessalonians had become dear to Paul during his stay with them. This emotion is expressed through the word ἀγαπητός, "one who is dearly loved."[105] This is a fairly common word for Paul to use in expressing or describing love within the Christian community. He uses it elsewhere,

---

101. BDAG, 1098–1100.
102. Bruce, *1 and 2 Thessalonians*, 32.
103. Wanamaker, *The Epistles to the Thessalonians*, 102.
104. Malherbe, *The Letters to the Thessalonians*, 147.
105. BDAG, 7.

usually in the vocative, to express his love for the churches (Rom 12:19; 1 Cor 4:14; 10:14; 15:58; 2 Cor 7:1; 12:19; Phil 2:12; 4:1). Paul also calls individuals "beloved" (Rom 16:5, 8, 9, 12; 1 Cor 4:17; Phlm 1, 16). In two cases in Romans a group of people is beloved to God (Rom 1:7; 11:28). Greed and honor were not Paul's motivation for his ministry among the Thessalonians; his motive was love.

2.5. Summary

Incorporating all the issues of textual criticism, grammar, punctuation, and translation discussed in this chapter results in the following translation of 2:5–8:

> [5] For we never came with flattering words (just as you know), nor with a motive of greed (as God is witness), [6] nor seeking honor from human beings, whether from you or from others [7] (though we could have insisted on our own importance as apostles of Christ), but we were infants in your midst. Like a nurse tenderly caring for her own children, [8] in the same way, longing for you, we were pleased to share with you not only the gospel of God, but also our very selves, because you had become beloved to us.

In 1 Thessalonians Paul sought to encourage and strengthen a young, struggling congregation. His words are designed to praise and uplift, while at the same time exhorting the Thessalonians to view their faith and their community in accordance with their relationship to Christ. In order to serve these goals Paul looks back on his ministry among the Thessalonians in 2:1–12, insisting that his motives were pure and therefore his gospel was trustworthy. By restoring their faith in him and in the gospel that he preached, Paul sought to restore hope to a congregation struggling with social hostility and other concerns such as the unexpected death of some of its members. As rhetorical analysis of 2:13–16 has suggested, part of Paul's strategy to strengthen the congregation was to create an insider-outsider dynamic, urging the Thessalonians to see themselves as aligned with the true gospel of God. Within that strategy Paul defends his own innocence as an infant and pictures his relationship to the Thessalonians as that of a nurse with her own children. These metaphors strengthen the bond between Paul and the church, create an "insider" identity for the Thessalonians, and in this way are intended to strengthen the Thessalonians's faith and hope in Christ.

3
Historical and Social Backgrounds of the Infant and Nurse Metaphors

The previous chapter established the text and context of 1 Thess 2:7, but more background information is needed in order to explore in greater depth the metaphors found in this verse. While the study of written metaphors is primarily a literary endeavor, historical research has a crucial role to play as well. Metaphors do not have meaning in a vacuum, but only within a cultural context in which the speaker and the hearer of the metaphor share a common understanding of the target and source domains. Therefore, in order to understand a metaphor employed outside of one's own culture, one must engage in research related to the metaphor's time and place.

What meanings would have been attached to infant and nurse metaphors in first century Greco-Roman culture, and how might those meanings have been received and understood in the specific context of the Thessalonian congregation? To begin to answer these questions, two types of historical background information will be explored in this chapter: (1) historical and social information relevant to understanding the infant and nurse images themselves; and (2) historical and social information relevant to understanding the community to which the metaphors were addressed. The first section will address historical aspects of infancy, motherhood, and nursing in the first century Greco-Roman world. In the second section, an exploration of the social world of the Thessalonians will include an analysis of their relationships to each other and to Paul, and a discussion of kinship and identity in the ancient Mediterranean world.

3.1. Historical and Social Background of the Metaphor

People living in twenty-first-century America do not have the same understanding of infants, motherhood, and nursing as those living in the first century Mediterranean world. Therefore, to understand what Paul may have meant by the metaphors in 1 Thess 2:7, it is necessary to employ historical and social research related to infants, nursing, and motherhood in the first century. A metaphor's entailments are those aspects of the source domain that the writer or speaker seeks to highlight in relation to the target domain. As men and women in the Roman Empire, what entailments would Paul and the Thessalonians have associated with infants, motherhood, and nursing? Historical research into this question is necessary to understand why Paul employed the metaphors and how the Thessalonians might have received them.

The Roman Empire consisted of various cultures, so practices and experiences surrounding birth, infancy, motherhood, and nursing would not have been uniform in all their details throughout the empire. However, it is possible to paint in broad strokes some aspects of what these experiences would have been like for most people in the Greco-Roman cultures of Paul's day. The dominant pagan culture will be the primary focus of this study, because research has led many scholars to conclude that Jewish life was not significantly distinct from its surrounding cultures in terms of family structures and ideals.[1] That is, aside from religious practices, Jewish families in Rome looked and behaved much like other Roman families, and Jewish families in Egypt like their Egyptian counterparts. The few areas in which Jewish customs may have been distinct from those of their neighbors will be noted.

3.1.1. Infants and Their Mothers in the Roman World

Girls in Greco-Roman cultures usually entered into their first marriage during their teenage years, and with matrimony came the expectation that they would become mothers, since the procreation of legitimate children was seen as the primary purpose of marriage in ancient Mediterranean

---

1. Shaye J. D. Cohen, "Introduction," in *The Jewish Family in Antiquity* (ed. Shaye J. D. Cohen; BJS 289; Atlanta: Scholars Press, 1993), 2; Dale B. Martin, "Slavery and the Ancient Jewish Family," in Cohen, *The Jewish Family in Antiquity*, 113.

cultures.[2] Understanding some details about maternity and infancy will help illumine some possible entailments of the infant and nurse metaphors in 1 Thess 2:7.

3.1.1.1. Childbirth

Giving birth was a dangerous endeavor in the ancient world for both the mother and the infant.[3] Infection was probably one of the primary causes of death during or shortly after labor.[4] In the ancient world most babies were born at home, and men, including doctors, were almost never present during labor and delivery. The laboring woman would have been surrounded by a number of other women offering encouragement and support, including relatives, slaves, and midwives.[5] On rare occasions male doctors were called in to assist with particularly difficult births. But even on occasions that required a doctor, modesty was still a consideration, as can be seen in the writings of second century Greek physician Galen, whose discussion of labor suggested that the doctor offered his advice to the midwife from the next room (*On the Natural Faculties* 3.3).[6]

Many midwives were slaves or freedwomen. Levels of training and expertise varied dramatically; some offered folk traditions while others had extensive education and training in their profession.[7] Soranus, a second century Greek physician who also practiced in Alexandria and Rome, stressed the importance of literacy, respectability, soundness of mind and body, sympathetic nature, and formal medical training in seeking a qualified midwife (Soranus, *Gynecology* 1.3–4). The midwife's role was to guide and support the mother through labor and delivery, as well as to direct the care of the newborn infant after the birth. Immediately after delivery the midwife would set the infant on the floor and inspect

---

2. Carolyn Osiek, Margaret Y. MacDonald, and Janet H. Tulloch, *A Woman's Place: House Churches in Earliest Christianity* (Minneapolis: Fortress, 2006), 20.
3. Historians estimate that each time a woman gave birth there was a 5–8 percent chance of infant death and a 2.5 percent chance of maternal death. See Valerie French, "Birth Control, Childbirth, and Early Childhood," *CAM* 3:1357.
4. Osiek, MacDonald, and Tulloch, *A Woman's Place*, 56.
5. Ibid., 53–54. See Soranus, *Gynecology* 1.67–69, in which he recommends the presence of three women to give physical and emotional support to the laboring woman, one on each side and one behind, with the midwife in front.
6. Osiek, MacDonald, and Tulloch, *A Woman's Place*, 54.
7. Ibid., 55.

it, making some determinations about the viability of the child (Soranus, *Gynecology* 2.10).[8] Immediately following a successful birth, friends of the father would gather to offer him their congratulations and share in a small party, while the women who had been present during labor continued to celebrate with the new mother.[9]

3.1.1.2. Controlling Family Size

Several different contraceptive methods were employed in the ancient world to prevent unwanted pregnancies.[10] Like modern parents, mothers and fathers in the ancient world had a variety of reasons to limit the number of children they had to raise. Poor families may not have been able to afford to raise many children. Wealthier families may have wished to limit the division of their property among many children and worried that money for multiple political careers and dowries would bankrupt them.[11] Some women may simply have wished to limit their number of pregnancies for a variety of personal reasons. When contraceptive methods were not used or failed to be effective, abortion was also practiced.[12] A woman might choose an abortion for the same reasons just noted in relation to contraception. Furthermore, she might have an abortion at the instigation of her father if she was unmarried, or at the instigation of her husband if he suspected that the pregnancy was the result of adultery.[13]

---

8. Beryl Rawson, *Children and Childhood in Roman Italy* (Oxford: Oxford University Press, 2003), 105.

9. Ibid., 106; Osiek, MacDonald, and Tulloch, *A Woman's Place*, 64. For one example of the gathering of the father's friends, see Gellius, *Attic Nights* 12.1.1–5. When the philosopher Favorinus receives news that the wife of one of his disciples has given birth, he says to his companion, "'Let us go,' he said, 'to see the boy and congratulate the father'" (*Attic Nights* 12.1, in Mary R. Lefkowitz and Maureen B. Fant, *Women's Life in Greece and Rome: A Source Book in Translation* [2nd ed.; Baltimore: Johns Hopkins University Press, 1992], 189). Upon arrival at the house Favorinus embraces the father and inquires as to the nature of the labor and the health of the mother and child.

10. See French, "Birth Control, Childbirth, and Early Childhood," *CAM* 3:1356. For Soranus's recommended methods of contraception, see *Gynecology* 1.60–62.

11. Lynn R. Cohick, *Women in the World of the First Christians: Illuminating Ancient Ways of Life* (Grand Rapids: Baker Academic, 2009), 51.

12. Osiek, MacDonald, and Tulloch, *A Woman's Place*, 51. For Soranus's recommendations, see *Gynecology* 1.64–65.

13. Rawson, *Children and Childhood in Roman Italy*, 114.

Women may also have sought abortions of their own volition for these same reasons. In general, evidence shows that abortion was accepted in Roman society, unless a woman obtained one without her husband's knowledge and permission.[14] This would infringe on the rights of the father to make life and death decisions concerning his children. The procedure, however, could be a dangerous one. Methods such as toxic potions or sticks inserted into the uterus carried a great deal of risk to the life and health of the pregnant woman.[15]

Even when contraceptives failed and abortion was not employed, ancient parents still had options if they did not want to, or felt they could not, accept the child into their family: infanticide and exposure were also practiced. Such methods were employed for the same reasons discussed earlier in connection with contraception and abortion, as well as on occasions when a newborn child was deformed or especially sickly. Ancient authors Cicero and Seneca were among those who advised that deformed infants be killed or left to die (Cicero, *Leg.* 3.8.19; Seneca, *Ira* 1.15).[16] These authors argued that allowing a severely deformed infant to live was not in the best interest of the family and society.[17] There is also some evidence that girls were exposed more frequently than boys, based solely on gender.[18] For example, in the year 1 BCE Hilarion wrote a letter to his wife Alis in Egypt instructing her that if she should happen to bear a child while he was gone, she should keep it if it was a boy but expose it if it was a girl (*Oxyrhynchus papyrus* 744, Lefkowitz and Fant). Some recent historians, however, argue that there is not enough evidence to conclude that such a distinction was common or widespread.[19]

Legally, the right to decide whether to kill, expose, or accept an infant into the family lay with the father.[20] However, others had input into the decision. The midwife who delivered the child would examine it and make a recommendation to the parents as to whether or not it should be raised,

---

14. Ibid., 115.
15. French, "Birth Control, Childbirth, and Early Childhood," *CAM* 3:1356.
16. See Osiek, MacDonald, and Tulloch, *A Woman's Place*, 53.
17. Rawson, *Children and Childhood in Roman Italy*, 116.
18. Cohick, *Women in the World of the Earliest Christians*, 40–41.
19. Rawson, *Children and Childhood in Roman Italy*, 117.
20. Mireille Corbier, "Child Exposure and Abandonment," in *Childhood, Class, and Kin in the Roman World* (ed. Suzanne Dixon; London: Routledge, 2001), 58. In the case of a slave mother, this right lay not with the child's father but with the master of the house.

based on its form and health (Soranus, *Gynecology* 2.10). Additionally, though the legal right lay with the father, it is difficult to imagine that, in reality, mothers would not have been deeply involved in this decision as well, exerting an authority of their own.[21] However the decision was made, it had to be within eight to nine days of the infant's birth, before the "social birth" of the child at its naming day.[22]

The abandonment or exposure of unwanted infants seems to have taken place with some frequency, and it was both legal and socially acceptable.[23] Some cities and towns had well-known places, often the trash dump, where infants were left to die or to be picked up by people other than their parents.[24] Most often, those retrieving abandoned infants were either slave traders or individuals looking for slaves. In a much smaller number of cases a child might be retrieved to be raised as a free child in another family.[25] Freeborn children who entered into slavery through abandonment could seek their freedom when they became adults if they had proof of their origins.[26] Such proof was surely difficult to produce in most cases, and often depended on amulets or other small objects that had been attached to the infant when abandoned.[27] Sometimes families kept track of where their exposed infants were taken and sought to reclaim them later, though they might be required to reimburse the foster family for the cost of the child's upbringing to that point.[28] While it was not official Roman law, many Greek cities required repayment of child-rearing costs when an abandoned child raised as a slave reclaimed his or her free status.[29]

Though abortion, infanticide, and exposure were widely employed and accepted in Greco-Roman society, these practices were not without critics. In fact, this is one of the few areas where Jewish family values may have differed from those of their neighbors throughout the empire. Josephus claimed that Jews believed all children who were born should be raised,

---

21. Osiek, MacDonald, and Tulloch, *A Woman's Place*, 52–53.
22. Corbier, "Child Exposure and Abandonment," 57–58.
23. Ibid., 66.
24. Osiek, MacDonald, and Tulloch, *A Woman's Place*, 53; Corbier, "Child Exposure and Abandonment," 62; Rawson, *Children and Childhood in Roman Italy*, 118.
25. Corbier, "Child Exposure and Abandonment," 67.
26. Ibid., 68.
27. Rawson, *Children and Childhood in Roman Italy*, 118.
28. Corbier, "Child Exposure and Abandonment," 69.
29. Rawson, *Children and Childhood in Roman Italy*, 118.

and that abortion was equivalent to infanticide (*Ag. Ap.* 2.202–203). Philo also condemned exposure and infanticide, observing that parents who engaged in them were breaking the laws of nature by murdering their children (*Spec. Laws* 3.112).[30] However, other sources provide occasional evidence that some Jewish families did abort or expose their children. It seems safe to conclude, however, that while individual Jewish families may have participated in abortion, infanticide, and exposure, these practices were not engaged as routinely among Jewish families as they were among their pagan neighbors.[31] As Christianity grew in the first centuries of the Common Era, Christian groups also saw opposition to abortion, infanticide, and exposure as something that set them apart from the larger culture.[32] While Jewish and Christian groups were the most outspoken opponents of such practices in the ancient world, it should not be assumed that no one else was ever troubled by them. For example, first century Roman Stoic philosopher Musonius Rufus taught that every child who was born should be raised and that poverty was not an adequate excuse for neglecting to feed and care for one's offspring (*Frag.* 15).[33]

3.1.1.3. The Infant's Early Life

While specific practices might have varied from culture to culture, in general the safe arrival of a wanted infant was a cause for celebration in the ancient Mediterranean world. As noted above, informal parties to congratulate the parents often occurred on the day of birth. Eight to nine days after birth infants were thought to enter a new stage of life, associated with the opening of their eyes and their ability to focus on people and objects.[34] This was considered a major transition and was marked by a naming day ceremony, in which the infant became a member of the family and of society.[35] Depending on the parents' culture, social status,

---

30. See Adele Reinhartz, "Parents and Children: A Philonic Perspective," in Cohen, *The Jewish Family in Antiquity*, 71.

31. Ross S. Kraemer, "Jewish Mothers and Daughters in the Greco-Roman World," in Cohen, *The Jewish Family in Antiquity*, 108.

32. Osiek, MacDonald, and Tulloch, *A Woman's Place*, 52.

33. See Trevor J. Burke, *Family Matters: A Socio-Historical Study of Kinship Metaphors in 1 Thessalonians* (JSNTSup 247; London: T&T Clark, 2003), 84.

34. Rawson, *Children and Childhood in Roman Italy*, 110.

35. Corbier, "Child Exposure and Abandonment," 57–58.

and wealth, this day might involve a religious ceremony and an extravagant party.[36]

Following birth, the midwife would supervise the care of the newborn for the first few days.[37] Newborn infants were typically swaddled for one to two months in order to keep their eyes safe from their hands and because it was thought to promote a strong and well-formed body (Soranus, *Gynecology* 2.14, 42). Whether the mother would breastfeed the child or employ a wet nurse was a major consideration, and will be discussed in detail in §3.1.2, below. While in many families the mother would have been the primary caregiver of the newborn infant, those who could afford it commonly employed a variety of nurses and other types of caregivers to tend to the infant's daily needs.

3.1.1.4. The Death of Young Children

In comparison to the developed world of the twenty-first century, infancy in the ancient world was a precarious state. While definite statistics cannot be known, historians estimate that 5 percent of babies who survived pregnancy, labor, and delivery died in their first month of life, 30 percent during their first year, and 50 percent by their tenth birthday.[38] Infection and disease were the main culprits, exacerbated by poor hygiene, dietary deficiencies, and limited medical knowledge and care.[39] The reality of sickness and death was such a central aspect of infancy and early childhood in the ancient world that it should be carefully considered in the interpretation of metaphors involving infants and children.

Some historians have argued that such high infant and child mortality rates had a negative effect on the attachment between parents and young children—indeed, that Roman parents were not very concerned with their young offspring, turning them over to other caregivers if they could afford it, until the children proved hearty enough to survive their first few years

---

36. Osiek, MacDonald, and Tulloch, *A Woman's Place*, 63; Rawson, *Children and Childhood in Roman Italy*, 111.
37. Rawson, *Children and Childhood in Roman Italy*, 104.
38. Ibid., 103–104; Osiek, MacDonald, and Tulloch, *A Woman's Place*, 65, 78.
39. Keith R. Bradley, "Wet-Nursing at Rome: A Study in Social Relations," in *The Family in Ancient Rome: New Perspectives* (ed. Beryl Rawson; Ithaca, N.Y.: Cornell University Press, 1986), 219.

of life.[40] If so, this can be understood as a defense mechanism against the grief that multiple infant and child deaths would generate. In support of this theory are several Roman authors who berated parents for lack of concern for their young children,[41] as well as the fact that there was no official Roman mourning for infants under one year of age. Mourning rituals for children became progressively more elaborate as the age of the child increased, until they reached the equivalent of those for an adult at about age ten.[42]

However, there is also anecdotal evidence of deep parental attachment to young children and deep sadness at their loss. While Plutarch's letter to his wife upon the death of their two-year-old daughter urges restraint and decorum in mourning for children, it also reveals the depth of sorrow that could be occasioned by the death of young children. In contrast to the detachment some historians suggest existed between Roman parents and young children, Plutarch writes: "Our affection for children so young has, furthermore, a poignancy all its own: the delight it gives is quite pure and free from all anger and reproach" (*Cons. ux.* 2, De Lacy and Einarson). Urging his wife not to banish memory of their daughter in an attempt to ease the pain of her loss, Plutarch writes these tender words: "But rather, just as she was herself the most delightful thing in the world to embrace, to see, to hear, so too must the thought of her live with us and be our companion, bringing with it joy in greater measure, nay in many times greater measure, than it brings sorrow" (*Cons. ux.* 3, De Lacy and Einarson). While Roman society in general may have frowned upon public mourning for infants and young children, it is clear that at least some parents were deeply distressed by their deaths, not only because those deaths might represent dashed hopes for support in old age and continuance of the family line, but also because of their love for the child who had died.[43]

---

40. Ibid., 216.
41. Ibid. See Plutarch, *Cons. ux.* 6; Tacitus, *Dial.* 28.4–29.2; and Gellius, *Attic Nights* 12.1.10.
42. Osiek, MacDonald, and Tulloch, *A Woman's Place*, 78.
43. Suzanne Dixon, *The Roman Mother* (Norman: University of Oklahoma Press, 1988), 114.

3.1.1.5. The Mother-Young Child Relationship

In many aspects of their relationships with small children, mothers and fathers in the Greco-Roman world were regarded as having similar roles. Parents were responsible for caring for the needs of their infants and young children and for providing for their moral guidance and education, and writers often did not distinguish between mothers and fathers when discussing these duties.[44] It was also recognized that parents who were irresponsible in their duties, whether mother or father, could have a detrimental effect on a child's moral and social development.[45] Another similarity between mothers and fathers, according to several ancient authors, was that love for their children was natural to both of them. Philo, for example, wrote that love between parents and their children was a matter of instinct, and therefore did not need to be included in the law (*Spec. Laws* 2.240). For Philo, parental love was a selfless love, seeking the good of the child without regard to one's own personal interests (*Spec. Laws* 2.236).

Despite these shared roles, some aspects of a mother's relationship to her young child were viewed as distinctive. Some sources associate mothers with indulgence and fathers with severity and discipline. These associations seem to have originated in Greek rather than Roman culture; Roman sources that predate strong Greek influence do not associate mothers as frequently with affection and indulgence, but more often picture them as the primary disciplinarians for young children, responsible for their moral development.[46] Yet even in Roman sources there is evidence of great affection between some mothers and their young children, and the arms or bosom of a mother are described by some Roman authors as a place of comfort to a young child.[47]

Several ancient authors discussed the differences between a mother's love and a father's love. Some saw maternal love as the stronger of the two. Aristotle, for instance, wrote that mothers love their children with a greater affection than fathers because parenthood "costs the mother more trouble" (*Eth. nic.* 8.7.7, Rackham). Mothers, he observed, take great pleasure in loving their children, ask nothing from them in return, and remain

---

44. Rawson, *Children and Childhood in Roman Italy*, 236.
45. Ibid., 221–22. See Tacitus, *Dial.* 29; and Juvenal, *Sat.* 14.
46. Dixon, *The Roman Mother*, 131.
47. Ibid., 130.

content only to see them prosper (*Eth. nic.* 8.8.3). Other authors thought that mothers and fathers loved their children with equal strength, but felt that mothers and fathers expressed their love in different ways. Seneca wrote the following on the difference between maternal and paternal love:

> Do you not see how fathers show their love in one way, and mothers in another? The father orders his children to be aroused from sleep in order that they may start early on their pursuits, even on holidays he does not permit them to be idle, and he draws from them sweat and sometimes tears. But the mother fondles them in her lap, wishes to keep them out of the sun, wishes them never to be unhappy, never to cry, never to toil. (*Prov.* 2.5, Basore)

According to this view, fathers express their love by urging children to improve themselves, while mothers express their love through physical affection and wishes for the child's comfort and happiness.

Plutarch also discussed the love of parents for their children, and a mother's love in particular. Plutarch wrote that one of the signs of a mother's natural love for her child is that, even as she is still in pain and shaken from giving birth to the child, she does not turn away from the infant but turns towards it and loves it (*Mor.* 496D). He also comments on the strength of a nursing mother's love for her infant, remarking that this is why a woman's breasts are up on her chest and do not hang down beneath her belly as in other animals, allowing her to "kiss and embrace and fondle the infant" as she feeds it (*Mor.* 496C, Helmbold). Many historians stress the practical reasons people would have desired to have children in the ancient world, such as continuation of the family line and provision for the parents' proper burial. Plutarch, however, expresses the view that "the end and aim of bearing and rearing of a child is not utility, but affection" (*Mor.* 496C, Helmbold).

3.1.2. Nursing and Wet Nurses in the Roman World

In whatever era or place a baby is born, one of the first parental concerns is to provide for the child's nourishment. In the Roman world, this would have meant either putting the child to the mother's breast or engaging another lactating woman to feed the child. These would usually have been the only two viable options, since it was generally understood that animal milk was not sufficient for a human baby's needs. Wet-nursing was considered a respectable job for a free, poor woman to engage in to make a living, but more often wet nurses were slaves who were instructed by their owners to nurse another infant.[48]

3.1.2.1. The Prevalence of Wet-Nursing

A variety of evidence points to the fact that wet-nursing was a very common practice in Roman society, and even the norm in many circles.[49] Numerous epitaphs have been catalogued in which nurses make dedications to their nurslings or vice versa.[50] Further evidence for its prevalence is found in the writings of Greco-Roman authors who discuss the practice as a common aspect of child rearing. In particular, writers who argue against the practice confirm its prevalence by their perceived need to speak against it.[51] For example, Tacitus's comments on the "Germanic" custom of maternal breastfeeding imply that such was not the normal practice in his own Roman culture (*Germ.* 20).

The use of wet nurses seems to have been particularly prevalent among the upper classes in Rome, who easily could have afforded a nurse or designated a slave for this purpose. However, there is also evidence that wet-nursing was practiced at lower social levels as well. For example, in one epitaph a freedman notes that his wife "nursed her children with her own breasts" (*CIL* VI.19128, Lefkowitz and Fant). One would not expect such a comment if it were the norm for their social class. Even poor free and freed women may sometimes have made arrangements for others to nurse their babies so that they could keep working.[52] Through no choice of their own, the infants of slave mothers were often nursed by another slave. From the wealthiest elite down to the lowest slave, it was not uncommon for infants in the ancient world to be nursed by women other than their mothers.

3.1.2.2. The Opinions of Elite Men

Several elite male writers expressed their opinions regarding maternal breastfeeding and wet-nursing. In general these men advocated for mater-

---

48. Bradley, "Wet-Nursing at Rome," 203.
49. Osiek, MacDonald, and Tulloch, *A Woman's Place*, 65.
50. See the extensive analysis of these epitaphs in Bradley, "Wet-Nursing at Rome."
51. Ibid., 201.
52. Rawson, *Children and Childhood in Roman Italy*, 124.

nal breastfeeding. One reason for doing so was that they observed a relationship between breastfeeding and the strength of affection mothers had for their infants.[53] Plutarch, for example, felt that wet-nursing interfered with mother-child bonding, and wrote that mothers ought to nurse their own children because they would do so with "a livelier affection and greater care" than a wet nurse (*Mor.* 3C, Babbitt). The philosopher and orator Favorinus felt that if a child was handed over to a nurse the nurse-child relationship would become the one filled with spontaneous, natural love, whereas the love the child expressed towards the parents would merely be a matter of etiquette and politeness (Gellius, *Attic Nights* 12.1.23).

Some also saw the pervasiveness of wet-nursing as a sign of the degeneration of society from its former glory days. Particularly in Roman circles some writers looked back on the "good old days" when Roman mothers were more virtuous and more directly involved with the daily care of their children. This idea is clearly expressed by Tacitus, who wrote "In the old days, every child born to a respectable mother was brought up not in the room of a bought nurse but at his mother's knee. It was her particular honour to care for the home and serve her children" (*Dial.* 28, Lefkowitz and Fant). Favorinus chastised women who had abortions and women who engaged wet nurses, accusing them of vanity, because they did not want their beauty to be compromised through pregnancy and breastfeeding, and of laziness, because they were not willing to care for their children and deprived them of their "natural" nourishment (Gellius, *Attic Nights* 12.1.8–9, Rolfe). Favorinus, Quintilian, and Tacitus all worried about the effects on society of placing children in the care of foreign or low-born women, who might corrupt the children through their incompetence, drunkenness, immorality, and poor speech (Gellius, *Attic Nights* 12.1.17–23; Quintilian, *Inst.* 1.1.4–5; Tacitus, *Dial.* 29.1).

From a Jewish perspective Philo expressed sentiments similar to those of the Greek and Roman writers, but with a different spin.[54] He wrote that the first two gifts of nature to a child, birth and breast milk, both come from the mother and the child should not be denied them. Philo called breast milk "the happily timed aliment which flows so gently fostering the tender growth of every creature" (*Virtues* 130, Colson). He also instructed that a mother and a newborn infant should be allowed to remain together.

---

53. Dixon, *The Roman Mother*, 135.
54. See Reinhartz, "Parents and Children: A Philonic Perspective," 69–71.

While many writers thought only of the good of the infant, Philo also considered the well-being of the mother. He wrote that separation from her infant would cause her emotional distress because affection was natural to her, as well as physical discomfort because her breasts would become engorged with milk (*Virtues* 128, Colson).

While these elite men expressed their opinions on maternal breastfeeding, it is clear that their advice was quite frequently ignored. The Roman author Gellius records an interesting story that illustrates this point. Gellius describes a birth in a senatorial family and the discussions of the men who had gathered to celebrate with the new father. Favorinus was present and he and the other men were sitting around discussing the reasons why women should nurse their own babies. In the midst of this discussion the mother of the woman who had just given birth emerged and told the men that her daughter was too weak to breastfeed as a result of the extremely difficult labor and delivery she had just undergone; this grandmother proceeded to make arrangements for engaging a wet nurse on behalf of her daughter (Gellius, *Attic Nights* 12.1.1–5, Rolfe).[55] This story illustrates both the limited influence that the opinions of philosophers like Favorinus had on this matter, as well as the likelihood that women retained control over it, despite the patriarchal structure of Greco-Roman society.

3.1.2.3. Choosing a Wet Nurse

With high rates of maternal mortality, sometimes wet-nursing was the only choice for the infant's survival because the mother was deceased. Free women who survived labor and delivery and who decided to employ a wet nurse rather than nurse their own children would have had a variety of reasons for doing so. As illustrated by Gellius's story above, wet-nursing was sometimes considered in the best interest of mothers who survived labor but were weakened by the ordeal. Additionally, ancient peoples were aware of the contraceptive effects of nursing; mothers who wished to conceive again quickly may have employed a wet nurse for this reason.[56] Lower class parents who could not afford to raise another child sometimes turned children over to foster parents, called *mammai* and *tatae*, and these

---

55. See discussion of this story in Rawson, *Children and Childhood in Roman Italy*, 106–8; Osiek, MacDonald, and Tulloch, *A Woman's Place*, 64–65.

56. Bradley, "Wet-Nursing at Rome," 215.

children would have been nursed by someone in their foster household.[57] Elite Roman women may have engaged wet nurses because they did not wish to restrict their normal activities and may have viewed nursing as an activity that was beneath them.[58] Historian Keith R. Bradley suggests that wet-nursing may have also served a self-protective function for upper class women; the practice would have placed some distance between mother and child, thus protecting the mothers against the "emotional trauma" of the repeated loss of their children due to high infant mortality rates.[59]

Unlike free women, slave mothers would not have been able to choose whether or not to nurse their own infants; this choice would have been the prerogative of their owners. Wet-nursing would have been automatic in cases when a slave mother died or was separated from her infant by sale to another household.[60] Also, slave infants acquired through the retrieval of abandoned babies would need wet nurses. Even if both mother and infant remained alive and in the same household, slave owners often directed that infants be nursed by women other than their mothers for reasons similar to those noted above in connection with free women. Perhaps the mother was too weak or ill from childbirth, or the owner wished the slave to conceive again more quickly.[61] In fact, slave owners may have encouraged their slaves to produce more children as a way to increase their slave holdings. Slave children born into the household were more economical, were expected to have greater loyalty to the household, and could be trained for specific purposes more easily than slaves purchased as adults.[62] Another reason a slave owner might instruct a slave other than the infant's mother to nurse it would be to free the mother to return to her usual work in the household.[63] A household with one slave designated as the wet nurse would continue to run more smoothly than households without a wet nurse. Whatever the reasons, it is clear that slave women themselves had no choice in the matter. Many of them may have wished to nurse their own children, but were not always given the opportunity.[64]

---

57. Dixon, *The Roman Mother*, 146.
58. Bradley, "Wet-Nursing at Rome," 215–16.
59. Ibid., 220.
60. Ibid., 210.
61. Osiek, MacDonald, and Tulloch, *A Woman's Place*, 100.
62. Bradley, "Wet-Nursing at Rome," 211–12.
63. Ibid., 212.
64. Ibid., 213.

In the case of parents free to decide for themselves, the selection of a nurse would have been influenced by several considerations. Soranus, who generally advised that a mother nurse her own infant as long as the mother's milk was of sufficient quality and quantity, urged very careful selection of a nurse in cases in which breastfeeding put too much strain on the mother or if she desired to bear more children (*Gynecology* 2.18). Soranus describes a good nurse as a woman between twenty and forty who has given birth two or three times and is healthy, sober, self-controlled, affectionate, not given to superstitions, and a practitioner of good hygiene (*Gynecology* 2.19–20). Quintilian, concerned for the upbringing of future orators, stressed the importance of the nurse's diction, and that she should be Roman, not a foreigner: "First of all, make sure the nurses speak properly. … These are the first people the child will hear, theirs are the words he will try to copy and pronounce. We naturally retain the most tenaciously what we learned when our minds were fresh" (*Inst.* 1.1.5, Russell).

Though from two or three centuries before the New Testament era, a letter attributed to the female Pythagorean philosopher Myia is notable for its detailed advice on the selection of a wet nurse and the manner in which the nurse ought to care for the infant. The author of the letter urges that the nurse be clean, not tending toward drowsiness or drunkenness, well able to refrain from sleeping with her husband, even-tempered, and moderate in talking and eating. She also indicates that the nurse should be Greek, not a foreigner. The nurse ought to care for the baby in accord with Pythagorean ideals of balance: she should nurse him at the proper times rather than at the baby's whim, show moderation in giving the infant foods other than milk, bathe the infant occasionally rather than continually, and ensure a temperate environment.[65]

Contracts governed wet-nursing arrangements, except when the nurse was a slave caring for an infant born within the same household. Several such contracts have been found in Egypt dating to Roman times (*Oxyrhynchus papyrus* 91; *BGU* 4.1106, 1107). Free nurses could contract for themselves, while slave nurses were subject to arrangements made by their owners. Contracts ranged in length from six months to three years. A common feature of such contracts was that the nurse was to refrain from sexual intercourse for the duration of the contract. This was intended to

---

65. Letter translated in Lefkowitz and Fant, *Women's Life in Greece and Rome*, 187–88.

prevent the nurse from becoming pregnant so that her attention would not be diverted from the infant entrusted to her care.[66] Soranus recommended gradual weaning, beginning around age eighteen months to two years (*Gynecology* 2.46–8), but there is evidence of this occurring at both earlier and later times, depending on culture and individual family practice.[67] After weaning it was a common practice for wealthy families to retain the nurse as a nanny for the child. For this reason nurses were often recognized as important role models and teachers for young children.[68]

3.1.2.4. The Nurse-Nursling Relationship

Despite the reservations of a few elite male authors, the figure of the nurse is generally regarded positively in Greco-Roman literature. Nurses are associated with storytelling and game playing, and are known for comforting, rocking, and singing to small children.[69] Both literary and nonliterary sources give evidence of strong affection between nurses and their charges. Fronto, for example, wrote that nurses often love their charges so much that they wish them to remain little children, lamenting their growth and transition to the outside world (Fronto, *Letter to Antonius Augustus* 1.5).[70]

Epitaphs are one source of information about the nurse-nursling relationship in instances in which a nurse commemorates her charge or vice versa. While such epitaphs are usually quite brief and therefore do not provide many details, they at least show that there was enough affection between some nurses and nurslings that they were moved to take the time and expense necessary to commemorate the other. In some cases nurses commemorate small children who have died. In other cases, adults commemorate their former nurses.[71]

The fact that some young children are commemorated by their nurses rather than by their parents may suggest that it was not uncommon for

---

66. Osiek, MacDonald, and Tulloch, *A Woman's Place*, 100.
67. Rawson, *Children and Childhood in Roman Italy*, 126.
68. Osiek, MacDonald, and Tulloch, *A Woman's Place*, 65.
69. Bradley, "Wet-Nursing at Rome," 221. See also Rawson, *Children and Childhood in Roman Italy*, 126.
70. See Dixon, *The Roman Mother*, 145.
71. See the detailed analysis of nurse inscriptions in chapter 2 of Keith R. Bradley, *Discovering the Roman Family: Studies in Roman Social History* (New York: Oxford University Press, 1991).

very young children to have a closer relationship with their nurses than with their parents. This may have been particularly true among wealthy Roman parents, who seem to have spent more time with their children once they were out of early childhood.[72] A letter of Seneca to a father who had just lost a young child illustrates this point. Seneca advises that the father ought not to be excessive in his grief because such a young child is closer to his nurse than to his father (*Ep.* 99).

In general, Roman society expected nurses and nurslings to feel affection for, and loyalty toward, one another.[73] Wealthy nurslings grown to adulthood often retained a patron-client type relationship with former nurses, granting them favors and burying them in family vaults.[74] Grateful owners of slave nurses who had served the family's children well sometimes granted them freedom and large gifts, such as farm land.[75] All in all, Greco-Roman literature presents an image of the nurse as a woman selflessly devoted to her charges and loyal to the family, who is generously rewarded for her good service. One must keep in mind, however, that such an image may be romanticized and not an accurate reflection of reality. There is evidence of great affection and loyalty in many cases. However, this was certainly not true for every nurse-nursling relationship. Epitaphs leave evidence of affectionate relationships; those that were not affectionate would not have left such evidence for us to find.[76] It is especially important to remember that most nurses were slaves and therefore had no choice about their engagement in wet-nursing. In such cases there were bound to be many positive, many negative, and many neutral relationships between nurses and nurslings.[77] Even free nurses may have felt constrained by poverty, and their feelings towards their nurslings were likely more complex than typically portrayed in literary sources.

For the most part, what we know of nurses comes from the writings of the elite and conveys only their perspective. It was in the best interest of the wealthy to praise the ideal of the dedicated and loyal nurse, since they would have hoped to have such women as part of their own households. How nurses themselves felt about their work and about the families

---

72. Dixon, *The Roman Mother*, 129.
73. Rawson, *Children and Childhood in Roman Italy*, 122–23.
74. Dixon, *The Roman Mother*, 145.
75. Rawson, *Children and Childhood in Roman Italy*, 123.
76. Bradley, "Wet-Nursing at Rome," 221.
77. Ibid.

and children for whom they worked is much more difficult to determine. Sandra R. Joshel uses the differing testimonies of mammies and their nurslings in the antebellum American South as a point of comparison to caution against simple assumptions of the mutuality of the affection between nurses and nurslings in ancient Rome.[78] Joshel presents evidence that some slaveholders were shocked by mammies who left or changed their behavior towards their owners with the advance of the Union army; they had assumed that they and their families had their mammy's complete love, loyalty, and devotion.[79] Some mammies clearly had affection for their charges, but their feelings were more complex than was typically portrayed by their owners. They may have cared for the children, but they also used their position to their advantage, exerting influence in the household to affect matters that concerned them, such as the protection of their own families from sale.[80]

One particularly interesting anecdote is the case of Louisa, a slave on a Georgia plantation liberated by the Union army. When the army occupied the plantation, Louisa continued to tend the white children who had been left in her care, but made no objection when the Union soldiers threatened to burn down her master's home. When questioned, she explained that she did not object to the burning of the house because of all the bad things that had happened there, such as the whipping of slaves nearly to death. As Joshel writes, "Louisa acted responsibly in terms of her charges, but her loyalties and feelings also were grounded in the slave community of which she was a member."[81] Similarly, Joshel argues, the loyalties of Roman nurses would have resided primarily with their own peer group rather than with their masters' or employers' families.[82]

There are significant differences between ancient Rome and the American South—comparisons must be made with extreme caution. However, Joshel's work is a helpful reminder that one ought not to make assumptions about the feelings of slaves based solely on the testimony of their masters. She makes several pertinent observations about Roman wet-nursing practices. First, she points out that wet-nursing as practiced in the

---

78. Sandra R. Joshel, "Nurturing the Master's Child: Slavery and the Roman Child-Nurse," *Signs* 12 (1986): 4–5.
79. Ibid., 12.
80. Ibid., 13.
81. Ibid., 14.
82. Ibid., 19.

Roman Empire entailed a coercive use of women's bodies—either direct compulsion via slavery or indirect compulsion through economic necessity.[83] Additionally, Joshel observes that all the elite men who argued against wet-nursing were concerned only for the well-being of the nursling; none articulated concern for the well-being of the nurse.[84] Joshel writes that for these men "the nurse symbolizes decadence, yet in reality she was a manifestation of imperial power—Rome's dominance over foreigners—and of the master's power over the slave."[85] Undoubtedly, there were many ancient nurses who did share lasting and affectionate relationships with those they nursed. Joshel does not argue that Roman nurses would have been without affection for their charges, but that, due to status difference, their feelings toward elite nurslings "would involve contradiction and ambivalence."[86] Such a view is probably more accurate than the romanticized view of the nurse found in some ancient literature.

In addition to the relationship between nurses and nurslings, there is also evidence of a special relationship that could exist between nonrelated children who were nursed by the same woman. In households large and wealthy enough to designate a slave as the family wet nurse or retain the services of a free nurse for the long term, slave children and free children often shared the same wet nurse.[87] The relationship between a nurse's charges and her own children was recognized through the term *conlacteus*. Such children would have been close in age, and were often companions and playmates in the household, until class distinctions asserted themselves as the children left early childhood.[88]

3.2. Historical and Social Background of the Thessalonian Community

What were the historical and social realities of life in first century Thessalonica that would have influenced Paul's use and the Thessalonians's reception of the infant and nurse metaphors? This section will blend historical and social scientific research to gain a picture of the group dynamics that stand behind Paul's presentation of himself as infant and nurse to the

---

83. Ibid., 5–6.
84. Ibid., 6.
85. Ibid., 7.
86. Ibid., 4.
87. Osiek, MacDonald, and Tulloch, *A Woman's Place*, 76.
88. Dixon, *The Roman Mother*, 128.

Thessalonian congregation. The study of social identity theories and kinship groups in the ancient Mediterranean will help illumine the nature of the Thessalonians's situation and their relationship to Paul. While there will be very little direct discussion of Paul's infant and nurse metaphors in this section, this information will provide a crucial background for the analysis of the metaphors in chapter 5.

3.2.1. Social Identity Theory

Rikard Roitto makes the case that modern cognitive-based sciences can be used in historical research because cognitive disciplines investigate the biologically-based structures of the human mind. Unlike some other kinds of modern psychology, research into how the human brain works can be applied to historical subjects because human biology gives us a common ground with those we study, even if their cultures were significantly different from our own.[89] This reasoning justifies the use of metaphor theory in biblical studies, as introduced in chapter 1, and also the use of cognitive-based theories of social identity.

Social psychologist Henri Tajfel, whose work in the 1960s and 1970s formed the foundation of social identity theory, defined "social identity" as the part of an individual's self-understanding that derives from membership in groups.[90] Tajfel analyzed how human beings form groups, the ways in which individual identity is formed through group membership and integrated with group identity, and how group membership affects individual and group behaviors. Many have built on, expanded, and altered his work in subsequent years. Social identity theory is a broad field with many facets and some competing theories. However, out of this mix emerge a few concepts that are particularly helpful for illuminating aspects of social identity within the Christian group in ancient Thessalonica.

---

89. Rikard Roitto, "Behaving Like a Christ-Believer: A Cognitive Perspective on Identity and Behavior Norms in the Early Christ-Movement," in *Exploring Early Christian Identity* (ed. Bengt Holmberg, WUNT 1/226; Tübingen: Mohr Siebeck, 2008), 94–96.

90. Esler, "'Keeping It in the Family': Culture, Kinship and Identity in 1 Thessalonians and Galatians," in *Families and Family Relations as Represented in Early Judaisms and Early Christianities: Texts and Fictions; papers read at a NOSTER Colloqium in Amsterdam, June 9-11, 1998* (ed. Jan Willem van Henten and Athalya Brenner; Leiden: Deo, 2000), 159.

Richard Jenkins identifies the basic concepts of *similarity* and *difference* as the core of social identity theory. Individual and collective identities are intertwined with each other and each "emerges out of the interplay of similarity and difference."[91] Group identity clearly entails similarity: people have to have something in common, however vague or trivial, before they can be considered a group. But similarity always implies difference—to say that a group's members are similar in a particular way implies that they are different from other people and other groups. As Jenkins writes: "To define the criteria for membership of any set of objects is, at the same time, also to create a boundary, everything beyond which does not belong."[92]

But what defines a group and how are groups formed? One outgrowth of social identity theory is self-categorization theory, which includes the concept that a group exists because group members think of themselves as a group.[93] While an outside observer can identify similarities between individuals and label them as a group, social identity theorists are most interested in groups that exist because people self-identify as members of the group; only with self-identification does group identity begin to form. Group self-categorization involves both the individual's identification with the group and group members' mutual recognition of each other as part of the group.[94] By thinking of themselves as a group, they "constitute that to which they believe they belong," making the group "real."[95] Shared identity is a product of shared cognition, which can only exist when group members think of each other as belonging to the group. Jenkins makes the important observation that collective self-identification with a group can derive from similar attributes and behaviors among a group of people, or vice versa; that is, similar attributes and behaviors can be produced by, and follow from, self-identification with a group.[96]

In daily life, people not only self-identify as members of groups, they also categorize others as members of different groups. The ability to place another individual into a known category gives one a sense of knowing

---

91. Jenkins, *Social Identity* (3rd ed.; London: Routledge, 2008), 37–38.
92. Ibid., 102.
93. Roitto, "Behaving Like a Christ-Believer," 96.
94. Ibid., 101.
95. Jenkins, *Social Identity*, 106.
96. Ibid., 103.

what to expect from that person, however illusory that sense might be.[97] Categorization of others is also crucial to group formation and group identity. A group's identity is formed in part by comparison to other groups, called "out-groups." In order to strengthen group identity, members tend to exaggerate similarity among in-group members and exaggerate differences between the in-group and out-groups.[98] This leads to stereotyping of both in-group and out-group members. Giving uniformly positive evaluation to in-group members and uniformly negative evaluation to out-group members strengthens bonds within a group and promotes group identity. This is why deviants within a group are often treated so harshly; the presence of a deviant threatens the group members' sense of in-group similarity and out-group contrast, and therefore the deviant threatens the identity of the group. Correcting or expelling the deviant restores group self-esteem by preserving the group's distinctiveness in comparison to outsiders.[99] Real or perceived persecution against a group strengthens the group's identity because it increases in-group and out-group stereotypes, creating an "us versus them" attitude that can solidify group members' identification with the group and force them to behave in accordance with that identification.[100]

The desire to strengthen group identity, and to avoid being labeled as a deviant, motivates group members to behave according to group norms.[101] According to social identity theorists, every group has an "in-group prototype," which can be defined as the "shared cognitive representation of the ideal group member."[102] The closer an individual group member adheres to the characteristics of the in-group prototype, the higher his or her status in the group will be. Individual members are dependent on the group for their understanding and evaluation of the world; to adhere to this consensus worldview means, according to the perspective of the group, to know the truth and to be right. Anyone viewed as a "prototypical group member" is seen by the group as manifesting group consensus. As Roitto

---

97. Ibid., 105.
98. Ibid., 112; Roitto, "Behaving Like a Christ-Believer," 105.
99. Roitto, "Behaving Like a Christ-Believer," 106.
100. Esler, "Keeping It in the Family," 160.
101. Roitto, "Behaving Like a Christ-Believer," 107.
102. Ibid., 102.

writes, "prototypicality is therefore the basis of a leader's influence within the group."[103]

Identity and behavior are closely tied together. People live out their daily lives in terms of their various identities and make decisions based on their own identities and the categories in which they place others; therefore identity has "practical consequences."[104] Within a group, behavior is associated with character traits and spiritual states and is therefore linked to identity.[105] Roitto gives a New Testament example of this kind of link. Speaking in tongues was regarded highly in some Pauline communities because that behavior was attributed to having the Spirit, and having the Spirit was one of the characteristics of the in-group prototype in Pauline communities.[106] Therefore, speaking in tongues was one of the behaviors associated with in-group identity, and enacting that behavior could raise one's status within the group.

3.2.2. Social Identity and Kinship in the Ancient Mediterranean World

An individual's identity is formed through interaction with the collective identities of the groups of which he or she is a member. In the ancient Mediterranean world, kinship groups were one of the most important types of collective identity, comprising the most basic categories to which individuals belonged.[107] Strong expectations existed regarding proper attitudes and behaviors towards kin and non-kin. Towards kin one was expected to feel affection, cooperate for the good of the family, and share available resources.[108] Within a family, brothers were understood to have a special relationship that involved love, closeness and support, hierarchy between older and younger, and cooperation for the benefit of the family.[109] In contrast to behavior toward kin, toward outsiders there tended to be an attitude of suspicion and competition, unless the outsiders proved themselves to be friends of the family.[110]

---

103. Ibid., 108.
104. Jenkins, *Social Identity*, 111.
105. Roitto, "Behaving Like a Christ-Believer," 105.
106. Ibid.
107. Esler, "Keeping It in the Family," 151.
108. Ibid.
109. Burke, *Family Matters*, 126.
110. Esler, "Keeping It in the Family," 151.

In the ancient Mediterranean world, an honor-shame society, increased honor for one member of a kinship group increased the honor of the whole family. Similarly, when one member was shamed the whole family was shamed.[111] Increasing one's honor and that of one's family involved challenge and competition because honor, like other resources, was understood as a "limited good." An increase in honor for one person usually meant a decrease for someone else.[112] A crucial point, however, is that challenge and competition were between families, rather than within a kinship group. Indeed, a family was dishonored when challenge and competition, rather than cooperation, occurred within the kinship group. Patricide and fratricide were the greatest sources of dishonor, and were considered sacrilegious.[113]

3.2.3. A Crisis of Identity at Thessalonica

A variety of groups would have comprised the social identity of residents of ancient Thessalonica. Kinship groups would have formed the foundation of identity, and daily interaction with business and other social groups would have been important as well. As part of a group-oriented culture, persons in the ancient Mediterranean could scarcely have imagined themselves apart from the groups to which they belonged. Clues in 1 Thessalonians suggest that church members were experiencing social difficulties as a result of their conversion, leading to strained or even severed ties to groups of which they had been a part. This had occasioned a crisis of identity in the Christian community at Thessalonica.

3.2.3.1. Persecution in Thessalonica: Biblical Evidence

Some scholars have argued that it is anachronistic to speak of persecution against Christians in the first century.[114] Indeed, to speak of widespread, severe persecution in this era would be inappropriate. However, one can speak of struggle and suffering experienced by Christians in the first century as a direct result of their conversion or participation in Christian

---

111. Ibid., 152.
112. Ibid., 154.
113. Ibid., 156.
114. E.g., Birger A. Pearson, "1 Thessalonians 2:13–16: A Deutero-Pauline Interpolation," *HTR* 64 (1971): 79–94.

activities and behaviors. Such persecution was not occasioned by decrees from government authorities or widespread violence, but rather by their daily interactions with friends, neighbors, and business associates. Difficulties and dangers arose from their choice of a way of life outside of the mainstream. Evidence for this kind of persecution in first century Thessalonica is found in the New Testament.

Persecution is mentioned repeatedly in 1 Thessalonians. Indeed, the suffering of the congregation is a major theme of the letter as a whole, especially the first three chapters. In the thanksgiving section of the letter Paul indicates that affliction (θλῖψις) was a reality for the Thessalonians from the earliest moments of their life in Christ, present even as they received the gospel with joy (1:6). In fact, Paul praises the Thessalonians for imitating him and his coworkers precisely because they have accepted suffering and persecution along with the word of God.[115] Indeed, this is what made them an example for all the churches in Macedonia, Achaia, and beyond (1:7–10).

Paul mentions this early opposition to the gospel in Thessalonica again in 2:2. Here the emphasis is less on the Thessalonians's courage to accept the gospel in the midst of opposition than on Paul's bravery to proclaim it. Having recently experienced suffering (προπάσχω) and mistreatment (ὑβρίζω) as a result of his preaching in Philippi, Paul and his coworkers nevertheless had the courage to proclaim the gospel in Thessalonica in the midst of similar opposition (ἀγών). This verse illustrates Paul's conviction that those who proclaim the gospel and those who receive it can anticipate persecution as the normal state of affairs. A Christian cannot expect to avoid suffering, but can expect the Spirit to provide joy and courage in the midst of it. Suffering and opposition do not deter those who proclaim the true gospel, because they speak not to please human beings but to please God (2:4).

Paul links imitation and suffering again in 2:14. This time Paul asserts that the Thessalonians had become imitators of the churches of Judea in their suffering. He speaks not of a generalized suffering that might have a variety of causes, but rather of specific suffering occasioned by opposition and persecution at the hands of their own people because of their faith in Christ. Jesus and the early believers were opposed and driven out by their

---

115. Donfried, *Paul, Thessalonica, and Early Christianity* (Grand Rapids: Eerdmans, 2002), 126.

3. HISTORICAL AND SOCIAL BACKGROUNDS   87

own people; the Thessalonians have experienced the same, yet exhibit the same faith in the midst of their suffering. God's wrath has overtaken those who opposed the church in Judea (2:16), and presumably Paul is implying that the Thessalonians can take comfort in the fact that their own persecutors will face the same fate.

Paul considered the suffering of the Thessalonians severe and was deeply worried about them and about their faith after he left Thessalonica. He wanted to return to them, but sent Timothy since he was unable to go himself (2:18). Timothy's mission was to strengthen (στηρίζω) and encourage (παρακαλέω) them in their faith, so that they would not be disturbed (σαίνω) by the affliction (θλῖψις) they were experiencing. As Robert Jewett observes, Paul was not worried about the Thessalonians's courage in the face of persecution, but about their faith. It seems that the very existence of the persecution was causing the Thessalonians to question the validity of their faith, as though their faith should exempt them from suffering.[116] Paul responds by noting that, far from casting doubt on the validity of their faith, suffering confirms their faith because it is to be expected. Paul reminds them in 3:3–4 that he had told them beforehand that they should expect to be oppressed (θλίβω). Indeed, this suffering is what they had been destined for (εἰς τοῦτο κείμεθα). Paul is encouraged by the good report he receives from Timothy, which comforts him in the distress (ἀνάγκη) and affliction (θλῖψις) that he himself continues to experience as he proclaims the gospel (3:7).

There is also evidence of persecution in Thessalonica elsewhere in the New Testament. While discussing the collection for Jerusalem in 2 Cor 8, Paul mentions the generosity of the Macedonian churches, a region of which Thessalonica was the capital. He writes that their generosity flowed not only out of their deep poverty but also in the midst of "a great ordeal of affliction" (ἐν πολλῇ δοκιμῇ θλίψεως). Paul does not elaborate on the nature of this affliction, but his language implies that the Thessalonian church and other churches in Macedonia were suffering from more than poverty.

The book of Acts also describes the persecution in Thessalonica experienced by Paul and his converts. The extent to which Acts can be relied on for historical information is debated. One ought to avoid both extremes—rejecting Acts entirely and accepting it uncritically—and carefully consider

---

116. Robert Jewett, *The Thessalonian Correspondence: Pauline Rhetoric and Millenarian Piety* (FF; Philadelphia: Fortress, 1986), 94.

its historical details on a case-by-case basis.[117] For this project, details such as whether or not Paul went to a synagogue first or whether the attack on Jason's house happened as described are not of critical importance. What is interesting for our purposes is the nature of the persecution described and the reason given for it. Paul's stay in Thessalonica is described briefly in Acts 17:1–9. After he has preached and debated in the synagogue for a few weeks and gathered new converts, some of the Jews of the city join forces with Gentiles in the marketplace and set the city against Paul, attacking Jason's house and bringing a group of believers before the city authorities. Luke attributes the Jews's actions to jealousy, but the charge that the mob makes against Paul and his associates to the city authorities is especially important. Unable to find Paul and Silas, the mob drags Jason and other believers before the city officials with the following accusation: "These people who have been disturbing the world have come here also, and Jason has welcomed them. And they are all acting contrary to the decrees of Caesar, saying there is another king, called Jesus" (Acts 17:6b–7). The mob accuses Paul and his coworkers and converts of causing a disturbance and acting against the emperor, specifically by proclaiming Jesus to be king. Spreading such a message was viewed as an act of sedition.[118] While one may doubt some details of Acts's presentation of Paul's time in Thessalonica, this accusation is a historically plausible explanation for the trouble that Christians faced in Thessalonica in the first century. According to Acts, Paul leaves town quickly after this incident. But as we know from Paul's letter to the congregation, troubles faced by Christians in Thessalonica did not end with Paul's departure.

3.2.3.2. Persecution in Historical and Social Perspective

The accusation of the mob in Acts 17 gives a historical clue to the kind of persecution Christians might have experienced in the first century. Early Christian ideas and behaviors could be viewed by non-Christians as antisocial, antireligious, and seditious. This clue from Acts is consistent with clues found in 1 Thessalonians, and details about the history of Thessa-

---

117. For a summary of the debate and a description of the "middle ground," see Joseph A. Fitzmyer, *The Acts of the Apostles: A New Translation with Introduction and Commentary* (AB 31; New York: Doubleday, 1998), 124–28.

118. Ibid., 596; Robert W. Wall, "The Acts of the Apostles: Introduction, Commentary, and Reflections," in *NIB* 10:239.

3. HISTORICAL AND SOCIAL BACKGROUNDS

lonica and concepts drawn from social identity theory clarify the picture even further.

Ancient Thessalonica was founded in 316 BCE and became the capital of Macedonia under Roman rule in 146 BCE. The city's support for Roman rulers, which led to exemption from tribute, as well as its location on the Via Egnatia, resulted in significant prosperity. Recognizing that they owed their prosperity to Rome, the citizens of Thessalonica were eager to honor the rulers of Rome and the Roman benefactors of the city.[119] Thessalonica's exceptionally active civic cult was one way to exhibit this honor. The goddess Roma was honored at Thessalonica along with the city's Roman benefactors. A temple to Caesar was built during the reign of Augustus. Coins minted in Thessalonica around 27 BCE honor Julius Caesar as a god, and consequently Augustus was honored as "son of god." Around the same time the head of Augustus replaced the head of Zeus on some Thessalonian coins.[120] The presence of such a strong civic cult in Thessalonica illustrates the way in which political, economic, and religious aspects of life were inextricably mixed in the Greco-Roman world.

Beyond the civic cult, one of the most important cults in Thessalonica at the time of Paul's ministry was the cult of Cabirus. Usually this cult revered multiple figures known collectively as "the Cabiri," but in Thessalonica the cult honored a single figure and had some unique characteristics.[121] In Thessalonica, Cabirus was a mythical savior figure, murdered by his brothers, and expected to return one day to help the poor and working class people of the city.[122] The story of Cabirus had several parallels to the message Paul preached about Jesus in Thessalonica. However, Cabirus, once a popular figure, had been integrated into the official civic cult by Paul's time. According to Jewett, a savior figure "perceived to have returned in behalf of the laborers of the city" but not under the control of the civic cult would have been perceived as subversive by the city's elite.[123]

---

119. Donfried, *Paul, Thessalonica, and Early Christianity*, 35.

120. Ibid., 36–37.

121. For information on the Cabirus cult in Thessalonica, see Bengt Hemberg, *Die Kabiren* (Uppsala: Almquist & Wiksells Boktryckeri, 1950), 205–210; Donfried, *Paul, Thessalonica, and Early Christianity*, 25–31; Jewett, *The Thessalonian Correspondence*, 127–32.

122. Jewett, *The Thessalonian Correspondence*, 128.

123. Ibid., 132.

What would it mean in ancient Thessalonica to "turn to God from idols" as Paul says his converts did in 1:9? Worship of the gods was intertwined with honoring Rome and the emperor, and further intertwined with social and business interaction; to withdraw from pagan rituals would be seen as a political act, one that would lead to social ostracism and possibly economic hardship as well.[124] Early Christians across the empire risked losing family and social contacts, business partners, and even patronage relationships as a result of their conversions.[125] In a city such as Thessalonica that viewed its economic and political prosperity as being tied to Rome, this kind of social persecution may have been even more severe; the Christian message would have been seen as a threat to the status quo, and refusal to participate in pagan rituals would have been regarded as antisocial behavior and therefore dangerous.[126]

While much of the difficulty that the Thessalonians faced probably stemmed from altered interactions with their families, neighbors, and business associates, it appears that the city authorities had also acted against Paul and were exerting pressure on the Thessalonian Christians in the city. According to Acts, once the mob alerts the authorities to the politically subversive nature of the Christian message, Paul and his coworkers have to leave town very quickly. While the Acts narrative does not make it clear to what extent the city authorities may have acted against Paul, Donfried suggests that Paul's references to Satan as obstructer and tempter in 2:18 and 3:5 may refer to the city authorities—that they had banned Paul from the city and were making things difficult for the church members who remained behind.[127] While such a conclusion can only be tentative, it is not difficult to find elements in 1 Thessalonians that the city authorities would have found politically subversive and dangerous to Thessalonica's positive relationship with Rome, for Paul uses politically laden terms in the letter. In common usage παρουσία (2:19; 3:13; 4:15; 5:23) referred to the arrival of Caesar or a king to a city, ἀπάντησις (4:17) referred to a group of citizens going out to meet a visiting dignitary, and

---

124. Esler, "Keeping It in the Family," 164–65.
125. Ben Witherington III, *1 and 2 Thessalonians: A Socio-Rhetorical Commentary* (Grand Rapids: Eerdmans, 2006), 42.
126. Wayne A. Meeks, "Social Functions of Apocalyptic Language in Pauline Christianity," in *Apocalypticism in the Mediterranean World and the Near East* (ed. David Hellholm; Tübingen: Mohr, 1983), 691.
127. Donfried, *Paul, Thessalonica, and Early Christianity*, 39.

κύριος (used twenty-two times in 1 Thessalonians) was a term applied to the Roman emperor.[128] Even more significant is Paul's attack on Rome's ability to provide true peace and security (εἰρήνη καὶ ἀσφάλεια) in 5:3. While commentators most often link this verse to Jer 6:14 and Ezek 13:10, it cannot be overlooked that these two terms appeared as a slogan in Paul's time in celebration of the *Pax Romana*.[129] A statement that those who put their trust in the peace and security of the empire will encounter "sudden destruction" (αἰφνίδιος ... ὄλεθρος) would not have been received well by Thessalonian authorities.

Scholars disagree about the severity of the persecution in Thessalonica. Donfried suggests that "those who have died" (κοιμωμένων) in 4:13 refers to church members who died as a result of persecution, and thus to martyrdoms.[130] Schlueter, on the other hand, finds violent persecution unlikely, but suggests that the Thessalonians would have suffered from "public insults, social ostracism and other kinds of non-violent opposition."[131] Either way, it is reasonable to conclude that life was not easy for the Thessalonian Christians. Whatever its severity, the suffering of the Thessalonian congregation would have been rendered all the more difficult because it was at the hands of their "own people" (τῶν ἰδίων συμφυλετῶν; 2:14). This was not an outside threat but a threat from within the very social, political, and economic networks in which they moved on a daily basis. Persecution at the hands of family, friends, and associates was a threat not only to their economic stability and political status, but also to their very identity.

3.2.4. Paul's Strategies for Addressing the Crisis

Prior to conversion, the Thessalonian church members would have been part of a variety of social, business, and kinship in-groups, and their individual identities would have derived largely from these collective identities. With such ties severed, or drastically altered at the very least, upon

---

128. Ibid., 34.

129. Abraham J. Malherbe, *The Letters to the Thessalonians: A New Translation with Introduction and Commentary* (AB 32B; New York: Doubleday, 2000), 292; Donfried, *Paul, Thessalonica, and Early Christianity*, 34.

130. Donfried, *Paul, Thessalonica, and Early Christianity*, 41–43.

131. Carol J. Schlueter, *Filling up the Measure: Polemical Hyperbole in 1 Thessalonians 2:14–16* (JSNTSup 98; Sheffield: JSOT Press, 1994), 52.

their conversion and withdrawal from pagan worship, the Thessalonian Christians would have experienced isolation and found themselves in need of a strong alternative community to fill the vacuum. Paul employs several strategies in 1 Thessalonians to ground the Thessalonians's identity in the church group, thereby filling the void left by other severed connections. These rhetorical strategies include in-group/out-group differentiation, kinship metaphors, and solidifying his own relationship to the community.

3.2.4.1. In-group/Out-group Differentiation

One way Paul seeks to strengthen the social identity of the Thessalonian church is by creating a strong sense of in-group similarity and out-group contrast.[132] The identification of the in-group begins in the very first verse of the letter, which is addressed to the assembly (ἐκκλησία) of the Thessalonians who are "in" (ἐν) God the Father and the Lord Jesus Christ.[133] The letter is addressed not to individuals but to an assembly, one that is distinct from other groups because of its relation to God and Christ. The fact that this in-group is partially defined by its difference from out-groups is emphasized throughout the letter. In 2:2 Paul writes that his proclamation of the gospel in Thessalonica had taken place in the midst of much opposition (ἐν πολλῷ ἀγῶνι). At the very founding of the congregation Paul claims that those on the outside were against them.

Such an insider-outsider distinction is even clearer in 5:5, where Paul distinguishes between the in-group members, whom he calls "children of light" (υἱοὶ φωτός) and "children of day" (υἱοὶ ἡμέρας), and out-group members, whom he identifies as "of the night" (νυκτός) and "of the darkness" (σκότους). Paul uses negative stereotyping of out-groups, whom he refers to in 4:12 simply as "those outside" (τοὺς ἔξω), as a rhetorical device to strengthen in-group identity in the Thessalonian congregation. This in-group identity is further strengthened by Paul's repeated reference to the persecution the Thessalonians are enduring. As social identity theorists observe, oppression, real or perceived, serves to strengthen group members' identity by creating an "us versus them" dynamic.[134] Therefore,

---

132. Wayne A. Meeks, *The First Urban Christians: The Social World of the Apostle Paul* (2nd ed.; New Haven: Yale University Press, 2003), 94–96.
133. Esler, "Keeping It in the Family," 162.
134. Ibid., 164. See also Meeks, *The First Urban Christians*, 96.

persecution at the hands of their former associates would have served to strengthen the Thessalonians's new identity within the Christian group.

3.2.4.2. Paul's Use of Kinship Metaphors

Considering the strength of kinship groups in ancient Mediterranean society and their key role in identity formation, it is not surprising that when Paul wants to strengthen the identity of a congregation and solidify the bonds between members, he pictures the local congregation as a kinship group.[135] Paul uses fictive kinship language in all of his letters, but this rhetorical strategy is especially prominent in 1 Thessalonians. For example, Paul employs the term ἀδελφοί to address his hearers fourteen times in the letter, more than he does in Romans, 2 Corinthians, Galatians, Philippians, or Philemon. Only in 1 Corinthians does Paul employ the term more frequently (twenty-two times), but, given the length of 1 Corinthians, it is employed with greater frequency in 1 Thessalonians.

Kinship language in 1 Thessalonians is not limited to the prominent vocative use of ἀδελφοί. Paul also uses other forms of ἀδελφός to refer to the Thessalonians in 4:6, 5:26, and 5:27. In addition, Paul uses the term to refer to Christians outside of Thessalonica (4:10), and he identifies Timothy as a brother in 3:2. As in his other letters, Paul uses family language to refer to God as father and Jesus as God's son. What is especially unique in 1 Thessalonians is the range of family metaphors Paul employs in chapter 2, in which he refers to himself and his coworkers as infants, nurse/mother, father, and orphans. Overall, kinship language permeates the letter.

It is important to remember that when Paul uses fictive kinship language he is employing metaphors. As cognitive-based disciplines, metaphor theory and social identity theory fit well together and overlap in many ways. Social identity involves the ways that groups influence our understanding of who we are. Metaphors are often integral to this process. Metaphorical language governs many aspects of our individual and group self-understanding, and Paul's use of fictive kinship language is a perfect example of the interaction of metaphor and identity.

As noted in chapter 1, metaphors carry cognitive content and are central to the way that human beings process information about the world around them. When Paul writes of the Thessalonian community as a

---

135. See Meeks, *The First Urban Christians*, 86–88.

family, he is not simply employing creative language, but is providing the Thessalonians with a way to think about themselves and each other, and implying a set of behaviors that follows logically from that perspective. When Paul addresses the Thessalonians as ἀδελφοί, he alters their understanding of each other through the interaction of the entailments of the source domain (brotherhood) with the target domain (the Thessalonian community). The ways in which community members are like siblings are highlighted by the metaphor, and the ways in which they are not like siblings are hidden by the metaphor. If the Thessalonians allow the metaphor to structure their thinking, then their attitudes and behaviors towards each other would be governed by kinship norms.

First of all, given the strong linkage between kinship and identity in the Greco-Roman world, Paul's use of ἀδελφοί and other kinship metaphors would provide a sense of group identity for the church, one that would distinguish them from outsiders.[136] In differentiating the community from out-groups, Paul seeks to ground their identity in Christ and remind them of who they are as a people called by God and living in the Holy Spirit.[137] To a community suffering from social ostracism and severed relationships, such language would have provided a new foundation of belonging. As Malherbe writes, "Disenfranchised by the larger society, the language of kinship is used to make them feel secure in a new fellowship."[138] However, though Paul's language is meant to comfort and encourage, it must be kept in mind that he does not seek to eliminate the Thessalonians's suffering. Indeed, as Wayne Meeks points out, Paul presents suffering itself as an identity marker for the Thessalonians. Living the way of the cross inevitably manifests itself in suffering, and this is one of the things that separate Christians from outsiders, thus strengthening solidarity within the familial in-group.[139] Meeks also describes the role of apocalyptic language in creating this in-group/out-group distinction. Apocalyptic language, which is found throughout 1 Thessalonians, emphasizes boundaries and creates an us/them dualism, thus strengthening the Thessalonians's identity within the Christian group.[140]

---

136. Campbell, *Paul and the Creation of Christian Identity* (LNTS 322; London: T&T Clark, 2006), 153.

137. Esler, "Keeping It in the Family," 171.

138. Malherbe, *The Letters to the Thessalonians*, 85.

139. Meeks, "Social Functions of Apocalyptic Language," 692.

140. Ibid., 700.

As an extension of such identity formation, the kinship metaphors bring all the expectations for attitudes and behaviors towards kin in the ancient Mediterranean world to bear on the Thessalonians's interactions with each other. As noted above, expectations for kin relationships involved affection, cooperation, and sharing of resources. If kinship metaphors filter the Thessalonians's view of one another, then these values will dominate their interactions. For example, in 4:6 Paul writes that no one should "trespass against or defraud his brother [or sister]." Such a statement indicates the expectation that if the Thessalonians think of each other as siblings they will not engage in challenge and competition with each other, for such behaviors are not appropriate within a family. In 4:9 Paul uses the term φιλαδελφία, a word found only five times in the New Testament. Sibling love is to characterize the Thessalonian church community. What should this look like in action? Paul gives a description in 4:11–12: "aspire to live peaceably and mind your own affairs and work with your hands, just as we instructed you, so that you conduct yourself properly towards outsiders and do not have need of anything." According to Esler, these verses provide an "image of a respectable non-elite family in a world of limited good, which lives quietly, engages in hard manual labor, presents a united and harmonious front to the outside world and looks after its own."[141] These family norms are what Paul seeks to instill in the Thessalonian community through the use of kinship metaphors.

3.2.4.3. Paul's Relationship with the Thessalonian Church

In addition to strengthening the Thessalonians's identity by fortifying their relationships to each other through kinship metaphors, Paul also seeks to strengthen their identity by reinforcing his own relationship with the Thessalonian church. Overall, 1 Thessalonians paints a picture of a close and warm relationship between Paul and this congregation. Paul continually affirms his affection for the congregation and the ways in which he gave himself to them, and, as Bruce points out, according to 2 Cor 8:5 these feelings were reciprocated.[142] However, reality may not have been as perfect as the letter portrays. As Donfried notes, it is logical to presume that some in the congregation may have been angry at Paul for stirring up

---

141. Esler, "Keeping It in the Family," 172.
142. F. F. Bruce, *1 and 2 Thessalonians* (WBC; Waco, Tex.: Word, 1982), 32.

trouble and then leaving them to deal with the consequences.[143] Such a reaction would explain why Paul felt the need to express his deep love for the congregation so frequently in 1 Thessalonians.

Whether or not members of the Thessalonian congregation were angry with Paul or doubting his love for them, Paul's expressions of love and statements defending his own conduct serve as a rhetorical device to strengthen the Thessalonians's faith because, for Paul, "the apostle and the gospel he preaches are one."[144] Paul viewed his character and the message he preached as thoroughly integrated; therefore, strengthening his relationship with the church and defending himself were ways to strengthen the Thessalonians's faith in the gospel. Put in social identity terms, Paul presented himself as the prototypical group member in order to "give credibility to his message."[145]

Throughout the letter, and especially in 2:1–12, Paul presents himself as the in-group prototype, behaving according to the norms of the Christian group. The thanksgiving in chapter 1 sets up what will follow in the letter, including Paul's emphasis on the integrity of his original preaching in Thessalonica. In 1:4–7 Paul states that the Thessalonians are clearly chosen by God, because the gospel that Paul and his coworkers preached did not come to them in word only, but with power and the Holy Spirit and conviction. This is connected in Paul's mind to "what kind of persons we became among you" (1:5). The integrity of the gospel message is linked in these opening verses of the letter to the integrity of those who preached it. Paul also introduces the theme of imitation in the thanksgiving section (1:6). Because the shape of Paul's life and his work as an apostle are tied so closely to the gospel, one of the primary ways the Thessalonians can ground their identity in the gospel is by imitating Paul. As Malherbe writes, Paul's repeated use of οἴδατε in the first two chapters of the letter serves to remind the congregation of "the qualities that make Paul trustworthy and worthy of imitation."[146] These themes become even clearer in 2:1–12, where Paul presents himself and his coworkers as the epitome of integrity, never stooping to trickery or greed, always being open and giving of themselves, and laboring hard to proclaim the gospel without laying a

---

143. Donfried, *Paul, Thessalonica, and Early Christianity*, 44.
144. Frank J. Matera, *New Testament Theology: Exploring Diversity and Unity* (Louisville: Westminster John Knox, 2007), 153–54.
145. Roitto, "Behaving Like a Christ-Believer," 108.
146. Malherbe, *The Letters to the Thessalonians*, 84.

burden on anyone. These verses portray Paul as the embodiment of the in-group prototype, and as such, Paul's life manifests group consensus, which increases his influence and authority within the group.[147] Therefore, the example of Paul's life strengthens the Thessalonians's grounding in the gospel message.

In addition to presenting himself as the in-group prototype, Paul also attempts to strengthen his relationship to the Thessalonian congregation through the use of highly emotional language that seeks to affirm and increase the warmth of feeling between Paul and the Thessalonians. In 2:17 Paul writes about his distress at being separated from the Thessalonians and describes himself and his coworkers as having "been made orphans" without them. He adds, "all the more, with great desire, we were eager to see your face." Following closely on this, Paul declares that the Thessalonians are their joy, their crown of boasting, and their glory (2:19–20). Chapter 3 also exhibits highly emotional language, in which Paul claims that Timothy's favorable report shows that their deep affection for the Thessalonians is reciprocated in the Thessalonians's affection for Paul and his coworkers (3:6). They all long to see each other. All this good feeling evokes in Paul an overflow of thanksgiving to God for them (3:9) and a deep desire for reunion (3:10–11). Paul's wish is that their love for each other "increase and abound" in the same way as his own love for them increases and abounds (3:12). While Paul expresses care and love for his churches in other letters, nowhere else does Paul's language overflow with such warmth and longing. This moving language serves to strengthen Paul's relationship with the Thessalonians, and if their connection to him is strong, their steadfastness to the gospel he preached to them will be as well—even in the midst of suffering.

3.3. Conclusion

Paul addressed the infant and nurse metaphors of 1 Thess 2:7 to a community struggling with persecution and a shaken social identity. Turning from idol worship had strained the ties that the Thessalonians shared with family, business, religious, and other social groups, threatening the foundation of their identity. Since kinship groups were fundamental to identity in the ancient Mediterranean world, Paul turns to kinship metaphors in

---

147. Roitto, "Behaving Like a Christ-Believer," 108.

order to solidify his relationship to the Thessalonians and strengthen their faith and identity in Christ. As kinship metaphors, the images of 1 Thess 2:7 tap into the world of childbirth, infancy, maternal affection, and the nurse-nursling relationship, applying these concepts to Paul's relationship to the Thessalonians. Historical knowledge of the world of infants, mothers, and nurses in the first century sheds light on the entailments of the infant and nurse metaphors. These entailments will be explored further in chapter 5. But first, the background of these metaphors will be illuminated further by an exploration of how other ancient authors used infant, mother, and nurse metaphors in the service of their rhetoric.

4
LITERARY BACKGROUND OF THE INFANT AND NURSE METAPHORS

Having considered the historical and social realities that stand behind Paul's presentation of himself to the Thessalonians as an infant and nurse, it is also important to consider the literary background of Paul's metaphors. In some cases, the passages discussed in this chapter may have directly influenced Paul's shaping of the infant and nurse metaphors. For example, Paul's familiarity with the Hebrew Scriptures was such that certain passages from those writings may have been in Paul's mind as he composed 1 Thess 2:7. In other cases Paul may have been unaware of the existence of these texts, but exploring them can still provide insight into how language such as Paul employs in 1 Thess 2:7 was used and understood in Greco-Roman cultures. With that aim, the following sections will investigate Jewish and Greco-Roman sources that employ images of infancy, nursing, and motherhood in rhetorical and metaphorical ways.

4.1. Infants and Innocence

4.1.1. Innocent of Right and Wrong

One of the most common attributes associated with infants in the ancient world was innocence.[1] An infant does not yet know right from wrong, and therefore cannot be guilty of a crime or give offense. Philo had such a view of infants, employing this idea in his allegorical interpretation of the nakedness of Adam and Eve: "The mind that is clothed neither in vice nor

---

1. Innocence is by no means the only attribute associated with infancy. See, for example, references to the foolishness of infants in Wis 12:24 and 15:14. Innocence is, however, a prominent theme, and the most relevant for interpretation of 1 Thess 2:7.

in virtue, but absolutely stripped of either, is naked, just as the soul of an infant, since it is without part in either good or evil, is bared and stripped of coverings: for these are the soul's clothes, by which it is sheltered and concealed" (*Alleg. Interp.* 2.53, Colson). The innocence of infants is one factor that led Philo to argue against infanticide. To those who argued that infanticide was not murder because of the child's young age, Philo countered that age does not matter. However, if one were to consider age, this would make infanticide even worse than other kinds of murder, because "in the case of adults quarrels and differences supply any number of reasonable pretexts, but with mere babes, who have just passed into the light and the life of human kind, not even a false charge can be brought against such absolute innocence" (*Spec. Laws* 3.119, Colson). Plutarch also viewed infants as innocent by virtue of being unable to comprehend right and wrong. Specifically, urinating on the altar of a god would be a grave offence for an adult, but an animal or infant cannot be held accountable for such an act, "since they are without any regard or understanding for such things" (*Mor.* 1045AB, Cherniss).

4.1.2. War and the Innocents

The innocent nature of infants was often used to heighten the rhetorical effect of literature describing the ravages of war. Many ancient authors viewed the killing of infants as unjust because they were innocent of whatever actions or circumstances had led to the armed conflict. For some, this became a rhetorical strategy to exhibit the depravity of enemies, who would kill *even* infants. Such themes are found repeatedly in biblical and apocryphal literature. For example, the desperate state of Zion following its destruction by the Babylonians is rendered all the more poignant by the description of infants and children dying of starvation: "My eyes are spent with weeping; my stomach churns; my bile is poured out on the ground because of the destruction of my people, because infants and babes faint in the streets of the city. They cry to their mothers, 'Where is bread and wine?' as they faint like the wounded in the streets of the city, as their life is poured out on their mothers' bosom" (Lam 2:11–12). Years later, when the Seleucids have become the enemy, the priest Mattathias begins his revolt with a speech lamenting the condition of Jerusalem, including the fact that "her infants have been killed in her streets, her youths by the sword of the foe" (1 Macc 2:9b). Such injustice against innocents provides powerful motivation to action. This type of rhetoric is directed toward God in

2 Macc 8:4, where Judas Maccabeus leads the faithful in imploring God to "remember also the lawless destruction of the innocent babies and the blasphemies committed against his name."

But it is not only the destruction of Israelite or Judean infants that is described in biblical literature. Revealing a darker side to this kind of rhetoric, a few authors report with satisfaction the killing of their enemies' infants. Such language usually serves to illustrate how complete the victory of Israel and its God was (or will be) over their enemies. Such is the Deuteronomistic perspective on the conquering of the promised land. God's instructions to the Israelites, given through Moses in Deut 20:16–17, are that they "must not let anything that breathes remain alive" in the towns that God is giving them for an inheritance, but "annihilate [חרם] them." Joshua carries out this charge faithfully, as can be seen in Joshua 10, in which the conquering of many cities is described with the repeated refrain, "Joshua … struck it and its king with the edge of the sword; he utterly destroyed [חרם] every person in it; he left no one remaining" (10:28–43). The killing of everything that breathes includes infants, of course, a point that is made explicit when God tells Saul, through Samuel, to "utterly destroy [חרם]" the Amalekites: "do not spare them, but kill both man and woman, child and infant, ox and sheep, camel and donkey" (1 Sam 15:3).[2] Such thorough destruction, even of infants and animals, illustrates the complete victory of the people, their complete possession of the land, and the complete eradication of false worship.[3]

In addition to looking back on the destruction of infants as representative of complete victory over past enemies, some of the prophets also envisioned the future destruction of the infants of Israel's enemies. In this case the killings represent not only victory, but also vengeance—the suffering inflicted on God's people by these nations would be experienced by them in turn. Nahum describes the defeat of Thebes at the hands of the

---

2. Saul does not completely follow this command, sparing the king and the best of the animals, but the command itself and God's displeasure when it is not carried out illustrate the point.

3. The *hiphil* of the root חרם is used in 1 Sam 15:3 as well as the passages from Deuteronomy and Joshua quoted in this paragraph. The term indicates complete extermination of the population and is also used in the context of holy war in Deut 2:34; 3:6; 7:2; and 13:15. Deut 20:18 gives one reason for such utter destruction of enemy populations: "so that they may not teach you to do all the abhorrent things that they do for their gods, and you thus sin against the LORD your God."

Assyrians: despite her strength, "even her infants were dashed in pieces at the head of every street" (3:10b). With the "you also" in verse 11, the prophet proclaims that this fate will now come upon the Assyrians themselves. Nineveh's defeat will be complete, and "all who hear the news about you clap their hands over you. For who has ever escaped your endless cruelty?" (3:19). The Assyrians will taste their own cruelty, typified by the killing of innocent infants.

Isaiah contains a similar theme, directed towards the Babylonians rather than the Assyrians. On the day of the Lord, God's wrath will come upon Babylon and, among other calamities, "their infants will be dashed to pieces before their eyes" (13:16a). The Medes, whom the Lord will use to execute his wrath, "will slaughter the young men; they will have no mercy on the fruit of the womb; their eyes will not pity children" (13:18). Once again, these graphic and violent sentiments arise from the desire for vengeance—God will bring upon the oppressors the very acts they themselves committed. This is clearly expressed in Ps 137:8–9: "O daughter Babylon, you devastator! Happy shall they be who pay you back what you have done to us! Happy shall they be who take your little ones and dash them against the rock!" Such a disturbing sentiment cannot be explained away or condoned, and can only be understood as expressing the feelings of a people who have already witnessed the destruction of their own infants and children at the hands of their enemies.

The innocence of infants in war also finds expression outside of biblical and apocryphal literature, in the writings of both Jewish and Greco-Roman authors. For example, Philo describes the treatment of Jews under Flaccus in Alexandria, stating that "whole families, husbands with their wives, infant children with their parents, were burnt in the heart of the city by these supremely ruthless men who showed no pity for old age or youth, nor the innocent years of childhood" (*Flaccus* 68, Colson). Ancient historian Diodorus Siculus takes similar aim against the forces of Agathocles when he writes that they killed not only men in their prime, but also the old, women, and "infant children borne in arms who had no consciousness whatever of the fate that was bearing down upon them" (*Bib. hist.* 20.72.2, Geer).

Whether the infants of one's own people or those of one's enemies are in view, it is the innocence of babies that renders these images so powerful. Little ones who have had no part in causing conflicts nevertheless suffer as a result of them. These images then become a powerful rhetorical tool, heightening the emotional impact of a passage and coloring the readers' feelings towards the issues and peoples under discussion. For example, the narrative drama of 3 Maccabees is heightened when the reader is told that the Jews, who think they are about to die at the hands of their enemies, included "parents and children, mothers and daughters, and others with babies at their breasts who were drawing their last milk" (5:49). Such danger to infants at the breast makes the miraculous intervention of God even more dramatic. Indeed, when praying for God's intervention, the priest Eleazar calls attention to the presence of infants, proclaiming to God that "the whole throng of infants and their parents entreat you with tears" (6:14). This is a rhetorical move meant to arouse God's compassion, and it has the same effect on the reader.

4.2. Nurses and Nursing Mothers

4.2.1. Nursing Mothers and Suffering

Given dangers in childbirth, dangers from illness, and dangers from war, the suffering or death of infants was common in the ancient world. The suffering of infants and the distress or grief that was experienced by their parents provided ancient authors with a source for metaphors and other rhetorical devices. As noted above, describing the mass death of infants in war was one common rhetorical move; however, authors also played on the more intimate aspects of the relationship between mother/nurse and child, and the suffering that was experienced as a result of separation or death. Dio Chrysostom, for example, uses the attachment between parents and infants, and the distress caused by separation, as a metaphor for human longing for the gods: "For precisely as infant children when torn away from father or mother are filled with terrible longing and desire, and stretch out their hands to their absent parents often in their dreams, so also do men to the gods, rightly loving them for their beneficence and kinship, and being eager in every possible way to be with them and to hold converse with them" (*Dei cogn.* 61, Cohoon).[4]

The book of Lamentations also plays on the emotional impact of language describing the suffering of infants and their mothers' grief. In attempting to convey the extreme distress of those living in Jerusalem after

---

4. Cf. 1 Thess 2:17 and Paul's use of the orphan metaphor to express his eager longing to see the Thessalonians.

its destruction by the Babylonians, the poet personifies Zion as a mother who has had to watch her children die. In Lam 2:18–19 the voice of the poet calls on Mother Zion to cry out to God on behalf of her children. In verses 20–22 she does so, lamenting that her children are lying dead in the streets and that things have been so bad that mothers have even eaten their own children to survive.[5] She ends with the lament, "those whom I bore and reared my enemy has destroyed." The pain of mothers who are unable to feed their children is expressed in 4:3–4. Even jackals offer the breast to their young, but the children of Zion suffer without their mother's milk: "The tongue of the infant sticks to the roof of its mouth for thirst; the children beg for food, but no one gives them anything." Within these words echo both the suffering of innocent infants and the distress of mothers unable to care for their children.

The haunting images of the suffering of infants found in Lamentations and other ancient literature are effective in moving readers because they tap into the innocent nature of infancy, the strong attachment between mother and child, and the distress that results when that attachment is severed. For this reason, images of safety and restoration for infants and small children are metaphors for hope equally as powerful as the images of suffering are for despair. The book of Isaiah plays on this theme. Considering the dangers to infants in the ancient world, words such as those of Isa 11:8 would offer an image of profound hope for the future: "The nursing child shall play over the hole of the asp, and the weaned child shall put its hand on the adder's den." Similarly, in Isa 65:17–25 the voice of God declares that he is about to create new heavens and a new earth, and that the sound of weeping will no longer be heard in Jerusalem. The first reason that weeping will be gone is that "no more shall there be in it an infant that lives but a few days" (65:20a). The distress caused by the suffering of innocent infants will be gone in the glorious future envisioned by the prophet.

4.2.2. Nursing as Life-Giving Provision

But motherhood and nursing are not all sorrow and grief, of course. Ancient authors also employed a variety of images that engage the positive aspects

---

5. See also the even more graphic description in Lam 4:10: "The hands of compassionate women have boiled their own children; they became their food in the destruction of my people." It is hard to imagine more effective language for conveying the utter desperation of a starving and destroyed people.

of the mother-child relationship. This included metaphorical images of breast milk as life and sustenance provided by mother or nurse. For example, in Deuteronomy the image of nursing describes God's provision for the people of Israel in the midst of "a howling wilderness waste" (32:10): God "fed him with produce of the field" and "nursed him with honey from the crags" (32:13). The nursing image in this context implies both the generosity and nurturing nature of God, as well as the total dependence of the people on God.

In Lamentations, Mother Zion was desolate, unable to provide milk for her children and forced to watch them die. In Isa 66:7–13, however, Mother Zion is restored to glory and her children are restored to her. Her milk flows freely, and the prophet urges all who love her to "nurse and be satisfied from her consoling breast; that you may drink deeply with delight from her glorious bosom. ... you shall nurse and be carried on her arm, and dandled on her knees" (66:11–12). The restoration of Jerusalem was certainly celebrated, but its rebuilding was not without hardship and frustration. The prophet urges those who would still mourn over Jerusalem to rejoice instead, and nurse from her overflowing bosom, where they will receive comfort. At the cognitive level, this metaphor is designed to inspire an attitude shift in the returning exiles, and acceptance of the Mother Zion metaphor would have led to an increased sense of community and a renewed commitment to rebuild their beloved city.

Philo called the earth "mother and nurse" and used the image of breastfeeding as a way to describe God's provision of plants for animals to eat:

> For he willed her at once to be both mother and nurse. For, even as in woman and all female kind there well up springs of milk when the time of delivery draws near, that they may furnish necessary drink of a suitable kind to their offspring, even so in like manner did the Creator bestow on earth, the mother of land animals, plants of all sorts, to the end that the new-born might have the benefit of nourishment not foreign but akin to them. (Philo, *Planting* 14–16, Colson)

Similarly, but from a Hellenistic perspective, Plutarch called the goddess Tethys, the spouse of Okeanos (father of all rivers, brooks, and streams), "the kindly nurse and provider for all things" (*Mor.* 364D, Babbitt). These writers personify the earth and its abundance as a nurse or nursing mother providing milk to her children. As Donfried points out, this reference to Tethys and references to the divine women who serve as nurses in the Dionysus mysteries suggest that when Paul uses τροφός in 1 Thess 2:7, "he is using a word that has definite connotations for the citizens of Thessalonica."[6]

When Wisdom is personified as a woman in Hebrew tradition, she is occasionally portrayed as a nurse, providing the milk of knowledge and insight to those who come to her. The version of the autobiographical poem in Sirach 51 discovered at Qumran describes the author's early pursuit of Wisdom in the following way: "When I was still young, before I had gone astray, I searched for her. She came to me in her beauty, and up to the end I kept investigating her. ... My foot tread on a straight path, for since my youth I have known her. I had hardly bent my ear, when I found much teaching. A wet-nurse[7] she became to me, to my teacher I give my honor" (11QPsª XXI 11–15). In this passage, drinking the milk of Wisdom represents how close a relationship the young man had with her and how directly she influenced him. Philo also pictured Wisdom as a nurse and mother, both of the whole world alongside God as Father (*Sobriety* 30–31), and particularly of "all who yearn after imperishable sustenance" (*Worse* 115, Colson).

4.2.3. The Affection and Comfort of Mother and Nurse

In addition to providing nutrition, a mother or nurse also gives affection and comfort to her little ones. This aspect of breastfeeding and motherhood was not lost on ancient writers in search of metaphors for comforting behavior. The Old Testament taps into the comforting aspects of nursing and motherhood to describe God's character. Though the Bible typically describes God in masculine terms, a few authors turn to maternal images to illustrate God's comfort. This theme is especially prominent in Second and Third Isaiah. The voice of God in Isa 46:3–4 says, "Listen to me, O house of Jacob, all the remnant of the house of Israel, who have been borne by me from your birth, carried from the womb; even to your old age I am he, even when you turn gray I will carry you. I have made, and I will bear; I will carry and will save." Second Isaiah presents God, who makes the

---

6. Karl P. Donfried, *Paul, Thessalonica, and Early Christianity* (Grand Rapids: Eerdmans, 2002), 28.

7. The Hebrew is ועלה, "and a nurse." This is the feminine participle of the root עול, which means "to give suck," and is also found in Gen 33:13; 1 Sam 6:7, 10; Ps 78:71; and Isa 40:11.

people, bears them from the womb, and carries them, as mother, midwife, and nurse to the people. As such, God takes care of the people in a way idols cannot; indeed, idols need to be made and carried themselves, rather than vice versa (see 46:1–2).

In addition to God's ability to create and carry the people of Israel, texts in Isaiah also compare God's love for and comfort of the people to that of a mother with her children. To those who feel forgotten by God, the prophet writes, "Can a woman forget her nursing child, or show no compassion for the child of her womb? Even these may forget, yet I will not forget you" (Isa 49:15). As strong as a mother's bond to her child is, God's bond to the people is even stronger. God's comfort is also compared to a mother's in Isa 66:13. As discussed in the previous section, the preceding verses describe Mother Zion as a nurse who provides abundant milk to her children. In verse 13 Mother Zion is identified with God, who says, "As a mother comforts her child, so I will comfort you; you shall be comforted in Jerusalem." In the book of Isaiah, a people rattled by the ravages of war, exile, and starvation are presented with maternal metaphors that tap into primal feelings of comfort, reassurance, and hope.

Another example is found in Hos 11:1–11. While the terms "mother" and "nurse" are not used, the images conjured by this passage call to mind the traditional roles of a mother more than a father. In addition to loving the child Israel (11:1), God taught him to walk, picked him up, and healed his wounds (11:3). God "was to them like those who lift infants to their cheeks" and God "bent down to them and fed them" (11:4). As the one who lifts the infant and bends down to feed him, God is a nursing mother to the people. Though the people have made God angry, the thought of giving them up causes God's heart to "recoil," and God's "compassion grows warm and tender" (11:8). Filled with a mother's love and compassion, God will not destroy the people.

Greco-Roman authors also build metaphors on the comforting presence of a nurse. Plutarch, for instance, was a great proponent of frank talk between friends. The time for a frank reprimand, however, is when one's friend is experiencing good fortune, not when he finds himself sick or in serious trouble. The latter is the time, rather, for gentleness and kind words. To illustrate his point, Plutarch writes, "When children fall down, the nurses do not rush up to them to berate them, but they take them up, wash them, and straighten their clothes, and, after all this is done, they then rebuke them and punish them" (*Mor.* 69C, Babbitt). The nurse's first instinct is to comfort, and only later to reprimand.

Dio Chrysostom also used metaphors of a nurse's care and comfort. Describing a philosopher addressing a king, he wrote, "Then Diogenes told it to him with zest and charm, because he wanted to put him in a good humour, just as nurses, after giving the children a whipping, tell them a story to comfort and please them" (*Regn. 4* 74, Cohoon). Sometimes a philosopher must handle a king like a nurse does her charge. Poets behave similarly: "Those comic poets, you see, being distrustful and timid, flattered the assembled multitude as one flatters a master, tempering their mild snapping with a laugh, just as nurses, whenever it is necessary for their charges to drink something rather unpleasant, themselves smear the cup with honey before they hold it out to the children" (*1 Tars.* 10, Cohoon). The skills of a nurse to soothe an infant or get a child to take medicine are apt metaphors for philosophers and poets who have to handle crowds and kings with care.

4.3. The Leader as Nurse

While many ancient texts employ mother and nurse images for a variety of purposes, two texts are particularly relevant as background for 1 Thess 2:7 because they place the leader of a group in the role of a nurse to the group's members. Whether or not Paul had these specific texts in mind as he wrote 1 Thessalonians, both provide a window into how nursing metaphors were used and understood in the ancient world, and both are intriguing not only in their similarities, but also in their differences from Paul's metaphor in 1 Thess 2:7.

4.3.1. Moses as Nurse to the Israelites

In Num 11 the people are complaining in the wilderness, tired of manna and remembering the good food they used to eat in Egypt. Both Yahweh and Moses become angry at the ungratefulness of the people. Moses then says to God, "Why have you treated your servant so badly? Why have I not found favor in your sight, that you lay the burden of all this people on me? Did I conceive all this people? Did I give birth to them, that you should say to me, 'Carry them in your bosom, as a nurse carries a sucking child,' to the land that you promised on oath to their ancestors?" (Num 11:11–12). Three things are particularly interesting about this passage and will be discussed in turn: (1) the image of Moses in the role of nurse, (2) the implication of God's motherhood, and (3) the negativity with which Moses views the role.

4.3.1.1. Moses as Nurse

Viewing the people as a burden, Moses reminds God that he (Moses) did not conceive or give birth to them and therefore he should not have to carry them in his bosom as a nurse carries a suckling. The word for "nurse" in verse 12 is אֹמֵן. The basic, literal meaning of this *qal*, masculine, substantive participle is "one who nourishes." The feminine form of the substantive refers to nurses elsewhere in the Hebrew Bible.[8] Since the word in Num 11:12 is masculine, some have argued that it should not be translated as "nurse" but rather as "foster-father."[9] But a closer look shows "foster-father" to be an inappropriate translation; everything about the context points to the meaning "nurse." The larger context is a controversy over eating. The people want to be fed. Who will feed them? Is Moses or God responsible for doing so? Focusing on the more specific context, Moses says that he did not conceive (הָרִיתִי) or give birth (יְלִדְתִּיהוּ) to the people. Thus maternal imagery is introduced into this larger feeding context. Because he is not a mother to the people, Moses also insists that he should not be asked to carry the people in his bosom as an אֹמֵן carries a suckling babe (הַיֹּנֵק). The carrying of infants was associated with nurses and nursing mothers (see Isa 46:3; 60:4; 66:12), and the image of a suckling child is also clearly associated with nursing.

Given the feeding imagery, maternal imagery, and the suckling babe, the context of Num 11:12 points entirely to the translation "nurse" or "wet nurse." Why, then, is the participle masculine? Because Moses, as a man, is imagining himself in the role of a breastfeeder. While the gender of the participle is different than in other occurrences of "nurse" in the

---

8. In 2 Sam 4:4, the young Mephibosheth is dropped by his אֹמֶנֶת in her haste to flee after the death of Saul and Jonathan. Since Mephibosheth is five years old at the time, it seems likely that, similar to Greco-Roman culture, nurses such as Mephibosheth's were employed as wet nurses for infants and continued to care for the children as they grew. This practice is further confirmed by Gen 24:59, which states that Rebekah's wet nurse (מֵנִקְתָּהּ) went with her at the time of her marriage. The feminine participle, אֹמֶנֶת, also appears in Ruth 4:16. After Obed is born Naomi takes the child to her bosom and becomes his nurse. While many interpret this symbolically, it is likely that the narrator intends us to understand that Naomi literally nursed Obed. Naomi is more than just an attentive grandmother: the women of the city proclaim, "A son has been born to Naomi" (Ruth 4:17). Naomi takes the child as her own, holding him to her bosom and becoming his nourisher.

9. See the entry for the word in BDB, 52.

Hebrew Bible, the meaning is the same. Various commentators argue this point persuasively.[10] Isaiah 49:23 may be a similar example: "Kings shall be your foster fathers, and their queens your nursing mothers." Where the NRSV translates "foster fathers," the Hebrew contains the plural form of the same masculine participle used for "nurse" in Num 11:12 (אֹמְנַיִךְ). At first glance "foster fathers" seems like a good translation since kings are men. However, since the word is in parallel construction with מֵינִיקֹתַיִךְ ("your nurses" or "your nursing mothers"), it is possible that the word should be understood to mean "nurses" here too, just as it meant "nurse" in Num 11:12. Indeed, the idea of the people of Israel nursing at the breasts of kings is not a foreign concept to the Isaiah tradition: "You shall suck the milk of nations, you shall suck the breasts of kings; and you shall know that I, the LORD, am your Savior and your Redeemer, the Mighty One of Jacob" (Isa 60:16). Isaiah 60:16, Num 11:12, and perhaps Isa 49:23 contain the image of a man breastfeeding an infant as a symbolic representation of care and provision. The terms used are masculine, but the meaning relates to nursing.

4.3.1.2. The Motherhood of God

In addition to the image of Moses, a man, as a nurse, another striking aspect of Num 11:12 is the implication of God's motherhood. With the emphatic "I" (two uses of אָנֹכִי), Moses insists *he* is not the mother and nurse of the people, which implies that God is.[11] God is the true mother of the community, the one who gave birth to them, and therefore God is the one who should carry and nourish them. God is usually imaged in masculine terms in the Hebrew Bible, but occasionally images of giving birth and nursing illustrate God's creation and ongoing care for the people in a way that masculine images could not.

---

10. Timothy R. Ashley, *The Book of Numbers*, (NICOT; Grand Rapids: Eerdmans, 1993), 210; Martin Noth, *Numbers: A Commentary* (trans. James D. Martin; OTL; Philadelphia: Westminster, 1968), 87; Katharine Doob Sakenfeld, *Journeying with God: A Commentary on the Book of Numbers* (Grand Rapids: Eerdmans, 1995), 73.

11. Jacob Milgrom, *Numbers* (The JPS Torah Commentary; Philadelphia: The Jewish Publication Society, 1990), 85; Noth, *Numbers*, 86; Sakenfeld, *Journeying with God*, 72.

4.3.1.3. Moses' negativity

The final relevant point about Num 11:12 is the negativity with which Moses views his potential role as mother and nurse to the people. Moses addresses God angrily, insisting that he did not give birth to the people and should not have to act as nurse to them. As commentator Jacob Milgrom points out, Moses uses the "derisive" term "this people," rather than calling them "my people." When God called the Israelites "this people" in Exod 32:9 and 33:12, Moses reminds God that they are "your people" (Exod 33:13).[12] "My people" implies closeness, while "this people" conveys distance. If Moses were to understand himself as nurse to the people this would place him in an intimate relationship with them—an intimacy Moses rejects at this point in the story. As we shall see in the next section, not all men in the ancient world were loath to see themselves as a nurse to the people in their care.

4.3.2. The Qumran Leader as Nurse

The Hodayot (1QH^a), or Thanksgiving Scroll, is a collection of poetry discovered at Qumran. The Hodayot psalms are similar to biblical psalms in many ways, but distinct in their predestinarian perspective, apocalyptic worldview, and focus on knowledge, mysteries, intelligence, wisdom, and insight. A subset of the Hodayot, known as the Hymns of the Teacher, are also distinct in their use of a first person perspective: the "I" of these psalms offers a highly personal reflection on his position as leader in relation to the rest of the community.[13] Some scholars have hypothesized that these psalms were written by the founding figure of the Qumran community, the historical Teacher of Righteousness. This cannot be known for certain, but what is clear is that the "I" in these psalms presents himself as having a unique leadership role in relation to the rest of the community. As such, according to Carol Newsom, these psalms would have had an important part to play in the formation of identity in the leader and in the community, not only at the time they were written, but in successive generations

---

12. Milgrom, *Numbers*, 85.
13. Esther G. Chazon, "Hymns and Prayers in the Dead Sea Scrolls," in *The Dead Sea Scrolls after Fifty Years: A Comprehensive Assessment* (ed. Peter W. Flint and James C. VanderKam; vol. 1; Leiden: Brill, 1998), 266.

as well.[14] In two of the teacher hymns, the speaker uses the image of a wet nurse: to describe himself in XV 23–25 and to describe God in XVII 36.

4.3.2.1. Reading 1QHª XV 23–25

1QHª XV 9–28 is a Hymn of the Teacher. It begins in the typical fashion of the Hodayot, with the words "I give you thanks, Lord." The author thanks God for strength and protection, for giving him the Holy Spirit, for placing him as a leader in the community, and establishing him in truth. The poem consists of two "refrains" that surround the main body of the psalm.[15] Both refrains contain metaphorical language that describes the relationship of the leader (the "I") to the rest of the community. In the first refrain the poet highlights the protective and supportive nature of his leadership by comparing himself to structures: "You placed me like a

---

14. Carol A. Newsom, *The Self as Symbolic Space: Constructing Identity and Community at Qumran* (STDJ 52; Leiden: Brill, 2004), 287–88. The precise nature of leadership and authority structures in the Qumran community is not clear. Leaders identified in the scrolls include various priests, the *paqid*, the *mebaqqer*, the *maskil*, and the Sons of Zadok. Some of these roles may have overlapped or referred to the same person. For references and analysis see Charlotte Hempel, "Community Structures in the Dead Sea Scrolls: Admission, Organization, Disciplinary Procedures," in *The Dead Sea Scrolls after Fifty Years: A Comprehensive Assessment*, (ed. Peter W. Flint and James C. VanderKam; vol. 2; Leiden: Brill, 1999), 79–84. Newsom, concerned with interpreting the "I" of the Hodayot teacher hymns, argues that the traditional notion of the Teacher of Righteousness as author of these psalms cannot be proven, but that the "I" represents the "leadership myth" of the current generation. Newsom refers to the leader of the community as a single individual and identifies this leader as the *mebaqqer*. See Newsom, *The Self as Symbolic Space*, 294–300. It should be kept in mind, however, that it is by no means clear that a single leader stood at the head of the community. The existence of such a leader cannot be established by analysis of the Damascus Document or the Community Rule. Nevertheless, a single, charismatic leadership voice does emerge in the "I" of the Hodayot. Since my primary objective in this section is not to reconstruct the nature of the historical Qumran community but rather to analyze the portrayal of leadership in the Hodayot through mother and nurse metaphors, I will follow Newsom in referring to the leader of the community in the singular, as the "I" of the teacher hymns. For more on community structures and hierarchy at Qumran, see David J. Chalcraft, "Towards a Weberian Sociology of the Qumran Sects," in *Sectarianism in Early Judaism: Sociological Advances* (ed. David J. Chalcraft; London: Equinox, 2007), 94–103.

15. Bonnie P. Kittel, *The Hymns of Qumran: Translation and Commentary* (Chico, Calif.: Scholars Press, 1981), 128.

4. LITERARY BACKGROUND

sturdy tower, like a high wall, you founded upon rock, my building and everlasting foundations as my base, all my walls are like a tested unshakeable wall" (XV 11b–12). After the main body of the poem, in which the leader reflects on the fate of his wicked enemies and entrusts himself to God's compassion and justice, the second refrain returns to metaphorical language for the leader's relationship to the community. The relevant section, XV 23b–25a, consists of four lines:

> You set me as a father to the sons of kindness
> and as an אומן to the men of portent.
>
> And they opened their mouths like a suckling babe [at the breast of its mother]
> and like a child taking delight in the bosom of its אומן.[16]

The root אמן appears here twice as a masculine substantive participle. This is the same participle found in Num 11:12. As in Num 11:12, some translators render this word as "foster father" and some as "nurse."[17] Here too, as in Num 11:12, a careful reading of the context and structure of the passage suggests that "nurse" is a more appropriate translation, despite the grammatically masculine gender of the participles.

The poetic lines of XV 23b–25a clearly form two couplets, each containing parallelism (see layout above). There are three characters in these lines who are in relationship with the community: the father, the mother and the אומן. Not insignificantly, we will run into this exact grouping of characters again when we turn to an analysis of 1QH^a XVII 29b–36 below. In XV 23b–25a the structure of the poetry links the אומן to the father in

---

16. My translation. Text in brackets indicates reconstructed text of an uncertain nature. Basic textual reading taken from Hartmut Stegemann, Eileen Schuller, and Carol Newsom, *1QHodayota* (DJD 40; Oxford: Clarendon, 2009), 199. The reconstructed reading in brackets is taken from Florentino García Martínez and Eibert J. C. Tigchelaar, *The Dead Sea Scrolls Study Edition* (Leiden: Brill, 1997), 1:178.

17. Those translating "foster father" or "guardian" include Svend Holm-Nielsen, *Hodayot: Psalms from Qumran* (Aarhus: Universitetsforlaget, 1960), 130; Michael O. Wise, Martin G. Abegg Jr., and Edward M. Cook, *The Dead Sea Scrolls: A New Translation*, rev. ed. (San Francisco: HarperSanFrancisco, 2005), 190. Those translating "nurse" or "wet-nurse" include Kittel, *The Hymns of Qumran*, 125; García Martínez and Tigchelaar, *The Dead Sea Scrolls Study Edition*, 1:179. Interestingly, Géza Vermès translates the first occurrence as "foster father" but the second as "nurse": Géza Vermès, *The Complete Dead Sea Scrolls in English* (New York: Allen Lane/Penguin, 1997), 276.

the first set of lines, and to the mother in the second set of lines. Thus we must look further than this simple parallelism to determine if this is a masculine image of a foster father or a feminine image of a wet nurse. In addition to the parallelism within each couplet, the couplets also relate to one another: the second couplet further explicates the relationship introduced in the first. In the first couplet the poet declares himself to be like a parental figure to the men of the community. Then this relationship is further developed in the second couplet by a description of how the community opens its mouth like a suckling babe. This explanation makes most sense if we translate אומן in the first couplet as "wet nurse" rather than as "foster father." In this case line two flows quite nicely into line three. Additionally, the translation "wet nurse" sets up a clearer parallelism in the second couplet than the translation "foster father" does: "suckling babe" is paired with "child," "breast" with "bosom," and "mother" with "wet nurse." We can conclude, then, that "wet nurse" is the best translation in this context, and that the three characters described by the poem are the father, the mother, and the wet nurse. Just as in Num 11:12, the participle is masculine not because the meaning is "foster father" but because the leader of the community, a man, is imagining himself in the role of a wet nurse.

4.3.2.2. The Leader as Wet Nurse

In addition to cognitive metaphor theory, Carol Newsom's work on the Hodayot provides a helpful lens for interpreting the nursing metaphor in 1QH^a XV 23–25. Especially relevant for this study is her treatment of the Hodayot and the effect that the reading of these psalms would have had on the construction of identity in both the leader and the community. As Newsom points out, when scholarly energies focus on whether or not the Teacher of Righteousness wrote these poems, "what tends to get left to one side is how these Hodayot functioned over time, as they were continually read or recited, to shape the ethos of the community and to address the perennial questions of sectarian life."[18] Thus, whatever the circumstances of their original composition, whenever these psalms were read at Qumran the community members would have identified with the "I" of the community hymns, and the leader with the "I" of the teacher hymns. But the teacher hymns also have a role to play in the formation of identity

---

18. Newsom, *The Self as Symbolic Space*, 288.

in the community members, for even though these hymns are addressed by the leader to God, they are intended to be "overheard" by the community.[19] The Hodayot of the leader "serve above all to construct a figure who is a compelling object of loyalty."[20] Thus, "these Hodayot are not simply compositions about a leader, whether historical or contemporary. They are themselves *acts* of leadership, verbal attempts to articulate a community through the self-presentation of the persona of the leader."[21]

Following Newsom's lead in reading 1QH^a XV, what appears at first to be a private conversation between the leader and God becomes a forum for shaping the community's identity and loyalty to the leader. If Newsom is correct that these psalms represent the persona of the current leader of the community in each generation, then each leader of the community would have his identity shaped by these words: "You set me as a father to the sons of kindness" (XV 23). As the community overhears these words, their own identity and understanding of their position in relation to the leader is also shaped. The authority of the leader in the community is solidified by this metaphor, in which the leader is compared to a father, and the community members to his children. As cognitive metaphor theory suggests, this metaphor organizes the thinking of the community about the leader by highlighting the ways the leader is similar to a father—we might think of discipline, the teaching of knowledge, and provision for physical and spiritual needs—and hiding the ways the leader is not like a father.

The authority of the leader is further strengthened by the introduction of the wet nurse metaphor. What changes when the metaphor shifts from father to wet nurse? For one thing, there is greater elaboration on the role into which the community is placed in this metaphor. They are now not only children, but helpless, suckling babies in the arms of a wet nurse. This metaphor invites the community to accept a point of view in which they are entirely dependent on the leader for all their needs. He is the mother or wet nurse, providing the milk to their open and waiting mouths. This metaphor is a highly effective one for conveying an imaginative picture of the Qumran community's understanding of the importance of knowledge and how knowledge is transmitted. The "I" of the teacher hymns understands himself to be the "source of instruction and transmitter of divine revelation. He is the conduit of the elect status God grants to the

---

19. Ibid., 303.
20. Ibid., 345.
21. Ibid., 299 (emphasis original).

community."²² What better image than breastfeeding to capture the idea that the leader is the provider of knowledge and the community members the receivers of knowledge? This is indeed an image with the power to be an "act of leadership," as Newsom describes it.²³ And once this metaphor achieves "truth status" in the community,²⁴ that is, once the community members begin to think of themselves as babies in relation to the leader, it has the power to change not only the thinking of the community members, but also their behavior towards the leader. In short, this metaphor inspires obedience and deference.²⁵

As I have described it, this metaphor creates a certain amount of distance between the leader and the community, by placing the leader firmly in a position of authority over the rest of the community. But that is not all there is to this rich metaphor. At the same time that it creates distance, it also creates intimacy, for one can hardly find a more tender, intimate image than that of a woman breastfeeding an infant. There is no question that the woman is powerful and the infant helpless, the woman the provider and the infant the receiver, yet the bond between woman and infant is strengthened through this exchange. She gives of her very self for the life of the infant. In the same way, the metaphor affirms the strong connection between the leader and the community. He has authority, but his authority is employed to give precious nourishment to his children. The bond between leader and community is strengthened each time this metaphor is read. In addition, the bonds between the community members are also strengthened, for this metaphor makes them into children nursed at the same breast. So, in addition to deference and obedience, the metaphor also inspires loyalty and trust.

A comparison to Num 11:12 is fruitful for further illuminating this passage. Of all the occurrences of אמן in the Hebrew Bible, Num 11:12 is the most similar in context and meaning to the wet nurse metaphor in XV

---

22. Matthew J. Goff, "Reading Wisdom at Qumran: 4QInstruction and the Hodayot," *DSD* 11 (2004): 287.

23. Newsom, *The Self as Symbolic Space*, 299.

24. George Lakoff and Mark Johnson, *Metaphors We Live By* (2d ed.; Chicago: University of Chicago Press, 2003), 139.

25. For sociological analysis of the hierarchical nature of the Qumran community, see Chalcraft, "Towards a Weberian Sociology of the Qumran Sects," 94–103. For the authority of priests in the community see John J. Collins, *Beyond the Qumran Community: The Sectarian Movement of the Dead Sea Scrolls* (Grand Rapids: Eerdmans, 2010), 60–65.

23b–25a. In both passages a leader of a community is pictured as holding the community in his bosom as a wet nurse with her children, in order to provide the community with some form of nourishment. But it is the difference between the two passages that is most intriguing. Moses feels that God's request for him to take this role in relation to the community is too much to ask. He does not wish to be a wet nurse to the community, implying that it is God who is the mother of the community, and therefore the one who ought to carry and nourish them. Despite the disavowal of the role of wet nurse by the great prophet Moses, it is this very role that the "I" of the Hodayot embraces with pride in relation to his community. It is God who has placed him as nurse to the community, and so, obedient to the will of God, he freely nourishes them with knowledge and wisdom. This is not to say that he denied Moses' insight that God was the true nourisher and mother figure of the community, for as I will note in the next section, the Hodayot teacher hymns also place God in the role of the wet nurse.

4.3.2.3. Reading 1QH^a XVII 29b–36

The masculine participle אומן appears also in 1QH^a XVII 36. As stated above, the same three characters from XV 23b–25a (the father, the mother, and the אומן) also make an appearance in 1QH^a XVII.[26] But here, it is God, rather than the leader of the community, who is compared to an אומן. The metaphor in this psalm is strikingly similar to the one in XV 23b–25a. In both cases a child, infant, or creature is being cared for in the bosom (בחיק) of an אומן. Based on the similarity of context, it seems likely that אומן in this psalm should be translated the same way as in XV 23b–25a (that is, as "nurse" rather than "foster father"), and further analysis of the specific context of XVII 36 bears this out.

Rather than boldly reflecting on his place of authority in the community, as the leader did in 1QH^a XV 9–28, the hymn in column XVII is an intensely personal reflection on the hardships that the poet has experienced throughout his life, and on God's compassion and protection that

---

26. The boundaries of this psalm are more difficult to determine than XV 9–28 because of some gaps in the text. Some scholars see XVI 4–XVII 37 as one very long poem (e.g., Newsom), while others think a new psalm starts at the beginning of column XVII (e.g., Wise, Abegg, and Cook). The question is not crucial for this analysis, since the passage with the nursing metaphor comes at the very end of the psalm. I will analyze the use of the participle in the context of column XVII.

have been with him through it all. This compassion and protection have been present from the very beginning of his life: "For you knew me from my father, and from the womb [you consecrated me, and from the belly of] my mother you dealt bountifully with me, and from the breasts of the woman who conceived me I had your compassion, and in the bosom of my wet nurse [אומנתי] was your great [kindness]" (XVII 29b–31a, my translation). The root אמן appears here as the feminine participle because it is not being used metaphorically to refer to a man as in Numbers 11:12 and 1QH^a XV 23b–25a, but to refer to a real woman. This passage contains reference to three real people from the poet's childhood: his father, his mother, and his wet nurse—the same group that appeared metaphorically in XV 23b–25a.

Following this reference to the parental figures of his childhood, the poet reflects for a few verses on how God has provided him with knowledge, the Holy Spirit, forgiveness, and compassion, beginning in his youth and continuing to the present day. And God's provision for him will continue until "old age" (XVII 34). Why is this special provision of God necessary? Because "my father did not know me, and my mother abandoned me to you" (XVII 35a). Abandoned and let down by the very people who should have cared for him in his youth, the poet has become completely dependent on the provision and compassion of God.[27] In fact, God takes on the very roles of those who failed to provide adequately for his physical and spiritual needs: "For you are a father to all the sons of your truth, and you rejoice over them like a woman who has compassion upon her suckling child, and like an אומן you nourish all your creatures in your bosom" (XVII 35b–36, my translation). The first line of this passage is clearly a reference to God as father. The second line compares God to a woman who has compassion on her own suckling child. This is the mother. In the third line we find again the masculine substantive אומן. According to the logic of the poem, the meaning "wet nurse" makes much more sense than "foster father," as God takes on the three roles from the poet's childhood that were introduced in XVII 29b–31a. This conclusion is further strengthened by the action of the אומן in this verse, who takes the creatures into the bosom (חיק) and nourishes or provides for them. Again, the participle is masculine not because the image is a masculine one, but because it is God who

---

27. Cf. Isa 49:15: "Can a woman forget her nursing child, or show no compassion for the child of her womb? Even these may forget, yet I will not forget you."

is imagined in the role of wet nurse, and there can be little doubt that the author thought of God in masculine terms.

4.3.2.4. God as Wet Nurse

1QH^a XV 23b–25a gives a very exalted position to the leader of the community. He is father, mother, and wet nurse to them. The community owes him respect and obedience, and as nurse he is imaged as their sole provider of protection, knowledge, and nourishment. But XVII 29b–36 broadens and deepens the reader's theological perspective. In this passage the reader sees that everything that the leader is and does in XV 23b–25a ultimately describes God and comes from God. While real parents and caregivers can let us down, God is true father, mother, and nurse to the community. As demonstrated above, the wet nurse metaphor in XV 23b–25a creates both a sense of distance and a sense of intimacy between the leader and the community. Likewise, God in this role is utterly distant and utterly intimate at the same time. In the Hodayot, God is typically portrayed as distant from all human beings: as the Holy One compared to the "dust" that is humanity.[28] But here God is also intimate with the community, with the compassion of a mother and the tender care of a nurse. The community owes to God both obedience and loyalty, fear and love. As wet nurse, God is the true source of all knowledge, including the knowledge that the leader provides to the community. God is the one who set the leader apart from his youth, and gives him his place in the community. Even as the community is nourished at the breasts of the leader, all, including the leader himself, are nourished at the breasts of God.

The image of God as wet nurse is a striking one within Hebrew tradition. On rare occasions the Old Testament does portray God with female images, particularly the role of mother: God has labor pains, gives birth, and cares for his children, when they are young, and until old age (see Deut 32:18; Isa 42:14; 46:3–4; and 66:13). Yet the Hebrew Bible is reticent to attribute the role of nursing to God. Two passages imply it but do not directly state it. Isaiah 49:15 presents a comparison rather than a metaphor: "Can a woman forget her nursing child, or show no compassion for the child of her womb? Even these may forget, yet I will not forget you."

---

28. "Dust" is a word used many times in the Hodayot to describe humanity. See, for example, VII 34, XIX 6, and XXIII 5.

This passage declares God's compassion to be greater than the compassion of a nursing mother, but does not image God as a nursing mother. The second passage that implies God's role as nurse is Num 11:12, as discussed above. This passage does not directly present God as a nurse, but it is implied in Moses' insistence that *he* should not have to be nurse to them. What is implicit in these two passages 1QH^a XVII 36 makes explicit.[29] God has the compassion of a mother with her suckling child, and as a wet nurse God nourishes his people in his bosom.

4.3.2.5. Summary

Qumran literature in general and the Hodayot in particular are androcentric documents. Women's perspective is absent, real women are infrequently mentioned in these documents, and female images are also rare—which makes the use of the wet nurse metaphor in 1QH^a XV and XVII all the more striking. While the Hodayot Scroll displays little concern for the lives of real women, the author harnesses the power of a feminine image. Even in the midst of an androcentric context, the metaphor of breastfeeding goes to the deepest levels of human experience and human emotion. It packs a powerful rhetorical punch.

Metaphors shape our thinking and influence our behavior. The wet nurse images in 1QH^a XV and XVII served as an invitation to the Qumran community to view reality in the way that the author did. Specifically, 1QH^a XV placed the community members in the role of infants and invited them to see the leader as their mother and wet nurse, providing them with knowledge and spiritual nourishment. The metaphor would also have emboldened the leader of each generation to exert authority and provide strong leadership for the community. 1QH^a XVII uses the same metaphor to a different effect. This metaphor reminds both leader and community members that God is the ultimate nourisher. The leader speaks to God in this psalm, but the community overhears as the leader declares that God

---

29. This may or may not mean that the author of the Hodayot had these Old Testament passages in mind while composing this hymn. Julie Hughes, in her study of scriptural allusions in the Hodayot, argues that Isa 40–66 is the main scriptural influence on the poem found in column XVII. For XVII 36 she draws particular attention to Isa 46:3–4 and 49:15, noting comparison to Num 11:12 in a footnote. See Julie A. Hughes, *Scriptural Allusions and Exegesis in the Hodayot* (STDJ 59; Leiden: Brill, 2006), 167.

is father, mother, and wet nurse to all the "sons of truth." These nursing images inspire confidence, trust, loyalty, and obedience toward the leader of the community and toward God. The community members are nourished at the breasts of the leader, all are nourished at the breasts of God, and both the community members and the leader are exhorted to behave in accordance with the view of reality these metaphors inspire.

4.4. Conclusion

Metaphors of infants, nursing mothers, and wet nurses were used to express a wide range of emotions and experiences in ancient literature. These metaphors illustrated the depths of suffering, the heights of hope, and the intimacy of close relationship. While, for the most part, these passages did not directly influence Paul's construction of the infant and nurse metaphors in 1 Thess 2:7, they all help illuminate the kinds of ideas ancient authors expressed through the use of infant and nurse metaphors. They also give clues about how metaphors such as Paul's might have been read and understood in their cultural context. As such they form an important background for the analysis of 1 Thess 2:5–8, to which the next chapter is dedicated.

5
Paul as Infant and Nursing Mother among the Thessalonians

As discussed in chapter 1, metaphor was one of Paul's rhetorical strategies, employed to convince his readers of his point of view. Metaphors are not merely fancy ways of speaking or writing but carry cognitive content and guide human thought processes; therefore, they play an important role in the construction of individual and social reality. When a metaphor describes an individual or the group to which he or she belongs, it has the power to create and shape identity. Since identity and behavior are linked, metaphors influence both the thoughts and the actions of individuals and groups.

After Paul left town, the Thessalonian believers faced the challenges of living in a counterculturalmanner, specifically the social ostracism that would have resulted from their withdrawal from pagan rituals honoring the gods and the Roman emperor. Given the very group-oriented Mediterranean culture, pressure and persecution from neighbors, severed family ties, and the collapse of business relations had led to a crisis of identity for the Thessalonians. Paul sought to fill the void left by broken connections with a vision of community centered in Christ. The purpose of 1 Thessalonians was to comfort, strengthen, and shape the congregation. Two of the strategies Paul employed to accomplish this purpose entailed (1) extensive use of kinship language and (2) strengthening his own relationship to the community as the reliable and trustworthy proclaimer of the gospel. With those aims in mind, Paul wrote the words of 2:5–8:

> For we never came with flattering words (just as you know), nor with a motive of greed (as God is witness), nor seeking honor from human

beings, whether from you or from others (though we could have insisted on our own importance as apostles of Christ), but we were infants in your midst. Like a nurse tenderly caring for her own children, in the same way, longing for you, we were pleased to share with you not only the gospel of God, but also our very selves, because you had become beloved to us.[1]

This chapter will explore the metaphors found in these verses and their function as part of an identity-shaping rhetorical strategy in 1 Thessalonians.

5.1. Analysis of the Infant Metaphor

Paul's presentation of himself as an infant to the Thessalonians has baffled many interpreters through the centuries, so much so that ancient copyists and modern commentators alike have been more comfortable substituting "gentle" as the descriptor of the apostle. However, evidence clearly supports "infants" as the best reading, as I demonstrated in §2.2, above. What did Paul intend to convey by referring to himself and his coworkers as infants, and how does the metaphor fit within Paul's overall rhetorical strategy in 1 Thessalonians?

5.1.1. Entailments of the Infant Metaphor

Metaphors give structure to our understanding of a target domain by highlighting certain aspects of it and hiding others. The aspects or characteristics of the source domain that are being applied to the target domain, and thus highlighted, are called entailments. In this case, Paul applies certain entailments of infants to himself and his coworkers to describe the nature of their behavior in Thessalonica. Most of these entailments were associated with the idea of innocence. Infants are simply not capable of certain things, and so the infant metaphor serves to highlight Paul's innocence in the face of certain charges.

5.1.1.1. An Infant's Behavior is Transparent

While it may, at times, be difficult to determine the reasons for an infant's cry, nevertheless infants are not capable of hidden motives; they do not

---

[1]. For an explanation of this translation, see §2.4 in the present study.

scheme and deceive, nor do they use flattery to get their way. Infants do not consider the feelings of others or how they might manipulate those feelings to their advantage, but express their joys and frustrations in a more direct manner, such as through laughing or crying. This is what Philo referred to as the "naked" soul of the infant, a "mind that is clothed in neither vice nor in virtue," but "stripped of coverings" (*Alleg. Interp.* 2.53, Colson). This makes "infant" an appropriate metaphor for Paul to use in defending himself against the charges that he used flattery and had hidden motives while preaching the gospel in Thessalonica. Through this metaphor Paul seeks to emphasize that all of his actions were done to please God, not human beings, and these actions were carried out with the directness of an infant. As Furnish writes, infants are "innocents who are utterly incapable of dissembling or chicanery."[2]

5.1.1.2. Infants Have Low Social Status

While infants were certainly valued and cared for in Greco-Roman society, they did not have equal social status with adults. This can be seen, for example, in the fact that there were no official Roman mourning rituals for infants under a year old, and it was not until a child reached age ten that rituals were equivalent to those for adults. Infants were accepted into society at their naming day, but were not truly considered full members of society until much later. They did not occupy an important place in society, making them an apt metaphor to express the idea that Paul did not seek honor from the Thessalonians or insist on his own importance. Infants are incapable of seeking honor and occupy the low end of the status spectrum.

5.1.1.3. Infants Are Innocent

The two entailments described above both point to the innocence of infants. Paul's innocence in the face of charges of deception and greed is a key theme of this section of the letter. He makes claims about the uprightness and purity of his actions and motives both before and after the infant metaphor (see 2:3–4, 10). Furthermore, Paul's upright behavior and that of his coworkers is introduced in 1:5, establishing it as an important theme

---

2. Victor Paul Furnish, *1 Thessalonians, 2 Thessalonians* (ANTC; Nashville: Abingdon, 2007), 59.

not just for chapter 2 but for the letter as a whole. In support of this theme Paul compares himself and his coworkers to infants.

Some interpreters have claimed that it makes no sense for Paul to compare himself to a baby. On the contrary, infants is a particularly apt metaphor to express Paul's blamelessness, because "little babies are not capable of using deceptive speech, having ulterior motives, and being concerned with receiving honor; in all these things they are innocent."[3] As we have seen, it is not only modern commentators who understand infants as innocent. Philo, Plutarch, and others wrote of the innocence of infants and their inability to deceive or commit an offense.[4] That Paul himself was aware of these connotations of infancy can be seen in 1 Cor 14:20, in which Paul uses the verbal form νηπιάζω to convey that one should be an infant, that is, innocent, with respect to evil. This connotation of innocence, of being incapable of deception and false motives, makes "infants" a powerful metaphor for Paul to use in dissociating himself from the behaviors described in 2:5–7a.

5.1.1.4. Infants Are Demanding?

Stephen Fowl believes "infant" to be the original reading in 1 Thess 2:7, but writes that this metaphor is "in distress."[5] By this he means that the metaphor is in danger of accomplishing the opposite of what Paul intends: Paul wishes to show that he was not a burden to the Thessalonians, but infants are actually quite demanding in their need for care and attention. Fowl claims that Paul realized this, which is why he so quickly followed the infant metaphor with the metaphor of the self-giving nurse: "by following his 'infant' metaphor with this metaphor of the nurse Paul constrains his initial metaphor in order to provide the right sort of contrast between his own behavior and that of a demanding apostle."[6]

There is no question that infants are demanding. In another context the demanding nature of infants could be an entailment of a different

---

3. Jeffrey A. D. Weima, "'But We Became Infants Among You': The Case for ΝΗΠΙΟΙ in 1 Thess 2.7," *NTS* 46 (2000), 563. See also Beverly Roberts Gaventa, *Our Mother Saint Paul* (Louisville: Westminster John Knox, 2007), 26.

4. See the discussion of the innocence of infants in §4.1, above.

5. Stephen E. Fowl, "A Metaphor in Distress: A Reading of ΝΗΠΙΟΙ in 1 Thessalonians 2:7," *NTS* 36 (1990), 469–73.

6. Ibid., 472.

metaphor. However, this need not be the case in 2:7. According to metaphor theory, not every aspect of the source domain is active in a given metaphor. For example, in the metaphor "God is a rock," the inert and lifeless nature of rocks is not what is being highlighted. This metaphor is not "in distress" because God is not lifeless and inactive. Rather, the inert nature of rocks is simply not active in this metaphor; instead, their solid and immovable nature is highlighted, their ability to provide shelter and a strong foundation. Paul did not need the nurse metaphor to "constrain" the infant metaphor; the infant metaphor was already constrained by what came before it. The context of Paul's claim that he did not flatter, have false motives, or seek honor puts the innocence, rather than the demanding nature, of infants in view.

5.1.2. What the Infant Metaphor Hides

It is important to remember that, while metaphors work by highlighting certain aspects of the target domain through the application of the entailments of the source domain, they also work by hiding other aspects of the target domain. As noted in §1.2.1, above, if someone applies a chess metaphor to war, the strategic aspects of war will be highlighted while aspects such as death and emotional trauma will be hidden. Thus, analysis of a metaphor should ask not only what the metaphor highlights but also what it hides.

When Paul calls himself an infant, what is being hidden? The primary aspect of Paul and his work as an apostle that is hidden by the metaphor is the fact that Paul chooses every word carefully in order to communicate his gospel message as effectively as possible. Even as he crafts the infant metaphor to convey his innocence and utter transparency, he is seeking to influence and persuade the Thessalonians to view him in a certain way. While one might debate the precise definition of flattery, Paul clearly praises the Thessalonians in the opening verses of the letter in order to predispose them to hear his arguments favorably. Every word, from the beginning to the end of the letter, is carefully crafted, a fact that is hidden by the metaphor of the innocent and guileless infant.

5.1.3. Implications for Gospel, Rhetoric, and Social Identity

Metaphors give structure to our understanding of the target domain; therefore, they have the power to influence attitudes toward the target domain and also behaviors in relation to the target domain. When Paul describes himself as an infant, he is presenting the Thessalonians with a new metaphor, and therefore a new way to understand him. This section will explore the ways in which the infant metaphor may have influenced the Thessalonians's thinking about Paul, the gospel, and their own identity.

5.1.3.1. What Is an Apostle?

According to Gaventa, one of the most important things the infant metaphor does is describe what an apostle is.[7] First Thessalonians is thought to be Paul's first extant letter, and therefore the appearance of ἀπόστολοι in 2:7 is the earliest occurrence of the word in the New Testament. Not only is it the earliest use, it is the only use of the word in this letter. Considering this, it is striking that, after identifying himself and his coworkers as apostles, the first thing Paul writes is that they were infants. This implies that "infants" may be an appropriate metaphor for describing Paul's understanding of exemplary apostles in general, not only himself and his coworkers during their particular ministry in Thessalonica. This section will explore the idea of apostles as infants in conversation with Paul's understanding of the role and character of apostles as described in his later letters. This will demonstrate that the infant metaphor in 1 Thess 2:7 is consistent with Paul's broader understanding of apostleship.

To apply the metaphor in a more general fashion implies that genuine apostles are not greedy, do not use flattery or deceptive practices to get their way, and do not seek honor from other people. Such an understanding of apostles fits well with 2 Cor 10–13, where Paul compares himself and his coworkers to those he considers false apostles. One of the things Paul emphasizes in this section of 2 Corinthians is that he did not lay a financial burden on the Corinthian congregation. It seems he had offended some members by not accepting their money, something that the "superapostles" were apparently willing to do. Paul defends the uprightness of his own choice in financial matters: "Was it a sin for me to humble myself in order that you might be exalted, because I preached the gospel to you without payment?" (2 Cor 11:7). In the next chapter Paul gives his reason for not laying a financial burden on the congregation: "And I will not be a burden, for I do not want to possess what is yours, but you. For children ought not

---

7. Gaventa, *Our Mother Saint Paul*, 26.

to save up for their parents, but parents for their children" (2 Cor 12:14). In this case Paul uses a metaphor that places him in the role of parent to illustrate his lack of greed, but the infant metaphor of 1 Thessalonians is equally effective for expressing the same idea. As an upstanding apostle, Paul has the innocence of an infant in financial matters. This is in contrast to false apostles, who seek financial gain through preaching.

Another difference, according to Paul, between himself and the superapostles in 2 Cor 10–13 is that these false apostles flash their credentials around while Paul and his coworkers remain humble in the presence of the congregation. The superapostles boast about their own background and abilities, but according to Paul, "it is not the one who commends himself that is approved, but the one whom the Lord commends" (2 Cor 10:18). Therefore Paul himself claims to be humble when present with his churches, making appeals "by the meekness and gentleness of Christ" (2 Cor 10:1). Boasters, on the other hand, are "false apostles, deceitful laborers, disguising themselves as apostles of Christ" (2 Cor 11:13). This contrast between boastful false apostles and humble true apostles in 2 Cor 10–13 again finds a parallel with the infant metaphor of 1 Thess 2:7. In Thessalonica Paul and his coworkers did not seek honor from the Thessalonians nor did they seek to deceive them through fancy words, but rather they were as humble and direct as infants.

In the past, interpreters have strongly resisted the idea that Paul would use the word "infants" to describe what apostles are like, but Gaventa rightly draws attention to the fact that Paul had an upside-down view of apostles that ran counter to then-prevalent cultural standards of honor, status, and even, at times, masculinity. To understand apostles of Christ, Gaventa writes, "one must employ categories that seem outrageous outside the context of Pauline paradox."[8] This upside-down view of apostles also finds support in 2 Cor 10–13. The superapostles brag about their credentials and show off their skills of oratory, but when Paul is pressured to produce his own boast, its content is of an entirely different nature:

> Are they ministers of Christ? I am talking like a madman—I am a better one: with far greater labors, far more imprisonments, with countless floggings, and often near death. Five times I have received from the Jews the forty lashes minus one. Three times I was beaten with rods. Once I received a stoning. Three times I was shipwrecked; for a night and a day

---

8. Ibid., 27.

> I was adrift at sea; on frequent journeys, in danger from rivers, danger from bandits, danger from my own people, danger from Gentiles, danger in the city, danger in the wilderness, danger at sea, danger from false brothers and sisters; in toil and hardship, through many a sleepless night, hungry and thirsty, often without food, cold and naked. And, besides other things, I am under daily pressure because of my anxiety for all the churches. (2 Cor 11:23–28 NRSV)

What qualifies Paul to claim that he is a "better" apostle is that he has been beaten, imprisoned, and exposed to many dangers, has toiled in labor, has been filled with anxiety, and has gone without food and other things essential to human life. This is the life of the true apostle. Paul writes, "If I must boast, I will boast of the things showing my weakness" (2 Cor 11:30).

Paul's culturally surprising view of true apostleship is grounded in the cross of Christ. The cross of Christ demonstrates that God works strength through weakness and power through powerlessness. Christ was "crucified in weakness, but lives by the power of God. For we also are weak in him, but we will live by the power of God with respect to you" (2 Cor 13:4). For those who pattern their lives on the cross, weakness, humility, and suffering are expected norms, as Paul reminded the Thessalonians repeatedly.[9] A similar idea finds expression in 1 Cor 1:27–29:

> God chose the foolish things of the world in order to shame the wise, and God chose the weak things of the world in order to shame the strong. God chose the low things of the world and the things that are despised and the things that are not, in order to nullify the things that are, so that no one might boast before God.

When Paul appeals for relief from the "thorn in the flesh," the Lord answers him, "'My grace is sufficient for you, for power is made perfect in weakness.'" Therefore, Paul boasts of weakness, "so that the power of Christ might dwell in me" (2 Cor 12:9). Paul concludes: "Therefore, I am well pleased with weakness, insults, distress, persecutions, and difficulties for the sake of Christ; for whenever I am weak, then I am powerful" (2 Cor 12:10).

As followers of Christ, genuine apostles are not held in high honor, praised for their oratory, or paid well for their labors; rather, they are

---

9. See my previous discussion of suffering and persecution in Thessalonica in §3.2.3, above.

humble, weak, beaten down, and scoffed at according to the world's standards. With this view of apostleship, as developed by Paul in his later letters to the Corinthians, it should not be surprising that Paul would describe apostles as infants. The weakness and low social status of infants in Greco-Roman society are the very things that make them an apt metaphor for true apostles of Christ. Paul says he "was orphaned" by separation from the Thessalonians in 2:17, and in like manner the infant metaphor in 2:7 places Paul and his coworkers in a lower position in relation to the Thessalonian congregation. This may be startling, but is consistent with Paul's theology of ministry. As Paul writes of the Corinthians in 2 Cor 13:9, "we rejoice when we are weak and you are powerful; this is also what we pray for—your maturation." Paul is willing to put himself in the role of infant for the sake of the maturation of his churches.

5.1.3.2. Defense of Paul Is Defense of the Gospel

In addition to illustrating what true apostles are like, the infant metaphor also serves as part of Paul's defense of the gospel that he had preached to the Thessalonians. One of the primary entailments of the infant metaphor is that infants are innocent; therefore, the metaphor serves to defend Paul against any charges and accusations that had been made against him in Thessalonica. Since, in Paul's mind, the apostle and the apostle's message are linked, in defending himself with the infant metaphor he also defends the gospel.[10]

In social identity terms, Paul's presentation of his innocence and integrity in 2:1–12 establishes him as the prototypical group member. Rhetorically, this accomplishes two things. First, it establishes Paul's right to speak with authority to the group; the basis of his authority is his own embodiment of the group's values and behavioral norms. Second, it establishes the behaviors described in this section as ideals worthy of imitation by the community. Having the innocence and guilelessness of infants becomes one of the norms of the group that distinguishes its members from outsiders who behave differently. Thus, Paul's defense in 2:1–12, including the infant metaphor, strengthens group identity by strengthening the notion of similarity among members in the group. A strengthened group identity

---

10. For further explication of the concepts and ideas referred to in this section, see §3.2, above.

would provide the motivation the Thessalonians need to persevere in their faith and in their loyalty to Paul's gospel in the face of daunting challenges, including even persecutions.

5.2. Analysis of the Nurse Metaphor

Immediately following the infant metaphor, Paul presents himself as a nurse who, in this case, is also a nursing mother. In this case, there is no dispute that the text does actually say "nurse"; nevertheless, many interpreters have struggled with how to interpret Paul's use of such a surprising metaphor. Scribes found "infants" so shocking that they altered the text. But, as Gordon Fee points out, the nurse metaphor is "equally astounding" and "unlike anything else in the Pauline corpus."[11] Metaphor theory and social identity analysis help illumine why a first century male would choose such a metaphor to describe himself and the meanings encompassed by this image.

As demonstrated in chapters 3 and 4 above, the practice of wet-nursing was common in the Greco-Roman world and the image of the nurse was employed with some regularity in ancient literature. Paul was by no means the originator of nursing metaphors. However, Paul did employ this image in a new and creative way in 1 Thess 2:7.[12] Creative metaphors are often grounded in conceptual metaphors that are already part of the author's culture, but they extend or combine conventional metaphors in new ways; this creativity gives new metaphors the power to provide a new perspective and a new understanding of the target domain. Paul's nursing metaphor is new and creative in several ways. First, it combines the separate conventional metaphors of parent and nurse into one, making the nurse herself a mother. The metaphor is also creative in taking advantage of the surprising effect of a male placing himself in a female role. Furthermore, the meanings found within the nurse metaphor are different from other contemporaneous, conventional uses of nurse metaphors: Paul's metaphor has less to do with the instruction and discipline of the nurse, and more to do with nursing as a self-giving action. These and other aspects of Paul's

---

11. Gordon D. Fee, *The First and Second Letters to the Thessalonians* (NICNT; Grand Rapids: Eerdmans, 2009), 65.

12. See chapter 1 of this study for background on the differences between conventional and creative metaphors.

metaphor will be illuminated through a closer analysis of the metaphor's entailments.

5.2.1. Entailments of the Nurse Metaphor

Readers of all ages, cultures, and life experience can immediately understand something of Paul's nurse metaphor based on the direct, common human experience of nursing—of an infant finding comfort and sustenance at the breast of a mother or nurse. Complex metaphors are often grounded in primary metaphors that are based in human experience of the world and shared across cultures. However, complex metaphors also make use of cultural information; therefore, it is necessary to study the entailments of a metaphor in cultures that differ from one's own, in order to understand the metaphor more fully.

5.2.1.1. Nursing Provides Comfort

This first entailment illustrates the way in which complex or creative metaphors are often grounded in primary metaphors shared across cultures. As discussed in §1.2.2.5, above, "affection is warmth" is one such metaphor, grounded in the primal human experience of infants and small children being comforted by the physical warmth of their parents' bodies as they are held close. From the very beginning of our lives, no matter our culture, affection and warmth are connected in our minds. Interestingly, one of the verbs Paul uses to describe the way in which he is like a nurse taps into exactly this primal human experience. The figurative meaning of θάλπω is "to care for" or "to cherish," but the literal meaning of this verb is "to make warm." As the mother's body keeps the infant warm and simultaneously provides comfort, so Paul and his coworkers warm and comfort the Thessalonians.

This comforting aspect of the nurse figure was also present in other uses of the nurse image in the ancient world, such as Plutarch's example of the nurse who comforts the injured child before scolding it, or Dio Chrysostom's metaphor of the nurse who tells a story to comfort her charges after giving them a whipping.[13] Yet Paul's metaphor differs from these in that there is no sense of scolding or discipline implied by the

---

13. For specific references and more examples, see chapter 4 of this study.

metaphor; Paul's words express only affection and comfort. Rhetorically, this is appropriate for the metaphor's context in 1 Thessalonians, in which Paul is not scolding his readers as he is sometimes disposed to do in other letters, but rather is intent on providing encouragement in the midst of difficult circumstances. Just as God's people who are beaten down by war, exile, and starvation are comforted by their Mother God (Isa 66:13), so the Thessalonians who are troubled by persecutions, insults, and ostracism are comforted by Mother Paul.

5.2.1.2. Nursing Provides Nourishment

One of the duties of mothers in the ancient world was to provide for their children's physical needs. While breastfeeding has many positive side effects, such as affection and comfort, its primary function is to provide nutrition to the infant. In this sense the metaphor implies not only that Paul sought to comfort the Thessalonians, but also that he sought to nourish them with the gospel. Paul and his coworkers gave the Thessalonians the milk of the gospel to nourish them in their infancy in Christ.

Breastfeeding differs from other forms of giving food, however, in that the nurse or nursing mother gives of her own body for the life of the infant. Paul clearly draws on this aspect of breastfeeding in his metaphor: "Like a nurse tenderly caring for her own children, in the same way, longing for you, we were pleased to share with you not only the gospel of God, but also our very selves, because you had become beloved to us" (1 Thess 2:7b–8). It was not only the gospel that they shared, but their "very selves." As Bruce points out, τάς ἑαυτῶν ψυχάς indicates not only that "we were willing to give (lay down) our lives for you" but also that "we were willing to give ourselves to you, to put ourselves at your disposal, without reservation."[14] The metaphor indicates that Paul held nothing back from the Thessalonians but gave of himself for their benefit.

This aspect of the metaphor has some interesting similarities to and differences from the nursing metaphor found in the Qumran Hodayot. Nourishment is one of the central entailments of the Qumran metaphor. The leader imparts knowledge to the community, just as he had received knowledge from God, and this is represented through the milk of the mother and nurse. The centrality of nourishment in this metaphor is made

---

14. Bruce, *1 and 2 Thessalonians*, 32.

explicit by the description of the community members: they "opened their mouths like a suckling babe at the breast of its mother, and like a child taking delight in the bosom of its wet nurse" (1QH^a XV 24–25). Paul's metaphor in 1 Thess 2:7 also places the community in the role of infants, but the Qumran metaphor does so more explicitly than Paul's, describing them as open-mouthed sucklings. The central focus, then, in this metaphor is on the reception of knowledge by the community. This aspect is not absent from Paul's metaphor, in which the nursing mother nourishes the community with the gospel; however, the emphasis in Paul's metaphor is less on the transmission of knowledge and more on the tender care of the mother-nurse for her children.

In this regard, the Qumran metaphor is more similar to 1 Cor 3:2 than to 1 Thess 2:7. In 1 Cor 3:2 the feeding aspect of the nursing metaphor is the most prominent entailment: "I gave you milk to drink, not solid food, for you were not yet able. But even now you are not yet able, for you are still fleshly" (1 Cor 3:2–3a). Here the emphasis is on the kind of knowledge that Paul was able to transmit to the Corinthians based on their maturity. As with the Qumran metaphor, the central focus is on the transmission of knowledge from the leader to the community. However, unlike both the Qumran metaphor and 1 Thess 2:7, 1 Cor 3:2 states that the community is not ready for the knowledge the leader wants to provide. Both the Hodayot image and Paul's image in 1 Thess 2:7 are wholly positive images of leader and community in harmony with each other. In these two metaphors there is no shame associated with being an infant in relation to the leader; the nursing relationship between the leader and the community is something to be celebrated. In 1 Cor 3:2, however, Paul implies that the community members ought to be ashamed of their need for milk and ought to mature to readiness for solid food.

5.2.1.3. The Nursing Mother Loves Her Child

While we ought not to romanticize the relationships between mother/nurse and child in the ancient world, it is nevertheless the case that love and affection were generally understood to be a part of these relationships. Inscriptional and literary evidence points to many cases of affection and loyalty between a wet nurse and her nurslings.[15] While in reality many

---

15. For primary source references and analysis, see chapter 3 of this study.

nurse-nursling relationships may have been ambivalent or characterized by resentment,[16] the societal ideal of the loyal and affectionate nurse is the image on which Paul draws for his metaphor.

But with the addition of ἑαυτῆς Paul strengthens the connotation of love and affection even further. This nurse is with *her own* children, making her a nursing mother. Several ancient authors commented on the strength of love between mothers and their children.[17] In fact, the greater affection and care of the mother for the child was the reason Plutarch thought mothers should nurse their own babies instead of hiring wet nurses (*Mor.* 3C). Paul may imply this greater level of affection and care when he adds the reflexive pronoun, making this metaphor a highly effective one for expressing his love and care for the Thessalonian community.

5.2.1.4. Breastfeeding Bonds the Mother and Infant

Among ancient authors, breastfeeding was understood to strengthen the natural bond of love between mothers and their infants. Both Plutarch and Favorinus recommended maternal breastfeeding for this reason (see Plutarch, *Mor.* 3C; Gellius, *Attic Nights* 12.1.23). Once again, this aspect of nursing makes the metaphor a particularly effective one for Paul. The idea of the bond between a mother and her nursing infant is part of Paul's rhetorical strategy to strengthen his relationship to the Thessalonians and thus their relationship to the gospel.

5.2.1.5. Nursing Mothers Are Acquainted with Suffering

As discussed in §3.1.1, above, childbirth was a dangerous endeavor in the ancient world, and the death of infants and young children was quite common. While the modern reader might miss connotations of suffering in maternal metaphors, the ancient reader would hardly fail to associate motherhood and suffering. With this in mind, Paul's nursing metaphor illustrates not only his love for the Thessalonian community but also his worry over them and anguish about them. The unweaned child was always in danger of illness and death, which was no doubt a cause of much anxiety to the nursing mother, who gave of her own body for the life of the

---

16. See my discussion of Joshel's work on slave nurses in §3.1.2.4, above.
17. For primary source references and analysis, see chapter 3.

5. PAUL AS INFANT AND NURSING MOTHER 137

infant but would nevertheless have understood the precarious nature of her infant's life and the fact that all her efforts in behalf of its health and growth might fail. This is the image Paul uses to illustrate his own worry over the stressful situation of the Thessalonian church and the precarious nature of their very young faith.[18] He is willing to give of himself for their life of faith, but is deeply concerned that his efforts may fail due to circumstances beyond his control. As he writes in 3:5, "For this reason, when I could endure it no longer, I sent to find out about your faith, in fear that somehow the tempter had tempted you and our labor had been in vain."

Another key to seeing suffering as part of Paul's nursing metaphor is to recognize that as Paul writes about nursing the Thessalonians he is separated from them by a great distance. Philo wrote that a nursing mother should never be separated from her infant because of the emotional distress and physical discomfort this would cause her (*Virtues* 128). Paul is not simply a nursing mother to the Thessalonians, but a nursing mother separated from her children. This is why, even in the midst of a metaphor of intimacy and connection, Paul expresses his longing (ὁμειρόμενοι) for them.

Paul's separation from the Thessalonians and his consequent longing for them and worry over them are themes elsewhere in the letter, especially in chapters 2 and 3. Paul's distress at the separation is so great that in 2:17 he describes himself as being orphaned from the Thessalonians. Like orphaned children, Paul and his coworkers "were especially eager, with great desire, to see your face." Yet they were distressed because Satan blocked them at every turn (2:18). For this reason Paul sent Timothy to strengthen the congregation and find out about their faith, in hopes of relieving their worry (3:1–5). Timothy's good report comforts Paul, but still he writes: "Night and day we pray most earnestly that we might see your face and complete what is lacking in your faith" (3:10).

This extreme longing and worry for the Thessalonians is also illustrated by the nursing metaphor in 2:7. Burke recognizes this aspect of the metaphor. He writes that picturing the Thessalonians as infants not yet weaned from Paul means the separation between them would have been "keenly felt"; therefore, the metaphor highlights both "the apostle's anxiet-

---

18. Cf. Paul's expression of his constant anxiety for all the churches as the climax of his list of apostolic sufferings in 2 Cor 11:23–28.

ies *and* the Thessalonians' vulnerability."[19] As a nursing mother Paul is in distress to be separated from his children. Additionally, the image of an unweaned infant separated from its mother is a striking one for illustrating the precarious state of the Thessalonians's young faith as they face ostracism and even persecution.

5.2.1.6. The Nurse Has Low Social Status

Similarly to the infant metaphor, the image of a wet nurse might seem at first a surprising choice for Paul because with it he places himself in a low-status role. Most nurses in Greco-Roman society were slaves, and those who were free would have been women of meager means. Margaret Aymer makes sure we do not miss this aspect of Paul's metaphor. Unlike the metaphors in Gal 4:19 and 1 Cor 3:1–2 in which a free, authoritative mother scolds her "recalcitrant children," the woman in 1 Thess 2:7 is a slave nurse: "In fact, in an unusually insightful metaphor for a free man who flippantly employs metaphors both of slavery and of maternity, Paul here identifies himself with a woman who has no control over her body or its functions."[20] In the first century Greco-Roman world, one could not get much lower on the social scale than a female slave nurse. As will be discussed further in this chapter and the next, the fact that Paul nevertheless associates himself with such a figure is not insignificant to understanding his character and his theology.

5.2.1.7. The Thessalonians Are "Wanted" Children

As illustrated in §3.1.1.2, above, there were many ways to deal with the problem of unwanted children in Greco-Roman society, including contraception, abortion, exposure, and infanticide. Presumably, even some children who survived those methods and were accepted as family members would still have felt unwanted if they had been accepted reluctantly or if there was disagreement among family members about whether they

---

19. Trevor J. Burke, *Family Matters: A Socio-historical Study of Kinship Metaphors in 1 Thessalonians* (JSNTSup 247; London: T&T Clark, 2003), 153.

20. Margeret Aymer, "'Mother Knows Best': The Story of Mother Paul Revisited," in *Mother Goose, Mother Jones, Mommie Dearest: Biblical Mothers and Their Children* (ed. Cheryl A. Kirk-Duggan and Tina Pippin; SemeiaSt 61; Atlanta: Society of Biblical Literature, 2009), 194.

should have been accepted or exposed at birth instead. Such is clearly not the case in Paul's nursing mother metaphor. This nursing mother not only wanted her children at birth but continued to care for them with deep affection.

Once again, knowledge that most nurses were slave women helps to deepen the metaphor's interpretation. It is important to remember that in most cases slave nurses had no choice over the use of their bodies for this purpose or over which infants they would nurse. In this regard Joshel's work on Roman nurses and American mammies is helpful for troubling the romantic picture of nurses found in the literature of elite Greek and Roman writers.[21] Roman nurses' feelings towards their charges were probably more ambivalent than portrayed in the literature, and the primary loyalty of these nurses would have resided with their own kin and other peers, rather than with their masters. This reality makes the addition of ἑαυτῆς to the metaphor striking. This is a nurse who normally has no choice over whom to suckle; but now she is with her own children and it is with them that her greatest loyalty and affection lie.[22]

Aymer presses this aspect of Paul's metaphor to the fullest: "To use an American-based metaphor, in 1 Thessalonians Paul and the apostles are not like the mother in the 'big house' but like the mammy back in the slave quarters who *finally* gets to nurse her own children."[23] Paul chooses the Thessalonians in the sense that he cares for them as his own children. There is no compulsion on him, no reluctance on his part. Rather he was "pleased" (εὐδοκοῦμεν) to share his very self with his beloved children (1 Thess 2:8). This circumstance makes the separation of Paul and the Thessalonians even more painful. Once again Aymer presses this point. It is as though the slave nurse, who finally was able to nurse her own children, has once again been forced away from her children to tend to others: "Mother Paul, the slave-nurse, longs for her children but cannot return to them."[24] Bradley's work on Roman wet nurses suggests that the prevalence of wet-nursing may have served to protect upper-class mothers from the emotional trauma of infant loss.[25] Paul the slave nurse desires no such

---

21. See the description and analysis of her work in §3.1.2.4 of this study.
22. Aymer, "'Mother Knows Best,'" 194.
23. Ibid, emphasis original.
24. Ibid.
25. Keith R. Bradley, "Wet-nursing at Rome: A Study in Social Relations," in *The Family in Ancient Rome: New Perspectives* (ed. Beryl Rawson; Ithaca, N.Y.: Cornell

emotional protection. He longs to nurse his own children, and willingly lives with the pain of separation, fully investing himself in the life and faith of the Thessalonians.

The aspect of choice and willingness that is part of Paul's metaphor makes for an interesting comparison to the nursing metaphors in the book of Numbers and in the Qumran literature. In strong contrast to Paul's metaphor, Moses in Num 11:12 is quite clearly not choosing the role of nurse to the people. He did not give birth to them and does not wish to nurse them. They are not his children, nor does he desire intimate association with them. In this sense God is like the master, forcing Moses the slave nurse to care for infants for whom he has no affection. By contrast, Paul accepts the Thessalonians as his own children and longs to be present with them. The role of nurse that Moses rejects in Num 11:12 Paul takes on gladly in 1 Thess 2:7. There is less contrast between Paul's metaphor and that found in the Hodayot. In 1QH^a XV 23–25 the leader glories in his roles of father, mother, and nurse to the community. Like Paul, he freely accepts his God-given role in relation to the community, and gladly nourishes them with knowledge and wisdom. The contrast between Paul and the Qumran leader lies in the emotional implications of the choice to be nurse to a community. While Paul's metaphor emphasizes Paul's deep emotional attachment to the Thessalonians, 1QH^a XV 23–25 gives no indication that the leader is affected emotionally by his relationship to the community. The leader definitely takes pride in his position, but whether the community is beloved to him is not evident in these verses.

5.2.1.8. The Nursing Mother Has Authority over Her Infants

Despite the fact that the nurse has low social status in Greco-Roman society, and that the entailments of the nursing image include intimacy and self-giving nurture, Paul's metaphor is complex in that there is also an element of authority to it. It is not an egalitarian image.[26] The nurse has a level of authority over her charges, and certainly the mother is above the infant in the family hierarchy. This is perhaps one of the reasons that the metaphor is so effective as part of Paul's rhetoric in 1 Thessalonians: it plays on a delicate balance between intimacy and authority.

University Press, 1986), 220. See also my discussion of Bradley's work on wet nurses at §§3.1.2.3–4 in this study.

26. Gaventa, *Our Mother Saint Paul*, 13–14.

One of the ways the authority of the mother or nurse was manifest in Greco-Roman society was that these women were understood to be role models for their children. Along with fathers, they were responsible for disciplining young children and for teaching moral living through both instruction and example. In this respect Paul's identification with a mother image fits well with his understanding of the apostle's role. Paul gave instruction to his churches, scolded them when he thought they did wrong, and even set himself up as an example to be imitated. This is illustrated throughout his writings and specifically with the Thessalonian church in 1 Thess 1:6: "You became imitators of us and of the Lord." He also reminds them in 4:1–2 that he and his coworkers, taking on a parental role in the community, had taught them how they ought to live to please God.

5.2.2. What the Nurse Metaphor Hides

Just as with the infant metaphor and all other effective metaphors, part of the power of the nurse metaphor comes from what it hides rather than what it highlights. The creators of metaphors always have aspects of the target domain that they are seeking to downplay as well as aspects they wish to emphasize. When Paul identifies himself as a nursing mother to the Thessalonians, what does the metaphor hide? There are many possible answers to this question, but two seem especially pertinent: Paul was an outsider to the community, and there may have been some trouble in his relationship with the Thessalonians.

The nursing metaphor creates a sense of intimacy that pictures Paul and the Thessalonians as members of the same family, as a mother with her children. This is effective as part of Paul's strategy to solidify his relationship with them and establish a new kinship group in which to ground their identity. However, it hides the fact that Paul is not actually one of them, but an outsider to Thessalonica. In a sense, this is why Paul's metaphors are necessary: to reorient the thinking of the Thessalonians to view themselves and Jesus' followers everywhere as their true family, regardless of their ethnic, national, kinship, or class identity. For this reason Paul tells them in 1:6–10 that their faith has become known everywhere the gospel has been preached, and he also calls attention to their connection to believers in Judea in 2:13–16. In a social world in which insider/outsider status based on kinship was important, Paul's nursing metaphor downplays his own outsider status and highlights the Thessalonians's connection to him, and through him to believers everywhere.

The nursing metaphor also downplays any disputes or tensions that may have existed between Paul and the Thessalonians. As noted in §3.2.4.3, above, scholars do not agree about the nature of the trouble that may have existed between Paul and various residents of Thessalonica, both within the believing community and outside of it. Some, such as Malherbe, feel that Paul's words in the letter reflect the conventional language of philosophers and do not necessarily imply an actual threat to Paul's authority in the community.[27] Donfried, however, is more convincing when he notes the likelihood that some in the community may have felt anger at Paul for stirring up trouble for them and then leaving town quickly.[28] This would have left Paul with the need to defend his actions and the gospel message he had preached.

Whatever the nature of these disputes or tensions, it is clear that Paul is not drawing attention to them as he often does with the Galatians or the Corinthians. Instead, he is attempting to smooth out and strengthen his relationship with the Thessalonian church. Part of his rhetorical strategy in the letter is to strengthen the bond between himself and the Thessalonians. Therefore he uses the image of a nursing mother with her infant, an image that implies intimacy and nurture and downplays any sense of tension or dispute.

5.2.3. Implications for Gospel, Rhetoric, and Social Identity

In exploring the nursing metaphor's entailments, I have already begun to trace some of the implications of this metaphor for Paul's presentation of the gospel and his rhetorical strategy in the letter. Three areas require further exploration: the nature of an apostle and his message, Paul's rhetoric of leadership, and the social identity of the Thessalonian community.

5.2.3.1. The Nature of an Apostle and His Message

As discussed in §5.1.3.1, above, Paul used the infant metaphor to illustrate what an apostle is. The nurse metaphor adds to the picture of what Paul believes an apostle should be. Based on the entailments related to

---

27. Abraham J. Malherbe, "Gentle as a Nurse: The Cynic Background to 1 Thess 2," *NovT* 12 (1970): 203–17.

28. Karl P. Donfried, *Paul, Thessalonica, and Early Christianity* (Grand Rapids: Eerdmans, 2002), 44.

5. PAUL AS INFANT AND NURSING MOTHER

nurses and nursing mothers explored above, an apostle is one who teaches by instruction and example, one who cares for and even loves those he teaches, and one who is willing to endure suffering for the benefit of those in his care. Also, as with the infant metaphor, the fact that the nurse was a woman of low social status in Greco-Roman society is not irrelevant to the picture of an apostle that the metaphor projects. This fits with Paul's willingness to endure hardship, boast in weakness, and humble himself to lift up his followers, especially as illustrated in 2 Cor 10–13. Like the infant metaphor, the nurse is another of the "outrageous categories"[29] Paul used to explain the nature of apostleship, which is defined by the humility, suffering, weakness, shame, and power of the cross of Christ.

In considering Paul's use of a parental metaphor to describe his work as an apostle, it is important to ask why he chose to employ a maternal image rather than a paternal one in this case. As a man, a father image would have been the more natural choice, and Paul makes this very choice elsewhere in his letters and even later in the same chapter (2:11–12). Why does Paul describe himself as a mother in 2:7? The answer may lie in the distinctions Greco-Roman culture made between the love and behavior of a mother and that of a father, as illustrated in the writings of ancient authors. Mothers were commonly associated with nurture, while fathers were commonly associated with instruction and discipline.[30] Seneca, for instance, wrote that fathers love their children by urging them on to noble pursuits and accomplishments through discipline, while mothers love their children by caressing them in the lap and wishing always for their comfort and happiness (*Prov.* 2.5).[31]

The theme of instruction is not absent from the nurse metaphor, since, along with fathers, nurses and mothers were also considered to be teachers and role models for their children. However, it would have been difficult for Paul to express the level of connection and intimacy implied by the nurse metaphor had he chosen a father metaphor instead; the associations of his audience with what fathers are like would not have supported this. One of Paul's rhetorical aims in 1 Thessalonians was to strengthen the emotional bond between himself and the Thessalonian community, as a way of fortifying their commitment to the gospel he had taught them.

---

29. Gaventa, *Our Mother Saint Paul*, 27.
30. Burke, *Family Matters*, 152.
31. For the full quote as well as other primary source references on the love of mothers and fathers, see §3.1.1.5 in this study.

Drawing on the cultural resources available to him, the level of affection, intimacy, and nurture that Paul wished to express to accomplish this end could be illustrated much more effectively through a maternal image than a paternal one.

A comparison of 1 Thess 2:7 and 2:11–12 confirms this understanding of the differences between maternal and paternal love in the ancient world. In 2:7 Paul chooses a mother image to express the deep level of self-giving love and affection he felt for the community. Only a few verses later Paul employs a father image. This metaphor could also be considered affectionate, but in a very different way: "Just as you know, we were with each one of you like a father with his children, exhorting you, and consoling, and imploring you to conduct yourselves in a manner worthy of God, who calls you into his own kingdom and glory" (1 Thess 2:11–12). Paul chooses a father image to express his action of urging and encouraging the Thessalonians toward a certain kind of behavior that would befit their identity as followers of Christ. The difference between 2:7 and 2:11–12 illustrates perfectly Seneca's distinction between fathers who show their love by insisting on their children's self-improvement, and mothers who show their love by physical affection and wishes for comfort and happiness. Paul presents himself to the Thessalonian community as a model of both of these kinds of love. Both maternal love and paternal love are needed to fully express Paul's idea of what an apostle should be. An apostle acts as both father and mother to his followers.

Aside from the fact that affectionate nurture was associated with mothers rather than with fathers in the ancient world, there are two further reasons why Paul may have chosen a maternal image rather than a paternal image in 2:7. The first reason is motherhood's association with suffering. Aristotle wrote that the affection of mothers is greater than that of fathers because parenthood "costs the mother more trouble" (*Eth. nic.* 8.7.7, Rackham). This makes a mother image more appropriate than a father image for expressing Paul's worry over the Thessalonians and his distress at being separated from them. The second reason is related to the nature of maternal and paternal authority over children. Aymer points out that Paul may choose a mother image in this case because, while fathers had legal power to control the affairs of their children, mothers had to rely on persuasion to exert influence over their children.[32] This distinction

---

32. Aymer, "'Mother Knows Best,'" 195.

makes motherhood a more appropriate metaphor for Paul's relationship with his communities, in which he had no legal power but sought to use his apostolic authority to convince them to believe and behave in the ways he thought appropriate.

One final question related to the nursing image's illustration of apostleship is whether or not Paul's maternal metaphor implies anything about the motherhood of God. In the Qumran literature, 1QH^a XVII 29b–36 explicitly identifies God as the true mother and nurse to the community, the true source of knowledge and the one who places the leader in the role of mother and nurse. In Num 11:12 Moses' language of rejection in reference to a nursing role implies that God is the true mother and nurse to the Israelites. Is the motherhood of God or Christ implied in any such way in 1 Thess 2:7? At first the answer would appear to be no. The motherhood of God is not explicitly mentioned by Paul nor does he ever directly imply it as Moses does. However, a careful look at Paul's rhetorical practices reveals that the motherhood of Christ might well be implied after all.

In all things Paul claimed to model his apostleship on Christ and the cross. Paul told his communities to imitate him because he imitated Christ. This idea is expressed quite simply in 1 Cor 11:1: "Be imitators of me, just as I also am of Christ." In her harsh critique of this aspect of Paul's rhetoric, Elizabeth Castelli writes that in this and other passages of imitation Paul places himself in the role of Christ to his communities and even confuses his own identity with that of Christ; he does this in order to cement his own privileged position of authority over his communities and in an effort to eradicate difference among church members.[33] Whether or not such a harsh critique of Paul's rhetoric is warranted will be explored further in the next chapter, but Castelli's point, that Paul bases his leadership of the communities on the role of Christ, is pertinent. For Paul, the true apostle models his life and ecclesial leadership on Christ and the cross.

Therefore, when Paul calls himself a nursing mother to the Thessalonians, one must ask if this also is patterned on Paul's understanding of the relationship of Christ to his followers. If Paul can "mother" the Thessalonians, is it not because Christ has first "mothered" him and all whom God has called to follow Christ? All the entailments of the nursing metaphor as Paul applies it to himself—comfort, nourishment, love, suffering, low

---

33. Elizabeth A. Castelli, *Imitating Paul: A Discourse of Power* (LCBI; Louisville: Westminster John Knox, 1991), 112–13.

status, and authority—can be applied also to the character and actions of Christ in relationship to his followers. Paul has given his very self to the Thessalonians, but for Paul it was first Christ "who loved me and gave himself up for me" (Gal 2:20). Because of his deep love for them, Paul is distressed by his separation from the Thessalonians and determined to come to them again. The love of Christ is even greater, such that one cannot be separated from it: "For I am convinced that neither death, nor life, nor angels, nor rulers, nor the things now present, nor the things to come, nor powers, nor height, nor depth, nor any other created thing will be able to separate us from the love of God that is in Christ Jesus our Lord" (Rom 8:38–39). Paul was willing to humble himself in order to lift his churches up, unafraid to appear as one of low social status. Christ was willing to humble himself to the "form of a slave," becoming "obedient to the point of death—even death on a cross" (Phil 2:7–8). Paul sought to teach his churches the wisdom of God rather than the wisdom of the world through example and instruction. Christ is the ultimate teacher of God's wisdom revealing the paradoxical power of God's weakness and foolishness: "Christ crucified, an offense to Jews and foolishness to Gentiles … who become for us wisdom from God, and righteousness and sanctification and redemption" (1 Cor 1:23, 30). While he does not explicitly say so, it is logical to conclude that Paul calls himself a nursing mother to the Thessalonians because he experienced Christ as mother-like in that he nurtured, nourished, taught, suffered, and gave his very self to Paul and to all believers.

5.2.3.2. The Rhetoric of Paul's Leadership

The nursing metaphor not only illumines Paul's understanding of an apostle in general, but also serves as an "act of leadership,"[34] for it gives expression to Paul's role as the founder and guide of the Thessalonian community. As illustrated in §3.2.4.3, above, Paul presents himself as the in-group prototype in 1 Thess 2:1–12. By demonstrating the ways in which he embodies the group's values and behavioral norms, Paul establishes his authority and influence in the group. The nurse image of 2:7 is part of this section and part of Paul's presentation of himself as the ideal group member. In this

---

34. Carol A. Newsom, *The Self as Symbolic Space: Constructing Identity and Community at Qumran* (STDJ 52; Leiden: Brill, 2004), 299.

sense Paul's metaphor is similar to that found in the Qumran Hodayot. In both cases a nursing image places the leader in the role of mother/nurse and the community in the role of suckling babes, thus shaping both the identity of the leader and the identity of the community. Within the metaphors, the bond between the leader and the community is strengthened at the same time that the authority of the leader is enhanced.

Both Paul and the Qumran Teacher believed that God had called them and placed them in a position of authority, and, unlike Moses, both took on the role of nurse to a community of people with willingness and pride. While both Paul's metaphor and the Qumran metaphor imply intimacy and affection, it is important to note that these images are also hierarchical. The mother/nurse has authority over her children/charges, and the flow of milk goes in only one direction. The leader is portrayed as providing knowledge and care to the community; the leader does not receive knowledge or care from the community.[35] There is no reciprocity. The metaphors portray the communities as helpless infants entirely dependent on the leader. The nursing mother metaphor of 2:7 serves to remind the Thessalonians that Paul is the one from whom they received the gospel, the source of their life and their hope for the future. They are dependent on him for their life in Christ in the same the way a nursing infant is dependent on its mother. As such they owe Paul respect and obedience.

Part of the reason Paul's act of leadership in 2:7 is so effective is that it is part of his emotional appeal to the Thessalonians. Paul uses highly emotional language throughout 1 Thessalonians to strengthen his bond to the community and convince them of his innocence and his affection for them. When Paul presents himself to the Thessalonians as a nurse tenderly caring for her own children, it is one of the most deeply emotional moments in the letter. There is no question that with this image Paul intends to strengthen the bond between himself and this community. Even as the image is a hierarchical one, it is also filled with intimacy, nurture, and love, implying that Paul would do anything for the Thessalonian church. This is an important aspect of Paul's act of leadership, because it invites the Thessalonians to view Paul as entirely trustworthy, one who has their best interests at heart. In this sense the metaphor of 2:7 is similar

---

35. This statement is meant only to imply that within this particular metaphor the knowledge and care flow only in one direction; it is not meant to imply that nowhere in Paul's letters is a community portrayed as contributing to Paul's knowledge or care.

to 2 Cor 12:14–15a:[36] "See, a third time I am ready to come to you. And I will not be a burden, for I do not want to possess what is yours, but you. For children ought not to save up for their parents, but parents for their children. And I will gladly spend and be spent for your sake." In both passages Paul takes the role of parent, but emphasizes the emotional aspect of parenting: parents' devotion to their children and their willingness to do anything for their children's health and well-being. In the case of 1 Thess 2:7 this is expressed as a willingness to give of his very self to the Thessalonian community; in the case of 2 Cor 12:14–15a it is expressed as a willingness to be utterly spent for the sake of the Corinthian community. In both cases the passages imply that the community members can have complete confidence in Paul's care for them, his leadership of them, and his commitment to the gospel he imparted to them.

5.2.3.3. The Social Identity of the Thessalonian Community

Metaphor has the power to shape identity when one finds oneself as the target domain of a metaphor. Paul's nursing metaphor places him in the role of mother and the Thessalonians in the role of infants. Therefore, if the metaphor becomes part of the Thessalonians's thinking about themselves, it has the power to shape their identity. This makes the nursing metaphor a particularly powerful one for Paul as he sought to ground the Thessalonians's group identity in the new Christian community rather than in older kinship, business, and civic ties. The metaphor affects the social identity of the community through in-group/out-group differentiation and the use of kinship language.

Group formation begins with self-categorization; that is, groups exist because people think of themselves as part of a group.[37] In this respect the nursing metaphor has a key role to play as part of Paul's rhetorical strategy because the image pictures the Thessalonians as part of a group—those who are nourished and cared for together by Paul as nursing mother. The metaphor invites the Thessalonians to think of themselves as a group of related infants. Once members identify as part of this group, group identity develops, including shared cognition and group behavioral norms.

---

36. Commentators Bruce and Furnish both make this comparison. See Bruce, *1 and 2 Thessalonians*, 32; Furnish, *1 Thessalonians, 2 Thessalonians*, 59.

37. See my exploration of this aspect of social identity theory in §3.2, above.

Categorization of others inevitably happens as part of the self-categorization process. Through the nursing metaphor, an insider-outsider status has been created: members of the Thessalonian church are part of this group and others are not. This continues the process of in-group/out-group differentiation. The more that members of a group can differentiate themselves from outsiders, the stronger their in-group identity will be. This is accomplished largely through the formation of stereotypes—exaggerating the similarities between in-group members and exaggerating the differences between in-group members and out-group members.

That Paul encourages this kind of thinking as a way to strengthen the Thessalonians's group identity can be seen at several points in his letter to them, especially in the "us versus them" dynamic which is stronger in 1 Thessalonians than in Paul's other letters.[38] The opening verses of the letter identify the Thessalonians as a group distinct from others, particularly as those chosen by God (1:4). In chapter 4 Paul reviews various group norms that distinguish the Christian group from others, such as avoiding fornication, controlling the body, and not exploiting a fellow believer (4:1-8). This also includes living a quiet life and behaving properly toward "those on the outside" (4:12). These outsiders are mentioned again in the next section, this time identified as "the rest of them who do not have hope" (4:13). The division between insiders and outsiders is even starker in 5:5, where Paul divides humanity into "children of light" and "children of darkness." The children of nursing mother Paul are children of light; the children of darkness are the outsiders, and "sudden destruction will come upon *them*" (5:3, emphasis added).

In addition to these verses dividing insiders and outsiders, 2:13-16 also has a key role to play in Paul's strategy of in-group identity formation among the Thessalonians. First of all, the passage stresses the persecution that the Thessalonians have endured. Real or perceived persecution strengthens group identity because it strengthens the us versus them dynamic, solidifying bonds between group members. The passage further strengthens the Thessalonians's group identity by identifying who the insiders are and who the outsiders are. The insiders are not only the Thessalonian church members, but also those to whom they are connected by faith and by persecution: the churches of Judea. The outsiders, on the other

---

38. Carol J. Schlueter, *Filling up the Measure: Polemical Hyperbole in 1 Thessalonians 2:14-16* (JSNTSup 98; Sheffield: JSOT Press, 1994), 121.

hand, are the persecutors: "your own compatriots" (2:14). Thus, the Thessalonians are to think of other Christ-believers as insiders, whether they live next door or halfway around the world, and they are to think of all nonbelievers as outsiders, even when those nonbelievers are their former kin and associates, their own compatriots. Within a few verses, Paul has turned the insiders into outsiders and the outsiders into insiders.[39]

The nursing metaphor in 2:7 also participates in Paul's strategy of in-group identity formation, for it creates a fictive kinship group: the children of Mother Paul. This serves both to strengthen the connection between Paul and the Thessalonians and to strengthen the connections the Thessalonian church members have with each other. Creating a sense of kinship would have been a particularly powerful way for Paul to strengthen these connections, given the central place of kinship ties to identity formation in ancient Mediterranean cultures.[40]

While discussions of fictive kinship language in Paul's letters often revolve around his use of ἀδελφοί to address his readers, the nursing metaphor in 2:7 creates a kinship relationship between Paul and the Thessalonians every bit as strong as that conveyed by addressing them as "brothers and sisters." As their mother, Paul presents himself as an insider to the Thessalonians, part of their kinship group. This serves to strengthen the bond between them and thus also to strengthen the Thessalonians's commitment to the gospel Paul preached and to ease any tensions or suspicions that church members may have had of Paul. As Wanamaker points out, it also serves the parenetic intention of this letter; by strengthening the positive relationship between Paul and the letter's recipients the metaphor encourages the Thessalonians to hear the rest of the letter "with sympathetic ears."[41]

In addition to creating a kinship tie between Paul and the Thessalonians, the metaphor also creates kinship among the Thessalonians by placing them in sibling relationship with each other. There are two possible ways of understanding the precise nature of this relationship, hinging

---

39. For general comments on early Christian identity as part of a worldwide movement, see Wayne E. Meeks, *The First Urban Christians: The Social World of the Apostle Paul* (2nd ed.; New Haven: Yale University Press, 2003), 107–110.

40. See my discussion of kinship in the ancient Mediterranean world in §3.2.2 of this study.

41. Charles A. Wanamaker, *The Epistles to the Thessalonians: A Commentary on the Greek Text* (NIGTC; Grand Rapids: Eerdmans, 1990), 102.

5. PAUL AS INFANT AND NURSING MOTHER

on one's interpretation of ἑαυτῆς in 2:7 as either a simple possessive or a reflexive pronoun. When understood as a simple possessive ("a nurse with her children"), the metaphor is that of a nurse with her charges, and therefore the children are not necessarily blood-related siblings. Even when interpreted in this fashion, however, the metaphor still creates a kin-like relationship among the Thessalonians as those who nursed at the same breast. Roman culture recognized this kind of bond, giving the term *conlactei* to nonrelated children nursed by the same woman.[42] These children were likely to be playmates in early childhood and their relationships were often characterized by closeness and affection, as evidenced by Roman inscriptions.[43]

However, for those who interpret ἑαυτῆς as a reflexive pronoun ("a nurse with her own children"), as I do, the bond that the metaphor creates among the Thessalonians is even stronger. Since the nurse is with *her own* children, those children are full kin to one another, blood-related siblings. Thus the metaphor serves Paul's overall rhetorical aim in 1 Thessalonians of getting the church members to think of one another as family. As Wanamaker states, the nurse metaphor "implicitly exhorted the readers to the sense of mutuality and love that would unite them into a cohesive community, thereby strengthening them to face a hostile environment."[44] If the Thessalonians think of one another as siblings, then all the cultural expectations of kinship relations will be brought to bear on their interactions, including affection, cooperation rather than competition, and the sharing of resources.[45] The encouragement of this kind of attitude and behavior would go far in strengthening the Thessalonians's sense of group identity, empowering them to stand firm in their countercultural practice of faith in the midst of persecution. Paul's language constitutes "a new family for those who are being disenfranchised from their families of

---

42. Beryl Rawson, *Children and Childhood in Roman Italy* (Oxford: Oxford University Press, 2003), 122.

43. Ibid.; Keith R. Bradley, *Discovering the Roman Family: Studies in Roman Social History* (New York: Oxford University Press, 1991), 149–55.

44. Wanamaker, *The Epistles to the Thessalonians*, 102.

45. Philip Francis Esler, "'Keeping It in the Family': Culture, Kinship and Identity in 1 Thessalonians and Galatians," in *Families and Family Relations as Represented in Early Judaisms and Early Christianities: Texts and Fictions; Papers Read at a NOSTER Colloqium in Amsterdam, June 9-11, 1998* (ed. Jan Willem van Henten and Athalya Brenner; Leiden: Deo, 2000), 151.

origin."⁴⁶ If this metaphor becomes part of the Thessalonians's thinking, they will regard one another as kin and treat one another as kin; thus their identity will be grounded in the Christian group rather than in previous kin and non-kin connections.

5.3. Conclusion

5.3.1. The Relationship between the Metaphors

This chapter has analyzed the infant and nurse metaphors in separate sections as separate metaphors. However, it remains striking that Paul refers to himself as an infant and, only six words later, as a nursing mother. This close proximity of the images is part of what has led many scholars to reject the reading "infants," and continues to raise the question of how the two images might be related to each other. While I maintain that these are two separate metaphors in two separate sentences, this does not rule out the possibility of any relationship between the metaphors. It is possible that they are related in that Paul's use of νήπιοι brought the world of infants to his mind, from which it was a natural progression for him to consider how apostles are not only like infants but also like their mothers.[47]

Beyond that speculative possibility, the two metaphors are clearly related in that they are both part of the same rhetorical strategy Paul employs in 2:1–12, in which he uses multiple family metaphors (infants, nursing mother, father, and orphans) to defend the trustworthy nature of his apostleship and his gospel. Gaventa comments on how these two metaphors operate together:

> Here Paul does use a mixed metaphor, perhaps even an inverted one, but for good reason. He is struggling to identify two aspects of the apostolic role. The apostle is childlike, in contrast to the charlatan who constantly works to see how much benefit he can derive from his audience. The apostle is also the responsible adult, in the first instance the nurse who tends her charges with care and affection.[48]

---

46. Gaventa, *Our Mother Saint Paul*, 27. See also Meeks, *The First Urban Christians*, 86–88.
47. Fee, *The First and Second Letters to the Thessalonians*, 71.
48. Gaventa, *Our Mother Saint Paul*, 27.

While I disagree with Gaventa's assertion that Paul presents a mixed metaphor, because the metaphors are more properly understood separately, nevertheless her comments on how these metaphors function together to describe the apostolic role are helpful. Paul is attempting to express a variety of aspects of what true apostles are like, including both their innocence and their nurturing qualities. In this sense the infant and nurse metaphors work together to illustrate the nature of apostleship more fully than each metaphor could do on its own. The fact that Paul uses such different images in such close proximity to describe the same target domain illustrates, according to Gaventa, his understanding of the complex and countercultural nature of apostleship: that "apostles of Christ are not to be understood in an ordinary way. To understand them, just as to understand the gospel itself, one must employ categories that seem outrageous outside the context of Pauline paradox."[49] Though in separate sentences, the infant and nurse metaphors still create a striking juxtaposition; not one that is nonsensical, as some have claimed, but one that serves to further Paul's rhetorical aims.

5.3.2. Summary

The various entailments of the infant and nurse metaphors operate on many different levels in the context of Paul's rhetorical aims in 1 Thessalonians. They emphasize Paul's innocence with regard to charges of deception and greed; as a defense of Paul's trustworthiness they are also a defense of his gospel message. The metaphors serve as an identity-shaping strategy, encouraging the Thessalonians to ground their identity in the Christian group rather than in previous kinship, business, and civic connections. They define what genuine apostleship entails in terms of affection, giving of the self, suffering, low status, and modeling of group norms. As such they strengthen Paul's authority in the community even as they solidify the deeply emotional bond between Paul and the Thessalonians and among the Thessalonian church members. The metaphors invite the Thessalonians to view Paul and one another through the lens of kinship. These images have the power to shape the way in which the Thessalonians experience themselves, Paul, and the gospel, and thus to strengthen the Thessalonians's confidence in their faith and their sense of group identity.

---

49. Ibid.

This confidence will enable them to stand firm in their faith in the midst of persecution and suffering. The next chapter will trace some of the broader implications of this interpretation of the infant and nurse metaphors for understanding 1 Thessalonians, Paul's rhetoric, his gospel and theology, his character, and the nature of his relationship to his churches.

6
THE METAPHORS, THE LETTERS, AND PAUL THE APOSTLE

Chapter 5 traced the entailments of the infant and nurse metaphors of 1 Thess 2:7 as interpreted through metaphor theory and social identity analysis in the context of Paul's larger rhetorical goals in the letter. This analysis helped illumine the ways that these metaphors work to encourage the Thessalonians to view Paul and one another through the lens of kinship, thus strengthening these relationships, encouraging behaviors appropriate to the kinship group, defining a new group identity for the Thessalonians grounded in the Christ-believing community, and solidifying the Thessalonians's confidence in Paul and in the gospel he preached. This final chapter will explore some of the implications of this analysis for the interpretation of 1 Thessalonians as a whole and for understanding the nature of Paul's letters, his theology, and his relationship to his churches.

6.1. The Metaphors, 1 Thessalonians, and Paul's Letters

This study has focused on the interpretation and implications of just a few verses of 1 Thessalonians, but it is important to consider what such a study might have to contribute to broader questions of interpreting the letter as a whole, as well as Paul's writings in general. This section will explore what a study of the infant and nurse metaphors contributes to debates surrounding the occasion and purpose of 1 Thessalonians, Paul's rhetoric, and the nature of his theology and gospel message.

6.1.1. The Occasion and Purpose of 1 Thessalonians

As noted in §2.1.1, above, the occasion and purpose of 1 Thessalonians is a matter of scholarly debate, particularly whether the letter should be characterized as primarily exhortation or consolation. Malherbe argues for the former, describing the letter as a whole as parenetic.¹ Donfried, on the other hand, argues for the latter, categorizing the letter as a *consolatio*.² However, since the letter contains both of these elements in significant measure, it seems unhelpful to argue for only one or the other. In this sense, Furnish is closer to the mark when he characterizes the letter as "paracletic," a term that encompasses "encouragement, assurance, consolation, and exhortation."³

A study of the infant and nurse metaphors illustrates the futility of trying to categorize the letter as either exhortation or consolation to the exclusion of the other. Both elements are found in these metaphors, and the metaphors help to illustrate Paul's purpose in writing the letter. The infant metaphor emphasizes Paul's innocence and therefore solidifies the Thessalonians's confidence in him and his gospel message. Thus the image could be categorized as exhortation because Paul is trying to persuade the Thessalonians to view him in a certain way. But it can also be categorized as consolation because Paul is attempting to comfort the Thessalonians in the midst of difficulties, and illustrating that their new faith rests on a solid foundation is part of that strategy. Similarly, the nurse metaphor participates in both the exhorting and consoling aspects of the letter. The metaphor of a nurse tenderly caring for her own children is a very consoling image, emphasizing Paul's longing for the Thessalonians and his willingness to give himself to them. This is clearly meant to be a comfort to the Thessalonian community. However, within that consolation is the more subtle exhortation for the Thessalonians to view Paul and one another through the lens of kinship, with all the expectations of attitude, affection, and behavior that this metaphor entails. In this sense both metaphors illustrate the many ways that exhortation and consolation are intertwined in 1 Thessalonians and the futility of trying to separate these strands from each other.

In addition to illustrating the futility of trying to separate exhortation and consolation in the letter, the metaphors also suggest an entirely different way of characterizing the purpose of 1 Thessalonians. An in-depth

---

1. Abraham J. Malherbe, *The Letters to the Thessalonians: A New Translation with Introduction and Commentary* (AB 32B; New York: Doubleday, 2000), 81.

2. Karl P. Donfried, *Paul, Thessalonica, and Early Christianity* (Grand Rapids: Eerdmans, 2002), 120.

3. Victor Paul Furnish, *1 Thessalonians, 2 Thessalonians* (ANTC; Nashville: Abingdon, 2007), 52.

study of these metaphors has demonstrated that they encourage the formation of Christ-centered group identity in the Thessalonian community. Rereading the letter in light of this metaphor study exhibits that the whole letter is driven by this identity-shaping strategy. Chapter 1 establishes the identity of group members as those who are "in God the Father and the Lord Jesus Christ" (1:1), chosen by God (1:4), and connected to Christ-believers everywhere (1:7–8). First Thessalonians 2:1–12 establishes the solid foundation of the group in the true gospel of God preached in an upright manner by apostles commissioned directly by God. This section and the rest of chapter 2 also highlight that the Thessalonians remain strongly connected to these true apostles and to persecuted believers everywhere. Chapter 3 further emphasizes persecution, contributing to a sense of in-group identity. First Thessalonians 4:1–12 and 5:12–28 review the group's behavioral norms, including purity and treating one another as kin. First Thessalonians 4:13–5:11 solidifies the identity of group members as those who live in the light rather than the darkness and who will be taken up to be with Christ forever—the ultimate in-group. Paul's purpose in writing the letter was to shape and strengthen the identity of the Thessalonian community, grounding it in the Christian group rather than in previous kin and non-kin connections, as a way to encourage them to stand strong in their new faith in the midst of social ostracism and persecution.

6.1.2. The Metaphors as Rhetorical Strategy

Recognition of the fact that language mediates our experience of the world[4] suggests that Paul's letter to the Thessalonians is an attempt to mediate their worldview through language. As part of this strategy Paul employs metaphors, which are powerful rhetorical tools because they function at the cognitive level.[5] Metaphors are rhetorical because, by using the source domain to highlight and hide various aspects of the target domain, they

---

4. Dirk Geeraerts and Hubert Cuyckens, "Introducing Cognitive Linguistics," in *The Oxford Handbook of Cognitive Linguistics* (ed. Dirk Geeraerts and Hubert Cuyckens; Oxford: Oxford University Press, 2007), 5. See the explanation of cognitive linguistics in §1.2 of this study.

5. See the extensive explanation of cognitive metaphor theory in chapter 1 of the present study.

have the power to cause shifts in attitude.⁶ This study has demonstrated the ways in which the infant and nurse metaphors are an attempt to influence the Thessalonians's thinking in relation to Paul, the gospel, and one another. Several of the specific aspects of how metaphors work, as discussed in §§1.2–3, above, are at play in the infant and nurse metaphors.

Lakoff and Johnson argue that metaphors are central to the ways our brains work and process information about the world, and therefore they are central to the construction of reality, especially an individual's perception of his or her social reality.⁷ In day-to-day life, it is largely conventional metaphors (such as "good is up" or "time is money") that guide our understanding of the reality we live in. However, new metaphors are significant for their power to change our perception of reality and provide new insights. As Lakoff and Johnson note, "new metaphors have the power to create new reality."⁸ This happens through a "feedback effect" in which the person encountering the metaphor initially accepts the truth of its implied entailments; subsequently, the metaphor begins to guide the person's thinking about the target domain, causing him or her to emphasize the entailments of the metaphor even more than before.⁹ This is a good description of how the infant and nurse metaphors could have influenced the thinking of the Thessalonians. On the one hand, if the Thessalonians did not agree with the metaphors' implied entailments (e.g., that Paul was innocent, or that he cared for them with deep love and affection) they would have rejected the metaphors out of hand and remained uninfluenced. However, if they accepted the basic entailments of the metaphors as true, then the metaphors would have begun to guide their thinking. Their perceptions of Paul, the gospel, and one another would have been changed as they thought of him as an infant and as their nursing mother. Thus the metaphors serve Paul's rhetorical goals, influencing the Thessalonians's view of him and their developing communal identity.

Another insight of metaphor theory is that metaphors have the power not only to affect attitudes but also to change behavior, since people act

---

6. Max Black, *Models and Metaphors: Studies in Language and Philosophy* (Ithaca, N.Y.: Cornell University Press, 1962), 41–42.

7. George Lakoff and Mark Johnson, *Metaphors We Live By* (2nd ed.; Chicago: University of Chicago Press, 2003), 146.

8. Ibid., 145.

9. Ibid., 142.

according to their understanding of reality.[10] This aspect of the persuasive power of metaphor can also be observed in Paul's metaphors in 1 Thess 2:7. While at first glance it might seem to be exclusively the thoughts and attitudes of the Thessalonians that are targeted by Paul's rhetoric in these metaphors, closer examination through metaphor theory reveals that the metaphors also seek to influence the behavior of the Thessalonian community. This is particularly true of the nurse metaphor, which pictures the Thessalonians as a kinship group. If the metaphor begins to guide their thinking they will not only think of one another as kin, but treat one another that way as well. In this sense the metaphor is connected to Paul's advice elsewhere in the letter, such as his admonitions that no one should wrong or exploit a brother or sister (4:6), that they love one another more and more (4:9–10), that they live a quiet, respectable life in the midst of outsiders (4:11–12), that they respect one another and live at peace with one another (5:12–13), and that they help one another and do good to one another (5:14–15). All these would be considered proper behaviors within a kinship group. These behaviors are also encouraged by Paul's metaphors in 2:7 because the metaphors call for the Thessalonians to think of one another as kin.

Paul's infant and nurse metaphors are rhetorical tools because they seek to influence how the Thessalonians view themselves, the world, and their place in it. They affect how the Thessalonians understand themselves in relation to others as insiders and outsiders, and thus shape the developing social identity of the congregation. A study of these metaphors reveals that metaphor in general, as understood through cognitive metaphor theory, should not be overlooked in analyses of Paul's rhetoric. Paul's many other metaphors should also be analyzed for their power to influence the thinking, behaviors, and identities of the communities to which he wrote.

6.1.3. The Metaphors as Theology

Two of the important insights of previous scholarship analyzing Paul's maternal metaphors, as highlighted in §1.1.1, above, are that these metaphors are connected to Paul's broader theology and to his proclamation of the gospel. Susan Eastman has argued that in Paul's letters the type of discourse he chooses is itself part of the gospel's expression: "the medium

---

10. Ibid., 158.

and the message are inseparable."[11] A study of 1 Thess 2:7 confirms the truth of this observation. Paul's use of family images, such as the infant and nurse metaphors, is not related to relationship building alone but is also an integral part of his proclamation of the gospel. The gospel is not merely communicated *through* words of connection and self-giving nurture; the gospel *is* a message of connection and self-giving nurture. When Paul presents himself as a nurturing mother who gives of himself to the Thessalonians, he expresses the heart of the gospel message—that God acted in Christ, who gave of himself for the sake of a new connection and intimacy with all people. As Christ gave of himself for Paul, so Paul does for the Thessalonians, and so they are to do for one another, because that is who they are in Christ. The infant and nurse metaphors do not simply decorate the text or increase its emotional impact; they serve Paul's proclamation of the gospel through their very form.

By serving Paul's proclamation of the gospel, the infant and nurse metaphors illustrate Gaventa's point that we cannot confine an exploration of Paul's theology only to certain "discrete portions" of Paul's letters, because "Paul's urgent need to announce and interpret what God has done in Jesus Christ pervades everything he writes."[12] Though 1 Thess 2:7 may not be the first place scholars typically go to explicate Paul's theology, in fact many of the ideas contained in the metaphors, as demonstrated in the exploration of their entailments in §§5.1.1 and 5.2.1, above, are theological. This includes the proper behavior of a true apostle called by God, the comfort and nourishment of the gospel, the suffering of Christ and his followers, the love shared among believers, and the nature of apostolic authority. The infant and nurse metaphors also illustrate the futility of attempting to separate Paul's letters into discrete theological and ethical portions. The metaphors give expression to the gospel at the same time that they imply proper behavior. Throughout Paul's letters his theology has behavioral implications and his ethical admonitions are grounded in the gospel message.[13]

---

11. Susan G. Eastman, *Recovering Paul's Mother Tongue: Language and Theology in Galatians* (Grand Rapids: Eerdmans, 2007), 6.

12. Beverly Roberts Gaventa, *Our Mother Saint Paul* (Louisville: Westminster John Knox, 2007), ix–x.

13. Victor Paul Furnish, *Theology and Ethics in Paul* (NTL; Louisville: Westminster John Knox, 2009), 208–27.

6.2. Maternal Metaphors and Paul the Apostle

Just as the infant and nurse metaphors show that Paul's letters cannot be separated neatly into theological and ethical sections, so they reveal that Paul himself cannot easily be put into any one category in terms of his role and identity as an apostle.[14] In the past, much feminist work on the letters has characterized Paul as either heroic or villainous in his attitude toward women. But a close study of Paul's maternal metaphors clouds this simplistic picture, whatever one's position on this much-debated question. Nevertheless, exploration of the feminist scholarly debate over the pros and cons of Paul's maternal metaphors may provide deeper insights into the implications of these metaphors.

As noted in §1.3, above, metaphors are rhetorical tools that can be wielded for good or ill by those with power, to provide new insight and wisdom or to obscure and control. Metaphors highlight what the speaker wants to highlight and hide that to which the speaker does not want to draw attention. The more power one has, the more dangerous one's metaphors can become.[15] Since Paul is generally considered to have had power within the communities he founded, it is important to analyze the role his metaphors played in his wielding of that power. Does his use of them reflect an authoritarian, dominating power or a shared, collaborative power?[16] Interpreters of Paul's letters in general and his maternal metaphors in particular have evaluated Paul's power relations with his communities quite differently.

6.2.1. The Authoritarian and Dominating Paul

Elizabeth Castelli, particularly in her work on imitation language in Paul's letters, is prominent among those who interpret Paul's personality as authoritarian and dominating. Castelli argues that when Paul urges his communities to imitate him, he sets himself up as an intermediary between believers and Christ and thus places himself above the members

---

14. Gaventa, *Our Mother Saint Paul*, 13.
15. Lakoff and Johnson, *Metaphors We Live By*, 157.
16. See the discussion of different kinds of power as "power-over," "power-to," and "power-with" in Kathy Ehrensperger, *Paul and the Dynamics of Power: Communication and Interaction in the Early Christ-Movement* (LNTS 325; London: T&T Clark, 2007), 17–33.

of his communities. In commenting on 1 Cor 11:1, Castelli makes the following observation:

> Paul's demand of imitation here is founded on the idea of non-reciprocity. That is, the community must imitate Paul as Paul must imitate Christ (who, presumably, must imitate God). The lines of relationship move in only one direction. Paul, by acting as intermediary between Christ and the gospel on the one hand, and the community on the other, has constructed a hierarchy which, above all else, undergirds and reinforces his own privileged position.[17]

In analyzing 1 Cor 11:1 and other passages featuring imitation language, Castelli concludes that Paul not only sets himself up as a higher authority, but also at times goes so far as to confuse his own position with that of Christ or God.[18] As such, Paul's imitation language functions as a "strategy of power"[19] that "reinscribes Paul's privileged position as natural."[20]

In a similar vein, Cynthia Briggs Kittredge analyzes obedience language in Paul's letters as evidence of the hierarchical nature of Paul's relationship to his communities. While much of the obedience language in the letters relates to obeying God, not Paul or other human leaders, Kittredge notes that metaphors for obedience to God draw on the relationships of the "classical kyriarchal family"—the hierarchical relations between parents and children, husbands and wives, and masters and slaves—without questioning the validity of such structures.[21] Additionally, in her analysis of Philippians, Kittredge observes, "Because of the parallelism constructed in the letter between God's activity and Paul's presence, a shift toward obedience to God is also a shift toward greater authority for Paul within the community."[22] Paul does use language of partnership in the letter, but by

---

17. Elizabeth A. Castelli, *Imitating Paul: A Discourse of Power* (LCBI; Louisville: Westminster John Knox, 1991), 112–13.

18. Ibid., 112.

19. Ibid., 15.

20. Ibid., 117.

21. Cynthia Briggs Kittredge, *Community and Authority: The Rhetoric of Obedience in the Pauline Tradition* (Harrisburg, Penn.: Trinity Press International, 1998), 6. One of Kittredge's main points in the work is that the assumptions behind these metaphors of obedience in Paul's undisputed letters should be seen as connected to the explicit directives in the disputed epistles for children to obey their parents, wives to obey their husbands, and slaves to obey their masters.

22. Ibid., 100.

presenting himself as a good example parallel to Christ, he identifies partnership as "unity with himself" and with his own opinions and directives.[23] Therefore, despite the use of language of partnership and self-emptying in Philippians, "Paul is capitalizing upon rather than transforming the conventional language of obedience."[24]

David Clines's analysis of Paul's masculinity is a very different type of analysis from that of Castelli and Kittredge, but nonetheless relevant for our consideration of domineering interpretations of Paul's character. Through a study of biblical literature, Clines identifies five elements central to the portrayal of masculinity in biblical texts: strength, violence, powerful and persuasive speech, male bonding, and womanlessness.[25] Clines analyzes the "fictional character Paul" who emerges in the undisputed epistles, the disputed epistles, and the book of Acts, rather than the "historical Paul," but his comments on passages in the undisputed epistles that illustrate these five elements of masculinity are relevant.[26] For example, Clines notes how Paul equates masculinity with strength as a desirable characteristic in 1 Cor 16:13: "Be on the alert, stand firm in the faith, act like men, be strong!"[27] Further, Paul identifies power as the test of apostolic validity in 1 Cor 4:19.[28] While some make much of Paul's discussions of power in weakness, Clines does not view these passages as meaning that weakness is desirable, but rather that Paul prefers strength and finds a way to turn even weakness into strength.[29] Overall, Clines's analysis paints a picture of a man who values strength and the power of persuasion, who values his male connections more than his female ones, and who is proud to live a "womanless" life of celibacy and independent action.

In the previous chapter, I showed how close analysis of the nursing metaphor, particularly in comparison to the Qumran metaphors, highlights the hierarchy implicit in the image. The mother may not have the

---

23. Ibid.
24. Ibid.
25. David J. A. Clines, "Paul, the Invisible Man," in *New Testament Masculinities* (ed. Stephen D. Moore and Janice Capel Anderson; SemeiaSt 45; Atlanta: Society of Biblical Literature, 2003), 182. Though Clines bases his elements on biblical literature, he claims that these elements of masculinity are cross-cultural and would also have applied to the Mediterranean cultures in which Paul moved.
26. Ibid.
27. Ibid.
28. Ibid., 183.
29. Ibid., 184.

same level of authority as the *pater familias* but nevertheless she has authority over her own children and thus the image is not an egalitarian one. The metaphor portrays Paul as provider and members of the community as dependent receivers. When this aspect of the metaphor is emphasized it can contribute to a picture of Paul as authoritarian and dominating. While Castelli, Kittredge, and Clines do not deal directly with Paul's maternal metaphors, their ideas can be brought into conversation with the metaphors. For instance, Castelli's argument that Paul's imitation language sets up Paul as an intermediary in a relationship in which the lines go only in one direction parallels the lack of reciprocity in the nursing image, for milk, too, flows in only one direction. Castelli claims that the language of imitation "reinscribes Paul's privileged position as natural,"[30] and one could argue that the nurse metaphor does the same thing. Similarly, Kittredge's interpretation of obedience language downplays the intimacy and affection of the nursing metaphor and emphasizes the fact that if Paul is the Thessalonians's mother then he ought to be obeyed and deferred to. Accepting Clines's interpretation of Paul as eminently masculine also reduces any focus on weakness or affection in the infant and nurse metaphors, highlighting rather the ways in which these metaphors enhance Paul's authority in the community.

Among those who advance an authoritarian view of Paul are several interpreters who do deal directly with Paul's maternal metaphors and who do not find them to be positive from a feminist perspective. In her commentary on 1 Thessalonians, Linda McKinnish Bridges describes the image of Paul that emerges from his letters in general as that of a "'dogmatic grouch,' who speaks with loud and authoritative voice, admonishing all of his churches to strict obedience to the gospel"; yet this grouchy Paul "stands in stark contrast to Paul the mother who cuddles and breastfeeds her children to full spiritual maturity."[31] Despite the fact that the nursing image of 2:7 would seem at first to alter the authoritative, dogmatic image of Paul, Bridges argues that upon closer analysis it actually serves to reinforce the androcentrism of the letter. Because Bridges believes that the Thessalonian community was an all-male artisan community,[32] Paul

---

30. Castelli, *Imitating Paul*, 117.

31. Linda McKinnish Bridges, *1 and 2 Thessalonians* (SHBC; Macon, Ga.: Smyth & Helwys, 2008), 49.

32. Ibid., 8–13. Bridges bases her idea of the all-male artisan community on the letter's emphasis on work and community living, the professional guild as a setting for

6. THE METAPHORS, THE LETTERS, AND PAUL THE APOSTLE   165

speaks to men as an authoritative male. The metaphor operates only in this all-male context, and would have been received differently had it also been addressed to women. Therefore, we should not suppose that such language had any positive effect on the lives or position of real women in the early church.[33]

While Clines does not directly address Paul's maternal metaphors in his article, Margaret Aymer, referencing Clines, is moved to ask, "What possible benefit could attend the *über*-masculine Paul that he should choose to 'metaphorize' himself, to use Gaventa's barbarism, as a mother?"[34] Aymer analyzes 1 Cor 3:2; Gal 4:19; and 1 Thess 2:7 and concludes that we should not think that Paul places himself in a position of weakness when he describes himself as a mother. Rather, interpreted in the context of the formidable image of the ideal Roman matron, "Paul's 'fictions' would likely have been understood by his assemblies as a statement of his relative, although not absolute, authority and power."[35] For instance, the breastfeeding image in 1 Cor 3:2 "suggests the dependency of the entire assembly on Mother-Mammy Paul for its existence and sustenance"; this powerful matron has the power to hold them accountable and has the right to expect obedience.[36] While it seems at first quite striking to hear a man speak of his own birth pangs, in the final analysis, according to Aymer, Gal 4:19 is an "exaggerated maternal entreaty," in which the powerful matron "cries out against the impiety of her children—who owe her their very lives—because they are 'putting her through childbirth' all over again."[37] Aymer also suggests that Paul's interpretation of the Sarah and Hagar story in the verses that follow, in which these women do not fare well, reveals that "we should not be under any illusions that Paul here is championing actual motherhood."[38] Aymer concludes: "Paul is playing on two recognized themes: the virtuous mother and the gentle but persuasive mammy/

---

concerns surrounding death, the male point-of-view of the letter, and the fact that the letter does not mention any women, whether collectively or individually.

33. Ibid., 49–51.
34. Margaret Aymer, "'Mother Knows Best': The Story of Mother Paul Revisited," in *Mother Goose, Mother Jones, Mommie Dearest: Biblical Mothers and Their Children* (ed. Cheryl A. Kirk-Duggan and Tina Pippin; SemeiaSt 61; Atlanta: Society of Biblical Literature, 2009), 187.
35. Ibid., 189–90.
36. Ibid., 192.
37. Ibid.
38. Ibid., 196.

nurse. But he retains the right to be mother and to define motherhood; not every mother counts in Paul's family."[39]

Bridges and Aymer recognize the unusual nature of Paul's maternal metaphors, but nevertheless conclude that they actually serve to reinforce the androcentrism of the letters and Paul's domination of his churches, rather than providing a liberating change from cultural stereotypes. A comment from Trevor Burke is relevant here. In his broader analysis of all the family metaphors of 1 Thessalonians, Burke concludes that they indicate that Christian communities did not start out as egalitarian and later degenerate into hierarchy; rather, Christian communities were never free of hierarchy.[40] Though both Bridges and Aymer recognize the startling nature of Paul's maternal metaphors, neither draws out the full implications of what it would have meant for a man of that culture to portray himself as a woman. This aspect of the metaphors is taken more seriously by those who view Paul's character in his ministry as collaborative and empowering rather than authoritative and dominating.

6.2.2. The Collaborative and Empowering Paul

Not all scholars share the view of Paul sketched above. Others see him in true partnership with his communities, seeking to empower them rather than dominate them. In one classic formulation of Paul's apostolic authority, John Howard Schütz argues that Paul is not personally powerful, but rather an instrument of power that comes from beyond him, a power that he "interprets and makes available" but that does not belong to him.[41] Paul only exerts power over the congregations when their members fail to "reflect and embody the power which originally he made available to them. Where they stand 'in' the gospel they stand in the same power he does and their authority is the same as his."[42] Subsequent generations, from the early church to the present day, failed to understand the nature of apostolic

---

39. Ibid., 197.

40. Trevor J. Burke, *Family Matters: A Socio-historical Study of Kinship Metaphors in 1 Thessalonians* (JSNTSup 247; London: T&T Clark, 2003), 256.

41. John Howard Schütz, *Paul and the Anatomy of Apostolic Authority* (NTL; Louisville: Westminster John Knox, 2007), 282.

42. Ibid.

authority in the church when they failed to separate "the power to which the apostle is subject and which he manifests, and his own person."[43]

Scholars who see Paul as collaborative and empowering take him at his word when he writes to the Corinthians, "not that we lord it over your faith, but we are fellow-workers with you for your joy" (2 Cor 1:24). Taking this perspective, Morna Hooker disagrees with Castelli's interpretation of Paul's imitation language. She argues that for the most part Paul calls his communities to imitate Christ along with him, rather than setting himself up as an intermediary. Paul does at times call on them to imitate him, but this is not a power play; rather, it flows from his understanding of the revelation of Christ both to himself and to other believers:

> The revelation of Christ which is given to Paul is stamped on him, so that he himself, by his life as well as by his words, becomes the means by whom Christ is revealed to the Gentiles. Paul's summons to his converts to imitate him was not the result of immodesty; rather it sprang from his conviction that the whole Christian community should reflect the love and compassion of Christ: there was no distinction here between apostle and community, except that the role of the apostle was to be a subsidiary model. The Gospel was to be proclaimed both by Paul and by the community, not simply through the preaching of the word, but in every believer's life.[44]

According to this view, anyone in whom Christ has been revealed can be a model to be imitated, as when Paul says the Thessalonians became imitators of the churches of Judea (1 Thess 2:14), or when he tells them that they themselves became a model for all the believers in Macedonia and Achaia (1:7). Paul is at times a more prominent model than others only because of his visibility as a founder and guide of the communities.

Kathy Ehrensperger has done an extensive study of power dynamics in Paul's letters, with conclusions that are also at odds with the portrait of an authoritarian Paul sketched by Castelli, Kittredge, and others. Ehrensperger argues that leadership in the early church was countercultural: "Paul's emphasis on mutuality, weakness and suffering, and his opposition to factionalism and boasting are indications of such an alternative

---

43. Ibid., 283.

44. Morna D. Hooker, "A Partner in the Gospel: Paul's Understanding of His Ministry," in *Theology and Ethics in Paul and His Interpreters: Essays in Honor of Victor Furnish* (ed. Eugene H. Lovering Jr. and Jerry Sumney; Nashville: Abingdon, 1996), 100.

power and leadership discourse in the context of a society which was dominated by competition for status, domination and control."[45] While some have argued that Paul's references to weakness and suffering are a hidden claim to power, Ehrensperger points out that this does not make sense in Paul's cultural context, in which the relation of authority to weakness would seem "at least paradoxical if not foolish."[46] Unlike Clines, Ehrensperger sees Paul's views on weakness and suffering as truly countercultural, rather than a desperate attempt on his part to gain more power for himself despite the personal weaknesses he cannot hide. For Ehrensperger, Paul's countercultural views on weakness and suffering are indicative of his countercultural relation to power.

To be sure, Ehrensperger does not deny that Paul has strong opinions and argues for them forcefully. However, she points out that "to adhere to one's convictions, and to argue from and for them, need not be the same, and should not be confused with, the imposition of one's will on others, contrary to their own will and interest."[47] Paul has great confidence in his own convictions, but lacks the power to coerce his followers to agree with his theology or copy his behavior. In terms of power dynamics in the communities, Ehrensperger reminds us that the members of Paul's communities were in a voluntary relationship with him.[48] There was "no force or domination, no violence or control"; rather, church members had chosen to enter the communities and chosen to learn from Paul as a teacher.[49] They could also choose to end the relationship at any time.

In Ehrensperger's view, Paul does not seek to create hierarchical communities in which one member (whether Paul or someone else) lords it over the others. Rather, Paul's presentation of the gospel message always reflects concern for the weakest members (e.g., 1 Cor 12:21–26 and Rom 14:15).[50] Ehrensperger notes the frequency of the word ἀλλήλους, arguing that it indicates the kind of community that Paul tried to build: they should love one another (Rom 12:10; 13:8; 1 Thess 3:12), bear one another's burdens (Gal 6:2), welcome one another (Rom 15:7), comfort one another (1 Thess 4:18), encourage one another (1 Thess 5:11), do good to

---

45. Ehrensperger, *Paul and the Dynamics of Power*, 97.
46. Ibid., 98.
47. Ibid., 187.
48. Ibid., 136.
49. Ibid., 181.
50. Ibid., 186–87.

one another (1 Thess 5:15), become servants to one another (Gal 5:13), and so on.[51] These are communities of mutuality that eschew surrounding cultural values of violence and domination.

Schütz, Hooker, and Ehrensperger do not directly address Paul's maternal metaphors (at least not in any extensive manner), but their views, too, can be placed in conversation with these metaphors. The view of Paul as collaborative and empowering places the metaphors in a different light than the authoritarian view. If Paul is in genuine partnership with his congregations, then his maternal metaphors can be understood as highly relational, affectionate illustrations of Paul's countercultural views. This perspective would emphasize the metaphors' entailments of comfort, nourishment, and love. This view would see the deep bond between mother and child as a provocative but nevertheless appropriate illustration of the deep bond between Paul and his communities. In addition, this perspective takes more seriously the aspects of suffering present in the metaphors, and the fact that in them Paul presents himself in low-status roles. Bruce, for example, writes that the nursing metaphor in 1 Thess 2:7 exhibits Paul as a servant to his people, taking the example of Jesus who emptied himself (Phil 2:7); Paul does not seek gain for himself but is eager to share everything with them.[52] This is a very different perspective from those who view Paul's maternal metaphors as a means by which he sought to increase his own status and domination of the churches.

One of the strengths of the interpretation of Paul's maternal metaphors from a collaborative point of view is that it takes seriously the startling nature of a first century Mediterranean male's portrayal of himself as female. These scholars recognize that the maternal metaphors need to be a part of any discussion of the androcentric or misogynistic nature of Paul's writings. While Sandra Hack Polaski does view Paul's writings as largely androcentric, nevertheless she recognizes that Paul "representing himself metaphorically 'in drag'" is relevant to a consideration of his attitudes towards gender roles.[53] Carolyn Osiek makes a similar observation when

---

51. Ibid., 196–97.
52. F. F. Bruce, *1 and 2 Thessalonians* (WBC; Waco, Tex.: Word, 1982), 33.
53. Sandra Hack Polaski, *A Feminist Introduction to Paul* (St. Louis: Chalice, 2005), 24–25.

commenting on Gal 4:19: "Perhaps a man willing to use such an image is not as alienated from women's experience as Paul is often made out to be."[54]

As noted in §1.1.1.3, above, Gaventa has emphasized the countercultural nature of Paul's maternal imagery, arguing that through these metaphors Paul brings on himself the shame of presenting himself as a "female-identified male."[55] This interpretation of gender inversion contrasts sharply with Clines, who presents Paul as always seeking to appear as masculine as possible. But Gaventa is not alone in her observations. Polaski maintains that through his maternal metaphors Paul presents himself in "a 'weak' and 'body-focused' female role."[56] In doing so, Paul is not conforming to "the strict rules of gender-appropriate behavior and attitudes" that characterized the cultures of which he was a part.[57] Calvin Roetzel also comments on this aspect of the metaphors, observing that they "may represent a significant social and biological inversion. … Becoming female in this metaphorical world was an act of denying both the self and the power constructions of the social world."[58] Thus Roetzel sees Paul's maternal metaphors not as strategies for increasing his own power and position, but rather as his "renunciation of the superordinancy socially prescribed for males."[59] Roetzel and others interpret Paul's maternal metaphors as a sign of his humility, his servanthood, and his rejection of the hierarchical nature of social relationships in ancient Mediterranean cultures.

6.2.3. Viewing Power through the Cross

As the two sections above illustrate, Paul's maternal metaphors in general, and 1 Thess 2:7 in particular, can be interpreted as promoting either hierarchy or true partnership, depending on one's preconceived notions of Paul's character.[60] Since evidence can be found in Paul's letters to sup-

---

54. Carolyn Osiek, "Galatians," in *Women's Bible Commentary* (ed. Carol A. Newsom and Sharon H. Ringe; exp. ed.; Louisville: Westminster John Knox, 1998), 426.
55. Gaventa, *Our Mother Saint Paul*, 14.
56. Polaski, *A Feminist Introduction to Paul*, 24.
57. Ibid., 25.
58. Calvin J. Roetzel, *Paul: A Jew on the Margins* (Louisville: Westminster John Knox, 2003), 16–17.
59. Ibid., 17.
60. Polaski, *A Feminist Introduction to Paul*, 80.

port both the hierarchical and collaborative points of view, it is logical to conclude that there is some truth to both perspectives. Therefore, to gain a more accurate picture of Paul the apostle, one needs to find a balance between these two understandings of his character.

Many have recognized that both hierarchical and egalitarian perspectives are present in Paul's letters. Scholars have attempted to express the tension between these two streams of Paul's thought in various ways. Furnish, for example, calls Paul "authoritative but not authoritarian in presenting his views,"[61] and Gaventa calls the apostle "the authority who does not conform to standard norms of authority."[62] Ehrensperger frames the paradox by placing Paul in the context of the Old Testament prophets; like them, "his apostleship does not depend on any human power, nor his own accomplishment, but only on God. This is a bold and humble statement at the same time. He claims to be commissioned by the God of Israel and at the same time he is merely a tool for God's purpose."[63]

Paul's maternal metaphors can help us find this middle ground between a view of Paul as authoritarian and a view of Paul as egalitarian. They can help us because they themselves resist categorization as either egalitarian or hierarchical. Paul's metaphorical mothers have authority over their children and Paul uses them to enhance his own authority in the communities. And yet, with these metaphors Paul eschews images of domination and paternal or political power, instead taking on the role of mother and even slave nurse, and using the images to encourage, comfort, and strengthen communities with whom he shared an intimate bond of affection. Neither the metaphors nor Paul himself can be easily categorized as authoritarian or egalitarian.

When trying to navigate the seeming contradiction between the hierarchical and egalitarian streams in Paul's thought, it is important to remember that Paul views power, like everything else, through the lens of the cross. The cross is power, but it is power expressed through weakness, through humility, and through love. The power of the cross is power exerted for the benefit of others, not the benefit of oneself. This is the most helpful light in which to view Paul's maternal metaphors. A mother has power over her children, but this power is used for the benefit of the child,

---

61. Victor Paul Furnish, *The Moral Teaching of Paul: Selected Issues* (3rd ed.; Nashville: Abingdon, 2009), 52.

62. Gaventa, *Our Mother Saint Paul*, 14.

63. Ehrensperger, *Paul and the Dynamics of Power*, 90.

not the benefit of the mother. For instance, Paul as nursing mother has more power than his children, but uses that power to nurture, nourish, and sustain them through difficult times, with the hope of eventually bringing them to maturity alongside himself. Since they are his beloved children, he does not use his position for his own gain, but is willing to give of his very self for their sake, the essence of the way of the cross.

At least, that is the ideal—that the mother uses her power only for love and the benefit of her children. There is danger of abuse in the system, however, and no doubt Paul sometimes fell short of his own ideal. This is why the critiques of Castelli, Kittredge, and others need to be taken seriously by those with feminist and egalitarian commitments. Despite the self-giving and loving way Paul frames his maternal metaphors, they do place him in a role of authority above his followers. That is why his maternal metaphors are such good illustrations of the fact that his thought contains both hierarchical and egalitarian streams. Burke holds that the infant metaphor of 1 Thess 2:7 "may modify his patriarchal role, but it does not deconstruct it altogether—after all Paul behaves in this letter as the father, not as the child!"[64] Similarly, one could say that by portraying himself as a nurse with her own children Paul destabilizes cultural gender and class hierarchies, but by no means diminishes his own authority within the group. The modern reader can appreciate the countercultural and self-giving aspects of Paul's maternal metaphors while exercising care not to let them become a model for reinscribing hierarchical or dominating power relations in modern relationships, including those of the family and those in the church.

6.3. Conclusion

This study has analyzed the infant and nurse metaphors found in 1 Thess 2:7 in the context of Paul's rhetorical aims in the letter as a whole. The primary tools for this analysis were metaphor theory and social identity theory, as described in chapters 1 and 3. It was of primary importance to establish the text, translation, and punctuation of 2:5–8, which was completed in chapter 2. This analysis determined that the original reading is "infants" rather than "gentle." I also concluded that it is not a mixed metaphor, for the infant metaphor relates to what precedes it, and the nurse

---

64. Burke, *Family Matters*, 157.

6. THE METAPHORS, THE LETTERS, AND PAUL THE APOSTLE 173

metaphor to what follows. Chapters 3 and 4 set these two metaphors in their historical, social, and literary contexts, laying the foundation for new insights into the meaning of the metaphors in their own historical and rhetorical locations. Chapter 5 explored these insights in depth, particularly through a study of the metaphors' entailments and of what they highlight and hide in relation to Paul and the gospel he preached. Chapter 6 explored the implications of these new insights for an understanding of the purpose and theology of 1 Thessalonians as well as Paul's relation to power and character as an apostle.

The primary conclusion of this study is that Paul's infant and nurse metaphors in 2:7 serve his overall rhetorical goals in the letter by presenting Paul to the Thessalonians as an innocent infant and an affectionate and trustworthy mother, and presenting the Thessalonians to one another as a kinship group. This serves both as a defense of Paul and his gospel message as well as an encouragement to the Thessalonians to ground their social identity in the Christian group. As a reassurance of the solid foundation of their faith and as an exhortation to see themselves as members of a new kinship group, the metaphors serve to strengthen the community in the midst of persecution and social hostility. At the same time they also define what a genuine apostle should be: trustworthy, affectionate toward followers, willing to give of oneself, willing to suffer, and accepting of low status. Thus the metaphors enhance Paul's authority in the community even as they solidify a deeply emotional bond between Paul and the community that is characterized by love, affection, and collaboration.

Bibliography

Aaron, David H. *Biblical Ambiguities: Metaphor, Semantics, and Divine Imagery*. BRLJ 4. Leiden: Brill, 2001.
Aasgaard, Reidar. "Like a Child: Paul's Rhetorical Uses of Childhood." Pages 249–77 in *The Child in the Bible*, edited by Marcia J. Bunge, Terence E. Fretheim, and Beverly Roberts Gaventa. Grand Rapids: Eerdmans, 2008.
———. "Paul as a Child: Children and Childhood in the Letters of the Apostle." *JBL* 126 (2007): 129–59.
Aland, Kurt, and Barbara Aland. *The Text of the New Testament: An Introduction to the Critical Editions and to the Theory and Practice of Modern Textual Criticism*. Translated by Erroll F. Rhodes. Grand Rapids: Eerdmans, 1989.
Aristotle. *The Nicomachean Ethics*. Translated by H. Rackham. LCL. Cambridge, Mass.: Harvard University Press, 1934.
Ascough, Richard S. *Paul's Macedonian Associations: The Social Context of Philippians and 1 Thessalonians*. WUNT 2/161. Tübingen: Mohr Siebeck, 2003.
Ashley, Timothy R. *The Book of Numbers*. NICOT. Grand Rapids: Eerdmans, 1993.
Aulus Gellius. *Attic Nights*. Translated by John C. Rolfe. 3 vols. LCL. Cambridge, Mass.: Harvard University Press, 1946.
Aymer, Margaret. "'Mother Knows Best': The Story of Mother Paul Revisited." Pages 187–98 in *Mother Goose, Mother Jones, Mommie Dearest: Biblical Mothers and Their Children*. Edited by Cheryl A. Kirk-Duggan and Tina Pippin. SemeiaSt 61. Atlanta: Society of Biblical Literature, 2009.
Balch, David L., and Carolyn Osiek, eds. *Early Christian Families in Context: An Interdisciplinary Dialogue*. Grand Rapids: Eerdmans, 2003.
Balla, Peter. *The Child-Parent Relationship in the New Testament and Its Environment*. WUNT 2/155. Tübingen: Mohr Siebeck, 2003.

Bauer, Walter, F. W. Danker, W. F. Arndt, and F. W. Gingrich. *A Greek-English Lexicon of the New Testament and Other Early Christian Literature.* 3rd ed. Chicago: University of Chicago Press, 2000.

Best, Ernest. *A Commentary on the First and Second Epistles to the Thessalonians.* HNTC. New York: Harper & Row, 1972.

Black, C. Clifton. "Rhetorical Criticism." Pages 256–77 in *Hearing the New Testament: Strategies for Interpretation.* Edited by Joel B. Green. Grand Rapids: Eerdmans, 1995.

Black, Max. *Models and Metaphors: Studies in Language and Philosophy.* Ithaca, N.Y.: Cornell University Press, 1962.

Blass, Friedrich, Albert Debrunner, and Robert W. Funk. *A Greek Grammar of the New Testament and Other Early Christian Literature.* Chicago: University of Chicago Press, 1961.

Booth, Wayne C. "Metaphor as Rhetoric: The Problem of Evaluation." Pages 47–70 in *On Metaphor.* Edited by Sheldon Sacks. Chicago: University of Chicago Press, 1979.

Bradley, Keith R. *Discovering the Roman Family: Studies in Roman Social History.* New York: Oxford University Press, 1991.

———. "Wet-Nursing at Rome: A Study in Social Relations." Pages 201–29 in *The Family in Ancient Rome: New Perspectives.* Edited by Beryl Rawson. Ithaca, N.Y.: Cornell University Press, 1986.

Bridges, Linda McKinnish. *1 and 2 Thessalonians.* SHBC. Macon, Ga.: Smyth & Helwys, 2008.

Brown, Francis, S. R. Driver, and Charles A. Briggs. *The Brown-Driver-Briggs Hebrew and English Lexicon.* Peabody, Mass.: Hendrickson, 1996.

Bruce, F. F. *1 and 2 Thessalonians.* WBC. Waco, Tex.: Word, 1982.

Bunge, Marcia J., Terence E. Fretheim, and Beverly Roberts Gaventa, eds. *The Child in the Bible.* Grand Rapids: Eerdmans, 2008.

Burke, Trevor J. *Adopted into God's Family: Exploring a Pauline Metaphor.* Downers Grove, Ill.: InterVarsity Press, 2006.

———. *Family Matters: A Socio-Historical Study of Kinship Metaphors in 1 Thessalonians.* JSNTSup 247. London: T&T Clark, 2003.

———. "Pauline Paternity in 1 Thessalonians." *TynBul* 51 (2000): 59–80.

Byrne, Brendan J. *Romans.* SP 6. Collegeville, Minn.: Liturgical Press, 2007.

Byron, John. *Slavery Metaphors in Early Judaism and Pauline Christianity: A Traditio-Historical and Exegetical Examination.* WUNT 2/162. Tübingen: Mohr Siebeck, 2003.

Campbell, William S. *Paul and the Creation of Christian Identity.* LNTS 322. London: T&T Clark, 2006.

Cantarella, Eva. *Pandora's Daughters: The Role and Status of Women in Greek and Roman Antiquity*. Baltimore: Johns Hopkins University Press, 1987.

Castelli, Elizabeth A. *Imitating Paul: A Discourse of Power*. LCBI. Louisville: Westminster John Knox, 1991.

Chalcraft, David J. "Towards a Weberian Sociology of the Qumran Sects." Pages 74–105 in *Sectarianism in Early Judaism: Sociological Advances*. Edited by David J. Chalcraft. London: Equinox, 2007.

Chazon, Esther G. "Hymns and Prayers in the Dead Sea Scrolls." Pages 244–70 in volume 1 of *The Dead Sea Scrolls after Fifty Years: A Comprehensive Assessment*. Edited by Peter W. Flint and James C. VanderKam. Leiden: Brill, 1998.

Classen, Carl Joachim. *Rhetorical Criticism of the New Testament*. WUNT 1/128. Tübingen: Mohr Siebeck, 2000.

Clines, David J. A. "Paul, the Invisible Man." Pages 181–92 in *New Testament Masculinities*. Edited by Stephen D. Moore and Janice Capel Anderson. SemeiaSt 45. Atlanta: Society of Biblical Literature, 2003.

Cohen, Shaye J. D. "Introduction." Pages 1–5 in *The Jewish Family in Antiquity*. Edited by Shaye J. D. Cohen. BJS 289. Atlanta: Scholars Press, 1993.

———, ed. *The Jewish Family in Antiquity*. BJS 289. Atlanta: Scholars Press, 1993.

Cohen, Ted. "Metaphor and the Cultivation of Intimacy." Pages 1–10 in *On Metaphor*. Edited by Sheldon Sacks. Chicago: University of Chicago Press, 1979.

Cohick, Lynn H. *Women in the World of the Earliest Christians: Illuminating Ancient Ways of Life*. Grand Rapids: Baker Academic, 2009.

Collins, John J. *Beyond the Qumran Community: The Sectarian Movement of the Dead Sea Scrolls*. Grand Rapids: Eerdmans, 2010.

Collins, Raymond F. *The Birth of the New Testament: The Origin and Development of the First Christian Generation*. New York: Crossroad, 1993.

———. *The Power of Images in Paul*. Collegeville, Minn.: Liturgical Press, 2008.

Collins, Raymond F., and Norbert Baumert, eds. *The Thessalonian Correspondence*. BETL 87. Leuven: Leuven University Press, 1990.

Corbier, Mireille. "Child Exposure and Abandonment." Pages 52–73 in *Childhood, Class, and Kin in the Roman World*. Edited by Suzanne Dixon. London: Routledge, 2001.

Cotrozzi, Stefano. "1 Thes 2:7—a Review." *FN* 12 (1999): 155–60.

Cousar, Charles B. *Reading Galatians, Philippians, and 1 Thessalonians: A Literary and Theological Commentary.* Macon, Ga.: Smyth & Helwys, 2001.

Crawford, Charles. "The 'Tiny' Problem of 1 Thessalonians 2,7: The Case of the Curious Vocative." *Bib* 54 (1973): 69–72.

Delobel, Joel. "One Letter Too Many in Paul's First Letter? A Study of (ν)ηπιοι in 1 Thess 2:7." *LS* 20 (1995): 126–33.

Dille, Sarah J. *Mixing Metaphors: God as Mother and Father in Deutero-Isaiah.* JSOTSup 398. London: T&T Clark, 2004.

Dio Chrysostom. Translated by J. W. Cohoon and H. Lamar Crosby. 5 vols. LCL. Cambridge, Mass.: Harvard University Press, 1932–1985.

Diodorus Siculus. Translated by C. H. Oldfather, Charles L. Sherman, C. Bradford Welles, and Russel M. Geer. 12 vols. LCL. Cambridge, Mass.: Harvard University Press, 1946–1989.

Dixon, Suzanne, ed. *Childhood, Class, and Kin in the Roman World.* London: Routledge, 2001.

———. *The Roman Family.* Baltimore: Johns Hopkins University Press, 1992.

———. *The Roman Mother.* Norman: University of Oklahoma Press, 1988.

Donfried, Karl P. "The Epistolary and Rhetorical Context of 1 Thessalonians 2:1–12." Pages 31–60 in *The Thessalonians Debate: Methodological Discord or Methodological Synthesis?* Edited by Karl P. Donfried and Johannes Beutler. Grand Rapids: Eerdmans, 2000.

———. "Paul and Judaism: 1 Thessalonians 2:13–16 as a Test Case." *Int* 38 (1984): 242–53.

———. *Paul, Thessalonica, and Early Christianity.* Grand Rapids: Eerdmans, 2002.

———. "The Theology of 1 Thessalonians as a Reflection of Its Purpose." Pages 243–60 in *To Touch the Text: Biblical and Related Studies in Honor of Joseph A. Fitzmyer, S. J.* Edited by Maurya P. Horgan and Paul J. Kobelski. New York: Crossroad, 1989.

Donfried, Karl P., and Johannes Beutler, eds. *The Thessalonians Debate: Methodological Discord or Methodological Synthesis?* Grand Rapids: Eerdmans, 2000.

Donfried, Karl P., and I. Howard Marshall. *The Theology of the Shorter Pauline Letters.* New Testament Theology. Cambridge: Cambridge University Press, 1993.

Eastman, Susan G. *Recovering Paul's Mother Tongue: Language and Theology in Galatians.* Grand Rapids: Eerdmans, 2007.

Ehrensperger, Kathy. *Paul and the Dynamics of Power: Communication and Interaction in the Early Christ-Movement*. LNTS 325. London: T&T Clark, 2007.

———. *That We May Be Mutually Encouraged: Feminism and the New Perspective in Pauline Studies*. New York: T&T Clark, 2004.

Esler, Philip Francis. *Conflict and Identity in Romans: The Social Setting of Paul's Letter*. Minneapolis: Fortress, 2003.

———. "'Keeping It in the Family': Culture, Kinship and Identity in 1 Thessalonians and Galatians." Pages 145–84 in *Families and Family Relations as Represented in Early Judaisms and Early Christianities: Texts and Fictions; papers read at a NOSTER Colloqium in Amsterdam, June 9-11, 1998*. Edited by Jan Willem van Henten and Athalya Brenner. Leiden: Deo, 2000.

Fauconnier, Gilles, and Mark Turner. *The Way We Think: Conceptual Blending and the Mind's Hidden Complexities*. New York: Basic Books, 2002.

Fee, Gordon D. *The First and Second Letters to the Thessalonians*. NICNT. Grand Rapids: Eerdmans, 2009.

———. "On Text and Commentary on 1 and 2 Thessalonians." Pages 165–83 in *Society of Biblical Literature 1992 Seminar Papers*. Edited by Eugene H. Lovering Jr. SBLSP 31. Atlanta: Scholars Press, 1992.

Felder, Cain Hope. "1 Thessalonians." Pages 389–400 in *True to Our Native Land: An African American New Testament Commentary*. Edited by Brian K. Blount, Cain Hope Felder, Clarice Jannette Martin, and Emerson B. Powery. Minneapolis: Fortress, 2007.

Ferguson, Everett. *Backgrounds of Early Christianity*. 3rd ed. Grand Rapids: Eerdmans, 2003.

Fitzmyer, Joseph A. *The Acts of the Apostles: A New Translation with Introduction and Commentary*. AB 31. New York: Doubleday, 1998.

Foster, Julia A. "The Motherhood of God: The Use of *hyl* as God-Language in the Hebrew Scriptures." Pages 93–102 in *Uncovering Ancient Stones: Essays in Memory of H. Neil Richardson*. Edited by Lewis M. Hopfe. Winona Lake, Ind.: Eisenbrauns, 1994.

Fowl, Stephen E. "A Metaphor in Distress: A Reading of ΝΗΠΙΟΙ in 1 Thessalonians 2:7." *NTS* 36 (1990): 469–73.

Francis, James M. M. *Adults as Children: Images of Childhood in the Ancient World and the New Testament*. Religions and Discourse 17. Oxford: Peter Lang, 2006.

French, Valerie. "Birth Control, Childbirth, and Early Childhood." *CAM* 3:1355–62.

Fronto, Marcus Cornelius. *The Correspondence of Marcus Cornelius Fronto.* Translated by C. R. Haines. LCL. London: Heinemann, 1919.

Furnish, Victor Paul. *1 Thessalonians, 2 Thessalonians.* ANTC. Nashville: Abingdon, 2007.

———. *The Moral Teaching of Paul: Selected Issues.* 3rd ed. Nashville: Abingdon, 2009.

———. *Theology and Ethics in Paul.* NTL. Louisville: Westminster John Knox, 2009.

Galen. *On the Natural Faculties.* Translated by Arthur John Brock. LCL. London: Heinemann, 1916.

García Martínez, Florentino, and Eibert J. C. Tigchelaar. *The Dead Sea Scrolls Study Edition.* Vol. 1. Leiden: Brill, 1997.

Gardner, Jane F. *Women in Roman Law and Society.* Bloomington, Ind.: Indiana University Press, 1991.

Gaventa, Beverly Roberts. "Apostles as Babes and Nurses in 1 Thessalonians 2:7." Pages 193–207 in *Faith and History: Essays in Honor of Paul W. Meyer.* Edited by John T. Carroll, Charles H. Cosgrove, and E. Elizabeth Johnson. Atlanta: Scholars Press, 1990.

———. "Finding a Place for Children in the Letters of Paul." Pages 233–48 in *The Child in the Bible.* Edited by Marcia J. Bunge, Terence E. Fretheim, and Beverly Roberts Gaventa. Grand Rapids: Eerdmans, 2008.

———. *First and Second Thessalonians.* IBC. Louisville: John Knox, 1998.

———. "The Maternity of Paul: An Exegetical Study of Galatians 4:19." Pages 189–201 in *The Conversation Continues: Studies in Paul and John in Honor of J. Louis Martyn.* Edited by Robert Tomson Fortna and Beverly Roberts Gaventa. Nashville: Abingdon, 1990.

———. "Mother's Milk and Ministry in 1 Corinthians 3." Pages 101–13 in *Theology and Ethics in Paul and His Interpreters: Essays in Honor of Victor Paul Furnish.* Edited by Eugene H. Lovering Jr. and Jerry L. Sumney. Nashville: Abingdon, 1996.

———. *Our Mother Saint Paul.* Louisville: Westminster John Knox, 2007.

———. "Our Mother St. Paul: Toward the Recovery of a Neglected Theme." Pages 85–97 in *A Feminist Companion to Paul.* Edited by Amy-Jill Levine and Marianne Blickenstaff. London: T&T Clark, 2004.

Geeraerts, Dirk, and Hubert Cuyckens. "Introducing Cognitive Linguistics." Pages 3–21 in *The Oxford Handbook of Cognitive Linguistics.* Edited by Dirk Geeraerts and Hubert Cuyckens. Oxford: Oxford University Press, 2007.

———, eds. *The Oxford Handbook of Cognitive Linguistics*. Oxford: Oxford University Press, 2007.
Gerber, Christine. *Paulus Und Seine "Kinder": Studien Zur Beziehungsmetaphorik der Paulinischen Briefe*. BZNW 136. Berlin: de Gruyter, 2005.
Getty-Sullivan, Mary Ann. *Women in the New Testament*. Collegeville, Minn.: Liturgical Press, 2001.
Gilliard, Frank. "The Problem of the Antisemitic Comma between 1 Thessalonians 2:14 and 15." *NTS* 35 (1989): 481–502.
Glancy, Jennifer A. *Slavery in Early Christianity*. Oxford: Oxford University Press, 2002.
Goff, Matthew J. "Reading Wisdom at Qumran: 4QInstruction and the Hodayot." *DSD* 11 (2004): 263–88.
Gorman, Michael J. *Cruciformity: Paul's Narrative Spirituality of the Cross*. Grand Rapids: Eerdmans, 2001.
Grady, Joseph E. "Metaphor." Pages 188–213 in *The Oxford Handbook of Cognitive Linguistics*. Edited by Dirk Geeraerts and Hubert Cuyckens. Oxford: Oxford University Press, 2007.
Grant, Michael, and Rachel Kitzinger, eds. *Civilization of the Ancient Mediterranean*. 3 vols. New York: Scribner's, 1988.
Gruber, Mayer I. *The Motherhood of God and Other Studies*. Atlanta: Scholars Press, 1992.
Hemberg, Bengt. *Die Kabiren*. Uppsala: Almquist & Wiksells Boktryckeri, 1950.
Hempel, Charlotte. "Community Structures in the Dead Sea Scrolls: Admission, Organization, Disciplinary Procedures." Pages 67–92 in volume 2 of *The Dead Sea Scrolls after Fifty Years: A Comprehensive Assessment*. Edited by Peter W. Flint and James C. VanderKam. Leiden: Brill, 1999.
Henten, Jan Willem van, and Athalya Brenner, eds. *Families and Family Relations as Represented in Early Judaisms and Early Christianities: Texts and Fictions; papers read at a NOSTER Colloqium in Amsterdam, June 9-11, 1998*. Leiden: Deo, 2000.
Holmberg, Bengt, ed. *Exploring Early Christian Identity*. WUNT 1/226. Tübingen: Mohr Siebeck, 2008.
———. "Understanding the First Hundred Years of Christian Identity." Pages 1–32 in *Exploring Early Christian Identity*. Edited by Bengt Holmberg. WUNT 1/226. Tübingen: Mohr Siebeck, 2008.
Holmberg, Bengt, and Mikael Winninge, eds. *Identity Formation in the New Testament*. WUNT 1/227. Tübingen: Mohr Siebeck, 2008.

Holm-Nielsen, Svend. *Hodayot: Psalms from Qumran*. Aarhus: Universitetsforlaget, 1960.
Holmstrand, Jonas. *Markers and Meaning in Paul: An Analysis of 1 Thessalonians, Philippians, and Galatians*. Stockholm: Almqvist & Wiksell International, 1997.
Holtz, Traugott. "On the Background of 1 Thessalonians 2:1–12." Pages 69–80 in *The Thessalonians Debate: Methodological Discord or Methodological Synthesis?* Edited by Karl P. Donfried and Johannes Beutler. Grand Rapids: Eerdmans, 2000.
Hooker, Morna D. "A Partner in the Gospel: Paul's Understanding of His Ministry." Pages 83–100 in *Theology and Ethics in Paul and His Interpreters: Essays in Honor of Victor Furnish*. Edited by Eugene H. Lovering Jr. and Jerry L. Sumney. Nashville: Abingdon, 1996.
Hopkins, D. Dombkowski. "The Qumran Community and 1QHodayot: A Reassessment." *RevQ* 10 (1981): 323–64.
Horgan, Maurya P., and Paul J. Kobelski, eds. *To Touch the Text: Biblical and Related Studies in Honor of Joseph A. Fitzmyer, S.J.* New York: Crossroad, 1989.
Hughes, Frank W. "The Rhetoric of Letters." Pages 194–240 in *The Thessalonians Debate: Methodological Discord or Methodological Synthesis?* Edited by Karl P. Donfried and Johannes Beutler. Grand Rapids: Eerdmans, 2000.
———. "The Social Situations Implied by Rhetoric." Pages 241–54 in *The Thessalonians Debate: Methodological Discord or Methodological Synthesis?* Edited by Karl P. Donfried and Johannes Beutler. Grand Rapids: Eerdmans, 2000.
Hughes, Julie A. *Scriptural Allusions and Exegesis in the Hodayot*. STDJ 59. Leiden: Brill, 2006.
Hurd, John C. "Paul Ahead of His Time: 1 Thess. 2:13–16." Pages 21–36 in volume 1 of *Anti-Judaism in Early Christianity*. Edited by Peter Richardson and David Granskou. SJC 2. Waterloo, Ont.: Wilfrid Laurier University Press, 1986.
Jasper, David. *Rhetoric, Power and Community: An Exercise in Reserve*. Louisville: Westminster John Knox, 1993.
Jenkins, Richard. *Social Identity*. 3rd ed. London: Routledge, 2008.
Jewett, Robert. *Romans: A Commentary*. Edited by Eldon Jay Epp. Hermeneia. Minneapolis: Fortress, 2007.
———. *The Thessalonian Correspondence: Pauline Rhetoric and Millenarian Piety*. FF. Philadelphia: Fortress, 1986.

Johanson, Bruce C. *To All the Brethren: A Text-Linguistic and Rhetorical approach to 1 Thessalonians*. ConBNT 16. Stockholm: Almqvist & Wiksell, 1987.

Josephus. Translated by H. St. J. Thackeray. 10 vols. LCL. Cambridge, Mass.: Harvard University Press, 1926.

Joshel, Sandra R. "Nurturing the Master's Child: Slavery and the Roman Child-Nurse." *Signs* 12 (1986): 3–22.

Juvenal and Persius. Translated by Susanna Morton Braund. LCL. Cambridge, Mass.: Harvard University Press, 2004.

Kim, Yung Suk. *Christ's Body in Corinth: The Politics of a Metaphor*. Minneapolis: Fortress, 2008.

Kirk-Duggan, Cheryl A., and Tina Pippin, eds. *Mother Goose, Mother Jones, Mommie Dearest: Biblical Mothers and Their Children*. SemeiaSt 61. Atlanta: Society of Biblical Literature, 2009.

Kittay, Eva Feder. *Metaphor: Its Cognitive Force and Linguistic Structure*. Clarendon Library of Logic and Philosophy. Oxford: Clarendon, 1987.

Kittel, Bonnie P. *The Hymns of Qumran: Translation and Commentary*. Chico, Calif.: Scholars Press, 1981.

Kittredge, Cynthia Briggs. *Community and Authority: The Rhetoric of Obedience in the Pauline Tradition*. Harrisburg, Penn.: Trinity Press International, 1998.

Koester, Helmut. "The Text of 1 Thessalonians." Pages 219–27 in *The Living Text: Essays in Honor of Ernest W. Saunders*. Edited by Dennis E. Groh and Robert Jewett. Lanham, Md.: University Press of America, 1985.

Kraemer, Ross S. "Jewish Mothers and Daughters in the Greco-Roman World." Pages 89–112 in *The Jewish Family in Antiquity*. Edited by Shaye J. D. Cohen. BJS 289. Atlanta: Scholars Press, 1993.

Krentz, Edgar. "1 Thessalonians: Rhetorical Flourishes and Formal Constraints." Pages 287–318 in *The Thessalonians Debate: Methodological Discord or Methodological Synthesis?* Edited by Karl P. Donfried and Johannes Beutler. Grand Rapids: Eerdmans, 2000.

Lakoff, George, and Mark Johnson. *Metaphors We Live By*. 2nd ed. Chicago: University of Chicago Press, 2003.

Lakoff, George, and Mark Turner. *More Than Cool Reason: A Field Guide to Poetic Metaphor*. Chicago: University of Chicago Press, 1989.

Lambrecht, Jan. "Thanksgivings in 1 Thessalonians 1–3." Pages 135–62 in *The Thessalonians Debate: Methodological Discord or Methodological Synthesis?* Edited by Karl P. Donfried and Johannes Beutler. Grand Rapids: Eerdmans, 2000.

Lamp, Jeffrey S. "Is Paul Anti-Jewish? Testament of Levi 6 in the Interpretation of 1 Thessalonians 2:13–16." *CBQ* 65 (2003): 408–27.

Lefkowitz, Mary R., and Maureen B. Fant. *Women's Life in Greece and Rome: A Source Book in Translation*. 2nd ed. Baltimore: Johns Hopkins University Press, 1992.

Lopez, Davina C. *Apostle to the Conquered: Reimagining Paul's Mission*. Paul in Critical Contexts. Minneapolis: Fortress, 2008.

Louw, Johannes P., and Eugene A. Nida. *Greek-English Lexicon of the New Testament: Based on Semantic Domains*. 2nd ed. New York: United Bible Societies, 1989.

Luckensmeyer, David. *The Eschatology of First Thessalonians*. NTOA 71. Göttingen: Vandenhoeck & Ruprecht, 2009.

Malherbe, Abraham J. "Gentle as a Nurse: The Cynic Background to 1 Thess 2." *NovT* 12 (1970): 203–17.

———. "God's New Family in Thessalonica." Pages 116–25 in *The Social World of the First Christians: Essays in Honor of Wayne A. Meeks*. Edited by L. Michael White and O. Larry Yarbrough. Minneapolis: Fortress, 1995.

———. *The Letters to the Thessalonians: A New Translation with Introduction and Commentary*. AB 32B. New York: Doubleday, 2000.

———. *Paul and the Thessalonians: The Philosophic Tradition of Pastoral Care*. Philadelphia: Fortress, 1987.

Marshall, I. Howard. *1 and 2 Thessalonians*. NCB. Grand Rapids: Eerdmans, 1983.

Martin, Dale B. "Slavery and the Ancient Jewish Family." Pages 113–29 in *The Jewish Family in Antiquity*. Edited by Shaye J. D. Cohen. BJS 289. Atlanta: Scholars Press, 1993.

Martyn, J. Louis. *Galatians: A New Translation with Introduction and Commentary*. AB 33A. New York: Doubleday, 1997.

Matera, Frank J. *New Testament Theology: Exploring Diversity and Unity*. Louisville: Westminster John Knox, 2007.

Meeks, Wayne A. *The First Urban Christians: The Social World of the Apostle Paul*. 2nd ed. New Haven: Yale University Press, 2003.

———. "Social Functions of Apocalyptic Language in Pauline Christianity." Pages 687–705 in *Apocalypticism in the Mediterranean World and the Near East*. Edited by David Hellholm. Tübingen: Mohr, 1983.

Merk, Otto. "1 Thessalonians 2:1–12: An Exegetical-Theological Study." Pages 89–113 in *The Thessalonians Debate: Methodological Discord or*

Methodological Synthesis? Edited by Karl P. Donfried and Johannes Beutler. Grand Rapids: Eerdmans, 2000.

Metzger, Bruce M. *A Textual Commentary on the Greek New Testament.* 2nd ed. New York: UBS, 1994.

Metzger, Bruce Manning, and Bart D. Ehrman. *The Text of the New Testament: Its Transmission, Corruption, and Restoration.* 4th ed. New York: Oxford University Press, 2005.

Meyers, Carol L., Toni Craven, and Ross Shepard Kraemer, eds. *Women in Scripture: A Dictionary of Named and Unnamed Women in the Hebrew Bible, the Apocryphal/Deuterocanonical Books, and the New Testament.* Boston: Houghton Mifflin, 2000.

Milgrom, Jacob. *Numbers.* The JPS Torah Commentary. Philadelphia: The Jewish Publication Society, 1990.

Moore, Stephen D., and Janice Capel Anderson, eds. *New Testament Masculinities.* SemeiaSt 45. Atlanta: Society of Biblical Literature, 2003.

Morris, Leon. *The First and Second Epistles to the Thessalonians: The English Text with Introduction, Exposition, and Notes.* NICNT. Grand Rapids: Eerdmans, 1959.

Moxnes, Halvor. "Body, Gender, and Social Space: Dilemmas in Constructing Early Christian Identities." Pages 163–81 in *Identity Formation in the New Testament.* Edited by Bengt Holmberg and Mikael Winninge. WUNT 1/227. Tübingen: Mohr Siebeck, 2008.

———, ed. *Constructing Early Christian Families: Family as Social Reality and Metaphor.* London: Routledge, 1997.

Nathan, Geoffrey S. *The Family in Late Antiquity: The Rise of Christianity and the Endurance of Tradition.* London: Routledge, 2000.

Newsom, Carol A. *The Self as Symbolic Space: Constructing Identity and Community at Qumran.* STDJ 52. Leiden: Brill, 2004.

Newsom, Carol A., and Sharon H. Ringe, eds. *Women's Bible Commentary.* Exp. ed. Louisville: Westminster John Knox, 1998.

Nguyen, V. Henry T. *Christian Identity in Corinth: A Comparative Study of 2 Corinthians, Epictetus and Valerius Maximus.* WUNT 2/243. Tübingen: Mohr Siebeck, 2008.

Noth, Martin. *Numbers: A Commentary.* Translated by James D. Martin. OTL. Philadelphia: Westminster, 1968.

Okeke, G. E. "1 Thessalonians 2. 13–16: The Fate of the Unbelieving Jews." *NTS* 27 (1980): 127–36.

Osiek, Carolyn. "Galatians." Pages 423–27 in *Women's Bible Commentary*. Edited by Carol A. Newsom and Sharon H. Ringe. Exp. ed. Louisville: Westminster John Knox, 1998.

Osiek, Carolyn, and David L. Balch. *Families in the New Testament World: Households and House Churches*. Louisville: Westminster John Knox, 1997.

Osiek, Carolyn, Margaret Y. MacDonald, and Janet H. Tulloch. *A Woman's Place: House Churches in Earliest Christianity*. Minneapolis: Fortress, 2006.

Pearson, Birger A. "1 Thessalonians 2:13–16: A Deutero-Pauline Interpolation." *HTR* 64 (1971): 79–94.

Perkins, Pheme. "1 Thessalonians." Pages 440–41 in *Women's Bible Commentary*. Edited by Carol A. Newsom and Sharon H. Ringe. Exp. ed. Louisville: Westminster John Knox, 1998.

Philo. Translated by F. H. Colson. 10 vols. LCL. Cambridge, Mass.: Harvard University Press, 1929.

Plutarch. *Moralia*. Translated by F. C. Babbitt. 16 vols. LCL. Cambridge, Mass.: Harvard University Press, 1927.

Polaski, Sandra Hack. *A Feminist Introduction to Paul*. St. Louis: Chalice, 2005.

Pomeroy, Sarah B. *Goddesses, Whores, Wives, and Slaves: Women in Classical Antiquity*. New York: Schocken Books, 1975.

Porter, Stanley E., and Dennis L. Stamps, eds. *Rhetorical Criticism and the Bible*. JSNTSup 195. Sheffield: Sheffield Academic, 2002.

Quintilian. Translated by Donald A. Russell. 5 vols. LCL. Cambridge, Mass.: Harvard University Press, 2001.

Rawson, Beryl. *Children and Childhood in Roman Italy*. Oxford: Oxford University Press, 2003.

———, ed. *The Family in Ancient Rome: New Perspectives*. London: Croom Helm, 1986.

Rehmann, Luzia Sutter. "To Turn the Groaning into Labor: Romans 8:22–23." Pages 74–84 in *A Feminist Companion to Paul*. Edited by Amy-Jill Levine and Marianne Blickenstaff. London: T&T Clark, 2004.

Reinhartz, Adele. "Parents and Children: A Philonic Perspective." Pages 61–88 in *The Jewish Family in Antiquity*. Edited by Shaye J. D. Cohen. BJS 289. Atlanta: Scholars Press, 1993.

Richard, Earl. *First and Second Thessalonians*. SP 11. Collegeville, Minn.: Liturgical Press, 1995.

Robinson, W. Peter, ed. *Social Groups and Identities: Developing the Legacy of Henri Tajfel*. Oxford: Butterworth-Heinemann, 1996.

Roetzel, Calvin J. *Paul: A Jew on the Margins*. Louisville: Westminster John Knox, 2003.

Roitto, Rikard. "Act as a Christ-Believer, as a Household Member or Both? A Cognitive Perspective on the Relation between the Social Identity in Christ and Household Identities in Pauline and Deutero-Pauline Texts." Pages 141–62 in *Identity Formation in the New Testament*. Edited by Bengt Holmberg and Mikael Winninge. WUNT 1/227. Tübingen: Mohr Siebeck, 2008.

———. "Behaving like a Christ-Believer: A Cognitive Perspective on Identity and Behavior Norms in the Early Christ-Movement." Pages 92–114 in *Exploring Early Christian Identity*. Edited by Bengt Holmberg. WUNT 1/226. Tübingen: Mohr Siebeck, 2008.

Runesson, Anders. "Inventing Christian Identity: Paul, Ignatius, and Theodosius I." Pages 59–92 in *Exploring Early Christian Identity*. Edited by Bengt Holmberg. WUNT 1/226. Tübingen: Mohr Siebeck, 2008.

Rydelnik, Michael A. "Was Paul Anti-Semitic? Revisiting 1 Thessalonians 2:14–16." *BSac* 165 (2008): 58–67.

Sacks, Sheldon, ed. *On Metaphor*. Chicago: University of Chicago Press, 1980.

Sailors, Timothy B. "Wedding Textual and Rhetorical Criticism to Understand the Text of 1 Thessalonians 2.7." *JSNT* 80 (2000): 81–98.

Sakenfeld, Katharine Doob. *Journeying with God: A Commentary on the Book of Numbers*. Grand Rapids: Eerdmans, 1995.

Samra, James George. *Being Conformed to Christ in Community: A Study of Maturity, Maturation and the Local Church in the Undisputed Pauline Epistles*. LNTS 320. London: T&T Clark, 2006.

Schlueter, Carol J. *Filling up the Measure: Polemical Hyperbole in 1 Thessalonians 2:14–16*. JSNTSup 98. Sheffield: JSOT Press, 1994.

Schmidt, Daryl. "1 Thess 2:13–16: Linguistic Evidence for an Interpolation." *JBL* 102 (1983): 269–79.

Schuller, Eileen M. "Prayer, Hymnic, and Liturgical Texts from Qumran." Pages 153–71 in *The Community of the Renewed Covenant: The Notre Dame Symposium on the Dead Sea Scrolls*. Edited by Eugene C. Ulrich and James C. VanderKam. Notre Dame: University of Notre Dame Press, 1994.

Schütz, John Howard. *Paul and the Anatomy of Apostolic Authority*. NTL. Louisville: Westminster John Knox, 2007.

Seneca. *Moral Essays*. Translated by John W. Basore. 3 vols. LCL. New York: G. P. Putnam's Sons, 1928.

Smith, Abraham. *Comfort One Another: Reconstructing the Rhetoric and Audience of 1 Thessalonians*. LCBI. Louisville: Westminster John Knox, 1995.

———. "The First Letter to the Thessalonians: Introduction, Commentary, and Reflections." *NIB* 9:671–737.

Soranus. *Soranus' Gynecology*. Translated by Owsei Temkin. Baltimore: Johns Hopkins University Press, 1956.

Soskice, Janet Martin. *Metaphor and Religious Language*. Oxford: Clarendon, 1985.

Stegemann, Hartmut, Eileen Schuller, and Carol Newsom. *1QHodayota*. DJD 40. Oxford: Clarendon, 2009.

Strange, W. A. *Children in the Early Church: Children in the Ancient World, the New Testament and the Early Church*. Carlisle: Paternoster, 1996.

Tajfel, Henri. *Differentiation Between Social Groups: Studies in the Social Psychology of Intergroup Relations*. European Monographs in Social Psychology 14. London: Academic Press, 1978.

———. *Human Groups and Social Categories: Studies in Social Psychology*. Cambridge: Cambridge University Press, 1981.

Tracy, David. "Metaphor and Religion: The Test Case of Christian Texts." Pages 89–104 in *On Metaphor*. Edited by Sheldon Sacks. Chicago: University of Chicago Press, 1979.

Van Rensburg, Fika. "An Argument for Reading νήπιοι in 1 Thessalonians 2:7." Pages 252–59 in *A South African Perspective on the New Testament: Essays by South African New Testament Scholars Presented to Bruce Manning Metzger during His Visit to South Africa in 1985*. Edited by J. H. Petzer and P. J. Hartin. Leiden: Brill, 1986.

VanderKam, James, and Peter Flint. *The Meaning of the Dead Sea Scrolls: Their Significance for Understanding the Bible, Judaism, Jesus, and Christianity*. San Francisco: HarperSanFrancisco, 2002.

Vermès, Géza. *The Complete Dead Sea Scrolls in English*. New York: Allen Lane/Penguin, 1997.

Wall, Robert W. "The Acts of the Apostles: Introduction, Commentary, and Reflections." *NIB* 10:3–368.

Wallace, Daniel B. *Greek Grammar Beyond the Basics*. Grand Rapids: Zondervan, 1996.

Walton, S. "What has Aristotle to do with Paul? Rhetorical Criticism and 1 Thessalonians." *TynBul* 46 (1995): 229–50.

Wanamaker, Charles A. *The Epistles to the Thessalonians: A Commentary on the Greek Text.* NIGTC. Grand Rapids: Eerdmans, 1990.

Watson, Duane F. *The Rhetoric of the New Testament: A Bibliographic Survey.* Blandford Forum: Deo, 2006.

Weatherly, Jon A. "The Authenticity of 1 Thessalonians 2.13-16: Additional Evidence." *JSNT* 41 (1991): 79-98.

Weima, Jeffrey A. D. "An Apology for the Apologetic Function of 1 Thessalonians 2:1-12." *JSNT* 68 (1997): 73-99.

———. "'But We Became Infants Among You': The Case for ΝΗΠΙΟΙ in 1 Thess 2.7." *NTS* 46 (2000): 547-64.

———. "Infants, Nursing Mother, and Father: Paul's Portrayal of a Pastor." *CTJ* 37 (2002): 209-29.

Wiedemann, Thomas. *Adults and Children in the Roman Empire.* New Haven: Yale University Press, 1989.

Williams, David John. *Paul's Metaphors: Their Context and Character.* Peabody, Mass.: Hendrickson, 1999.

Wise, Michael O., Martin G. Abegg Jr., and Edward M. Cook. *The Dead Sea Scrolls: A New Translation.* Rev. ed. San Francisco: HarperSanFrancisco, 2005.

Witherington, Ben, III. *1 and 2 Thessalonians: A Socio-Rhetorical Commentary.* Grand Rapids: Eerdmans, 2006.

Yarbrough, O. Larry. "Parents and Children in the Jewish Family of Antiquity." Pages 39-59 in *The Jewish Family in Antiquity.* Edited by Shaye J. D. Cohen. BJS 289. Atlanta: Scholars Press, 1993.

Yeo, K. K. "The Rhetoric of Election and Calling Language in 1 Thessalonians." Pages 526-47 in *Rhetorical Criticism and the Bible.* Edited by Stanley E. Porter and Dennis L. Stamps. JSNTSup 195. Sheffield: Sheffield Academic, 2002.

Ancient Sources Index

Old Testament/Hebrew Bible

Genesis
- 24:59 — 109 n. 8
- 33:13 — 106 n. 7
- 35:8 — 55 n. 88

Exodus
- 32:9 — 111
- 33:12 — 111
- 33:13 — 111

Numbers
- 11:11–12 — 108–11, 113, 114, 116–17, 118, 120, 120 n. 29, 140, 145

Deuteronomy
- 2:34 — 101 n. 3
- 3:6 — 101 n. 3
- 7:2 — 101 n. 3
- 13:15 — 101 n. 3
- 20:16–17 — 101
- 20:18 — 101 n. 3
- 22:6 — 56
- 32:10 — 105
- 32:13 — 105
- 32:18 — 119

Joshua
- 10:28–43 — 101

Ruth
- 4:16 — 109 n. 8
- 4:17 — 109 n. 8

1 Samuel
- 6:7 — 106 n. 7
- 6:10 — 106 n. 7
- 15:3 — 101

2 Samuel
- 4:4 — 109 n. 8

1 Kings
- 1:1–4 — 56
- 22:17 — 24

2 Kings
- 11:2 — 55 n. 88

2 Chronicles
- 22:11 — 55 n. 88

Job
- 3:21 — 57
- 39:14 — 56 n. 90

Psalms
- 62:2 Symmachus — 57
- 78:71 — 24, 106 n. 7
- 95:7 — 24
- 100:3 — 24
- 119:176 — 24
- 137:8–9 — 102

Isaiah
- 11:8 — 104
- 13:8 — 2 n. 3, 5 n. 13
- 13:16a — 102
- 13:18 — 102

Isaiah (cont.)		3:11	102
26:17–19	5 n. 13	3:19	102
40:11	24, 106 n. 7		
42:14	119	Deuterocanonical Books	
45:7–11	5		
46:1–2	107	Wisdom of Solomon	
46:3	109	12:24	99
46:3–4	106, 119, 120 n. 29	15:14	99
49:15	107, 118 n. 27, 119, 120 n. 29		
49:23	55 n. 88, 110	1 Maccabees	
53:6	24	2:9b	100
60:4	109		
60:16	110	2 Maccabees	
65:17–25	104	8:4	101
66:6–9	5 n. 13		
66:7–13	105	3 Maccabees	
66:12	109	5:49	103
66:13	107, 119, 134	6:14	103

Jeremiah		Dead Sea Scrolls	
6:14	91		
23:1–4	24	1QH[a]	
50:6	24	VII 34	119 n. 28
50:17	24	XV 9–28	112–13, 117
		XV 11b–12	112–13
Lamentations		XV 23–25	**112–17**, 118, 119, 135, 140
2:11–12	100		
2:18–19	104	XVII 29b–36	113, **117–20**, 145
2:20–22	104	XIX 6	119 n. 28
4:3–4	104	XXIII 5	119 n. 28
4:10	104 n. 5		
		11QPs[a]	
Ezekiel		XXI 11–15	106
13:10	91		
34:1–31	24	Ancient Jewish Writers	

Hosea		Josephus, *Against Apion*	
11:1–11	107	2.202–203	67
13:12–13	5 n. 13		
		Philo, *Against Flaccus*	
Micah		68	102
4:9–10	2 n. 3, 5 n. 13		
		Philo, *Allegorical Interpretation*	
Nahum		2.53	99–100, 125
3:10b	101–2		

Philo, *On Planting*
14–16   105

Philo, *On Sobriety*
30–31   106

Philo, *On the Special Laws*
2.236   70
2.240   70
3.112   67
3.119   100

Philo, *On the Virtues*
130   73
128   74, 137

Philo, *That the Worse Attacks the Better*
115   106

New Testament

Matthew
9:36   24
10:2   54 n. 83
10:5–15   53 n. 79

Mark
3:14   54 n. 83
6:7–13   53 n. 79
6:34   24

Luke
6:13   54 n. 83
10:1–12   53 n. 79

John
10:1–18   24

Acts of the Apostles
1:15–26   54 n. 83
14:14   54 n. 83
17:1–9   88
17:6b–7   88

Romans
1:1   54 n. 83
1:7   60
1:9   50
1:29   49 n. 69
2:20   39
8:22   1 n. 2, 2, 4, 5, 7
8:23   5
8:38–39   146
9–11   32, 34
11:28   60
12:10   168
12:19   60
13:8   168
14:15   168
15:7   168
16:1–16   6
16:5   60
16:7   54 n. 83
16:8   60
16:9   60
16:12   60

1 Corinthians
1:1   54 n. 83
1:23   146
1:27–29   130
1:30   146
3:1–2   39, 138
3:2   1 n. 2, 2, 5, 135, 165
3:10   38
4:9–13   54 n. 83
4:14   60
4:17   60
4:19   163
5:10–11   49 n. 69
6:10   49 n. 69
7:2   57
9:1   54 n. 83
9:1–19   53 n. 79
10:14   60
11:1   145, 162
11:1–16   6
12:21–26   168
13:11   39, 42

1 Corinthians (cont.)		6:2	168
14:20	39, 126	6:14	51 n. 76
15:8	1 n. 2, 2, 38		
15:58	60	Ephesians	
16:13	163	4:14	35
		4:19	49 n. 69
2 Corinthians		5:3	49 n. 69
1:23	50	5:29	56
1:24	167		
3:1–4	51	Philippians	
6:3–10	51 n. 76	1:8	50
7:1	60	1:18	49
8	87	2:7	169
8:5	95	2:7–8	146
9:5	49 n. 69	2:12	60
10–13	128–31, 143	3:8	51 n. 76
10:1	129	4:1	60
10:18	129		
11:5–33	54 n. 83	Colossians	
11:7	128	1:23	42
11:7–9	53 n. 79	3:5	49 n. 69
11:13	129		
11:21–33	51 n. 76	1 Thessalonians	
11:23–28	129–30, 137 n. 18	1	96
11:30	130	1:1	92, 157
12:9	130	1:2–10	29, 30
12:10	130	1:4	29, 149, 157
12:12	54 n. 83	1:4–7	96
12:14	128–29	1:5	29, 48, 49, 96, 125
12:14–15a	148	1:6	86, 96, 141
12:14–16	53 n. 79	1:6–8	29
12:16	52	1:6–10	141
12:19	60	1:7	167
13:4	130	1:7–8	157
13:9	131	1:7–10	86
		1:9	90
Galatians		1:9–10	29
1:1	54 n. 83	2	93
1:19	54 n. 83	2:1–12	27, **30–32**, 32, 60, 96, 131, 152, 157
2:20	146		
3:28	6	2:2	48, 49, 86, 92
4:1–3	39	2:3–4	48, 125
4:12–5:1	3	2:4	86
4:19	1 n. 2, 2–5, 7, 37, 138, 165, 170	2:5–8	**43–47, 47–60**, 123–24, 172, 173
5:13	169		

ANCIENT SOURCES INDEX 195

2:7	1 n. 2, 2, 5, 7, 27, 39, 43, 106, **124–54**, 159, 159, 160, 164–65, 169, 170, 172, 173	5:3	1 n. 2, 2, 91, 149
		5:5	92, 149
		5:11	168
2:8	57, 139	5:12–13	159
2:9	52	5:12–28	157
2:10	50, 125	5:14–15	159
2:11	57	5:15	169
2:11–12	143, 144	5:23	90
2:13–16	**32–34**, 60, 141, 149–50	5:26	93
2:14	86, 91, 150, 167	5:27	93
2:16	87		
2:17	39–42, 97, 103 n. 4, 131, 137	2 Timothy	
2:18	87, 90, 137	2:24	35, 42
2:19	90		
2:19–20	51, 97	Philemon	
3	157	1	60
3:1	54	16	60
3:1–5	137		
3:2	93	Hebrews	
3:3–4	87	5:13	35
3:4	49	13:20	24
3:5	90, 137		
3:6	97	1 Peter	
3:7	87	2:25	24
3:9	97		
3:10	137	Greco-Roman Literature	
3:10–11	97		
3:12	97, 168	Aristotle, *Nicomachean Ethics*	
3:13	90	8.7.7	70, 144
4–5	28	8.8.3	71
4:1–2	141		
4:1–8	149	Cicero, *De legibus*	
4:1–12	157	3.8.19	65
4:4	57		
4:6	93, 95, 159	Dio Chrysostom, *First Tarsic Discourse*	
4:9	95	10	108
4:9–10	159		
4:10	93	Dio Chrysostom, *Kingship*	
4:11–12	95, 159	4 74	108
4:12	92, 149		
4:13	91, 149	Dio Chrysostom, *Man's First Conception of God*	
4:13–5:11	157		
4:15	90	61	103
4:17	90		
4:18	168		

Diodorus Siculus, *Bibliotheca historica*
20.72.2 — 102

Fronto, *Letter to Antonius Augustus*
1.5 — 77

Galen, *On the Natural Faculties*
3.3 — 63

Gellius, *Attic Nights*
12.1.1–5 — 64, 74
12.1.8–9 — 73
12.1.10 — 69 n. 41
12.1.17–23 — 73
12.1.23 — 73, 136

Hilarion, *Oxyrhynchus papyrus*
744 — 65

Juvenal, *Satires*
14 — 70 n. 45

Musonius Rufus, *Fragments*
15 — 67

Plutarch, *Consolatio ad uxorem*
2 — 69
3 — 69
6 — 69 n. 41

Plutarch, *Moralia*
3C — 73, 136
69C — 107
48E–74E — 48
364D — 105
496C — 71
496D — 71
1045AB — 100

Quintilian, *Institutio Oratoria*
1.1.4–5 — 73
1.1.5 — 76

Seneca, *De ira*
1.15 — 65

Seneca, *De Providentia*
2.5 — 71, 143

Seneca, *Epistulae morales*
99 — 78

Soranus, *Gynecology*
1.3–4 — 63
1.60–62 — 64 n. 10
1.64–65 — 64 n. 12
1.67–69 — 63 n. 5
2.10 — 64
2.10 — 66
2.14, 42 — 68
2.18 — 76
2.19–20 — 76
2.46–8 — 77

Tacitus, *Dialogus de oratoribus*
28 — 73
28.4–29.2 — 69 n. 41
29 — 70 n. 45
29.1 — 73

Tacitus, *Germania*
20 — 72

Early Christian Writings

John Chrysostom, *Epistulae ad Olympiadum*
8.12.37–41 — 41

Modern Authors Index

Abegg, Martin G., Jr.   113 n. 17, 117 n. 26
Aland, Barbara   37
Aland, Kurt   37
Ashley, Timothy R.   110 n. 10
Aymer, Margaret   3 n. 9, 138, 139, 139 n. 22, 144, 165–66
Best, Ernest   41, 53 n. 80
Beutler, Johannes   30 n. 9
Black, C. Clifton   21
Black, Max   **9–11**, 13, 14, 158 n. 6
Bradley, Keith R.   68–69 nn. 39–41, 72 nn. 48 and 50–51, 74 n. 56, 75, 75 nn. 58, 60, and 62–64, 77 nn. 69 and 71, 78 nn. 76–77, 139, 151 n. 43
Bridges, Linda McKinnish   164–65, 166
Bruce, F. F.   2 n. 4, 36 n. 29, 40 nn. 44 and 45, 48, 49 n. 68, 52 n. 78, 54 n. 83, 59, 95, 134, 148 n. 36, 169
Burke, Trevor J.   67 n. 33, 84 n. 109, 137–38, 143 n. 30, 166, 172
Campbell, William S.   25 nn. 79 and 81, 94 n. 136
Castelli, Elizabeth A.   6 n. 18, 34 n. 26, 145, 161–62, 164, 167, 172
Chalcraft, David J.   112 n. 14, 116 n. 25
Chazon, Esther G.   111 n. 13
Clines, David   163, 164, 165, 168, 170
Cohen, Shaye J. D.   62 n. 1
Cohick, Lynn R.   64 n. 11, 65 n. 18
Collins, John J.   116 n. 25
Collins, Raymond F.   1 n. 1
Cook, Edward M.   113 n. 17, 117 n. 26
Corbier, Mireille   65 n. 20, 66 nn. 22–26 and 28, 67 n. 35
Cotrozzi, Stefano   38 n. 39
Crawford, Charles   38 n. 39
Cuyckens, Hubert   8 nn. 27–28, 157 n. 4
Dixon, Suzanne   69 n. 43, 70 nn. 46–47, 73 n. 53, 75 n. 57, 77 n. 70, 78 nn. 72 and 74, 80 n. 88
Donfried, Karl P.   28–29, 30 n. 9, 30–31, 33 n. 17, 86 n. 115, 89 nn. 119–21, 90, 91, 91 nn. 128–29, 95, 105, 142, 156
Eastman, Susan   3, 4, 5, 7 n. 25, 159–60
Ehrensperger, Kathy   6 n. 18, 161 n. 16, 167–69, 171
Ehrman, Bart D.   36 n. 30, 37, 43 n. 52
Esler, Philip Francis   25 n. 79, 81 n. 90, 83 n. 100, 84 nn. 107–8, 84–85 nn. 110–13, 90 n. 124, 92 nn. 133–34, 94 n. 137, 95
Fant, Maureen B.   64 n. 9, 65, 76 n. 65
Fee, Gordon D.   36 n. 29, 44 nn. 54 and 56, 47, 47 n. 60, 132, 152 n. 47
Felder, Cain Hope   36 n. 29, 39
Fitzmyer, Joseph A.   88 nn. 117–18
Fowl, Stephen E.   44 n. 54, 126–27
French, Valerie   63 n. 3, 64 n. 10, 65 n. 15
Furnish, Victor Paul   2 n. 4, 8 n. 26, 28, 36 n. 29, 48 n. 66, 50 n. 71, 54 n. 84, 57 n. 96, 125, 149 n. 36, 156 n. 13, 171
García Martínez, Florentino   1 n. 2, 113 nn. 16–17
Gaventa, Beverly Roberts   3, 4, 6–7, 36 n. 29, 37–38, 37 n. 36, 41 n. 49, 44, 52 n. 78, 54 n. 83, 126 n. 3, 128, 129, 140 n. 26, 143 n. 29, 152–53, 152 n. 46, 160, 161 n. 14, 170, 171
Geeraerts, Dirk   8 nn. 27–28, 157 n. 4

Gilliard, Frank 34 n. 21
Goff, Matthew J. 116 n. 22
Gorman, Michael J. 7 n. 23
Hempel, Charlotte 112 n. 14
Holmberg, Bengt 25 n. 79, 89 n. 121
Holm-Nielsen, Svend 113 n. 17
Holmstrand, Jonas 33
Hooker, Morna 167, 169
Hughes, Julie 120 n. 29
Hurd, John C. 33 n. 18
Jenkins, Richard 25 n. 80, 82, 82 n. 95, 83 nn. 97–98, 84 n. 104
Jewett, Robert 87, 89, 89 nn. 121–22
Johnson, Mark **11–19**, 116 n. 24, 158, 159 n. 10, 161 n. 15
Joshel, Sandra R. 79–80, 136 n. 16, 139
Kittel, Bonnie P. 112 n. 15, 113 n. 17
Kittredge, Cynthia Briggs 162–63, 164, 172
Koester, Helmut 37
Kraemer, Ross S. 67 n. 31
Lakoff, George **11–19, 19–20**, 22, 116 n. 24, 158, 159 n. 10, 161 n. 15
Lamp, Jeffrey S. 33 n. 19
Lefkowitz, Mary R. 64 n. 9, 65, 76 n. 65s
MacDonald, Margaret Y. 63 nn. 2 and 4–7, 64 nn. 9 and 12, 65 n. 16, 66 nn. 21 and 24, 67 n. 32, 68 nn. 36 and 38, 69 n. 42, 72 n. 49, 75 n. 61, 77 nn. 66 and. 68, 80 n. 87
Malherbe, Abraham J. 2 n. 4, 8 n. 26, 28 n. 1, 28–29, 30, 36 n. 29, 37, 41, 49 n. 69, 51 n. 75, 52, 54 n. 84, 56 n. 91, 57, 57 n. 96, 58, 58 n. 98, 59, 91 n. 129, 94 n. 138, 96, 142, 155–56
Marshall, I. Howard 40 n. 45
Martin, Dale B. 62 n. 1
Martyn, J. Louis 3 n. 9, 5, 7 n. 25
Matera, Frank J. 96 n. 144
Meeks, Wayne A. 92 nn. 132 and 134, 93 n. 135, 94, 150 n. 39, 152 n. 46
Metzger, Bruce Manning 36 n. 30, 37, 37 n. 32, 43 n. 52
Milgrom, Jacob 110 n. 11, 111
Morris, Leon 40 n. 44, 41 n. 49

Newsom, Carol 111, 112 n. 14, 113 n. 16, 114–16, 117 n. 26, 146 n. 34
Nguyen, V. Henry T. 25 nn. 79 and 82
Noth, Martin 110 nn. 10–11
Osiek, Carolyn 63 nn. 2, and 4–7, 64 nn. 9 and 12, 65 n. 16, 66 nn. 21 and 24, 67 n. 32, 68 nn. 36 and 38, 69 n. 42, 72 n. 49, 75 n. 61, 77 nn. 66 and 68, 80 n. 87, 169–70
Pearson, Birger A. 33 n. 16, 85 n. 114
Polaski, Sandra Hack 3, 6, 169, 170, 170 n. 60
Rawson, Beryl 64 nn. 8–9 and 13, 65 nn. 14, 17 and 19, 66 nn. 24, 27, and 29, 67 n. 34, 68 nn. 37–38, 70 n. 44–45, 72 n. 52, 77 nn. 67 and n. 69, 78 nn. 73 and 75, 151 n. 42
Rehmann, Luzia Sutter 3 n. 9, 7 n. 25
Reinhartz, Adele 67 n. 30, 73 n. 54
Richard, Earl 2 n. 4, 33 n. 16, 36 n. 29, 40 nn. 43 and 45, 48, 53 n. 80, 57 n. 97
Richards, I. A. 9
Robinson, W. Peter 25 n. 80
Roetzel, Calvin J. 3 n. 9, 170
Roitto, Rikard 81, 82 nn. 93–94, 83, 83 nn. 98–99 and 101–2, 84, 84 n. 105, 96 n. 145, 97 n. 147
Sailors, Timothy B. 35 n. 28, 42 n. 51, 44 nn. 54 and 57, 45 n. 59
Sakenfeld, Katharine Doob 110 nn. 10–11
Schlueter, Carol J. 33 n. 17, 34, 91, 149 n. 38
Schmidt, Daryl 33 n. 16
Schuller, Eileen 113 n. 16
Schutz, John Howard 166–67, 169
Stegemann, Hartmut 113 n. 16
Tajfel, Henri 25 n. 80, 81
Tigchelaar, Eibert J. C. 1 n. 2, 113 nn. 16–17
Tulloch, Janet H. 63 nn. 2 and 4–7, 64 nn. 9 and 12, 65 n. 16, 66 nn. 21 and 24, 67 n. 32, 68 nn. 36 and 38, 69 n. 42, 72 n. 49, 75 n. 61, 77 nn. 66 and 68, 80 n. 87

Turner, Mark	**19–20**, 22
Van Rensburg, Fika	44 n. 54
Vermes, Geza	113 n. 17
Wall, Robert W.	88 n. 118
Wallace, Daniel B.	58 n. 100
Wanamaker, Charles A.	8 n. 26, 36 n. 29, 38, 40 n. 45, 48 n. 67, 50, 50 n. 71, 53 nn. 80 and 82, 54 n. 84, 59, 150, 151
Weatherly, Jon A.	33 n. 18
Weima, Jeffrey A. D.	35 n. 28, 36, 41, 41 nn. 49 and 50, 42, 43 n. 52, 44 nn. 54 and 57, 45 n. 59, 47, 126 n. 3
Wikgren, Allen	37 n. 32
Winninge, Mikael	25 n. 79
Wise, Michael O.	113 n. 17, 117 n. 26
Witherington, Ben, III	3 n. 4, 36 n. 29, 40 n. 45, 52 n. 78, 90 n. 125

Subject Index

1 Thessalonians
  authenticity of 2:13–16, **32–34**
  occasion, purpose, and dating of, **28–29, 155–57**
  Paul as sole author of, 8 n. 26, 54 n. 84
  punctuation of 2:5–8, **43–47**
  translation of 2:5–8, **47–60**
androcentrism, 2, 6, 120, 166, 169
apostles, 53–54, 54 nn. 83–84, 96, 141
  authority/power of, 161–72
  Paul's view of "true" apostles, 5–6, 54 n. 83, 128–31, 142–46, 152–53, 157, 160, 173
authority/power
  and the cross, 7, 130–31, 145, 171–72
  of nursing mothers, 6, 140–41, 144–45, 147
  of Paul, 7, 30–31, 40, 131, 144–45, 146–48, 153, 161–72
breastfeeding. *See* nurses and nursing in the ancient world
cognitive metaphor theory. *See* metaphor
Dead Sea Scrolls, **111–21**
  God as nurse in Hodayot, **117–21**
  leader as nurse in Hodayot, **111–17**, 120–21, 134–35, 147
  leadership at Qumran, 112 n. 14, 114–16
family. *See* kinship; mothers in the ancient world; parent-child relationships in the ancient world
feminist interpretation, **6–7**, 161–72
fictive kinship. *See* kinship
Hodayot. *See* Dead Sea Scrolls

identity, 25, 28, 114–15, 146–47. *See also* rhetorical strategies for shaping identity
  and behavioral norms, 83–84, 95, 149, 157
  Christ-centered identity, 28, 29, 31–32, 60, 148, 152, 153, 156–57, 173
  group identity, 25, 148–52, 153
  in-group prototype, 83–84, 96, 97, 131, 146
  in-groups and out-groups, 82–83, 141, 148, 149, 157
  leadership within groups, 83–84
  and metaphor, **24–26**, 141, 148
  and persecution, 83, 92, 149
  self-categorization theory, 82–83, 148
  similarity and *difference*, 82, 83, 131
  social identity, 1, 7, **81–84**
  stereotyping, 83, 149
imitation language, 29, 86, 96–97, 131, 141, 145, 161–62, 164, 167
infants in the ancient Mediterranean world, **62–71**
  contraception and abortion, 64, 66–67, 138
  infant/child mortality, 68–69
  infanticide and exposure, 65–67, 75, 138
  innocence of, **99–103**, 104, 124–26, 131
  Paul as infant, **124–32**, 156
  social status of, 125
Jewish family life, 62, 66–67
kinship, 5, 84–85, 141, 153, 156, 173
  and behavioral norms, 95, 157, 159

-201-

kinship (*cont.*)
  fictive kinship, 93–95, 150
  sibling relationships, 84, 95, 150–52
maternal imagery, 1, **2–8**
  and apocalypticism, 4–5
  and authority/power, 6–7, 140–41, 144–45, 147, 161–72
  as egalitarian, 6, **166–70**, 171
  and feminist interpretation, **6–7**, 161–72
  God as mother/nurse, 105, 106–7, 110, 117–21, 145–46
  as hierarchical, 6, **161–66**, 171
  men as nurses in biblical literature, 109–10, 140
  Moses as nurse, **108–11**
  and Paul's proclamation of the gospel, **4**, **159–60**
  and Paul's theology, **4–6, 159–60**
  Qumran leader as nurse, **111–17**, 120–21, 134–35, 147
metaphor, 8–9, 11
  and behavior, **14–17**, 19, 21, 23, 24, 26, 94, 116, 120–21, 158–59
  cognitive metaphor theory, 1, 4, 7, **8–21**, 81, 93–94, 115, 123, 126–27
  and the conceptual structures of the mind, **11–13**, 14, 20, 22–24, 94
  conventional metaphors, **11–13**, 22–23, 158
  and culture, 61
  entailments, **13–14**, 21, 24, 62, 94, 124–27, 133–41, 145–46, 158, 169
  experiential basis of, **17–18**
  highlighting and hiding, **13–14**, 18, 21, 23, 24, 62, 94, 115, 124, 126–27, 141–42, 157–58, 161
  and identity, **24–26**, 93, 94, 148
  as language that mediates reality, 8, 11, 14, 17, 18–19, 21, 24, 120–21, 157–58
  Max Black's interaction view of, 10–11
  new and creative metaphors, **18–20**, 21, 23, 132, 158

  and persuasion/rhetoric, 1, 11, **21–26**, 105, 120–21, **157–59**
  and power/authority, 11, 18, 21, 22–24, 132, 141, 148, 153, 157–59, **161–72**
Moses as nurse to the Israelites, **108–11**, 116–17
mothers in the ancient world. *See also* parent-child relationships in the ancient world
  maternal authority, 6, 140–41
  maternal breastfeeding, **72–74**
  maternal love, 70–71, 104, 135–36
  a mother's role as distinct from a father's, 70, 143–44
nurses and nursing in the ancient world, **71–80**
  breast milk as nourishment, **104–6**, 134–35
  choosing and employing a wet nurse, 74–77
  comfort/affection of nursing, **106–8**, 116, 133–36
  conlacteus/children nursed at the same breast, 80, 116, 151
  elite male opinion of, **72–74**, 80
  the Greek word τροφός, 55–56
  the nurse-nursling relationship, **77–80**
  the prevalence of wet-nursing, 72
  the social status of nurses, 71–72, 78–80, 138–40, 169
  and suffering, **103–4**, 136–38, 144
parent-child relationships in the ancient world. *See also* mothers in the ancient world
  attachment affected by child mortality, 68–69, 75, 139
  a father's love, 71, 143–44
  foster parents, 74–75
  parental love, 70, 135–36
  parental responsibilities, 70, 141
Paul
  authority/power of, 161–72

SUBJECT INDEX

Paul *(cont.)*
  counter-cultural message of, 51, 167–69, 170
  defense of himself and the gospel, 30–32, 60, 96, 125, 131–32, 142, 152, 153, 173
  imitation of, 29, 86, 96–97, 131, 141, 145, 161–62, 164, 167
  as infant, **38–42, 124–32**
  masculinity of, 2, 6–7, 129, 132, 163–66, 169–70
  as nurse, **132–54**
  as orphan, 38–42
  as sole author of 1 Thess, 8 n. 26
persecution of the Thessalonian church, 29, 31, 60, **85–91**, 173
  biblical evidence for, 86–88
  as expected consequence of accepting the gospel, 86, 87, 94, 130
  as expressed in 2:13–16, 32, 33–34, 86–87, 149–50
  historical and social reasons for, 88–91
  as reinforcement of Christ-centered identity, 92–93, 94, 157
  severity of, 91
  social nature of, 86–87
  as a threat to Christ-centered identity/faith, 87, 91
persuasion. *See* rhetoric
power. *See* authority/power
punctuation of 1 Thess 2:5–8, **43–47**
Qumran. *See* Dead Sea Scrolls
rhetoric, 1, 21–26, 28–29, 157–59. *See also* rhetorical strategies for shaping identity
rhetorical strategies for shaping identity, **91–97**, 157
  emotional language, 97, 147–48
  in-group/out-group differentiation, 34, 60, **92–93**, 94, 131, 141, 149, 157
  kinship metaphors, **93–95**, 123, 141, 148, 150–52, 173
  relationship building, **95–97**, 123, 136, 142, 147–48, 150
social identity theory. *See* identity
textual criticism of 1 Thess 2:7, 27, **35–43**
Thessalonian church. *See also* persecution of the Thessalonian church
  crisis of identity, 85, 123, 151–52
  Paul's initial visit, 48
  Paul's relationship to, 60, **95–97**, 141–42, 150, 153, 173
  as young in faith, 28, 60, 137–38
Thessalonica, city of, 85, 89, 90
translation of 2:5–8, **47–60**
wet nurses. *See* Nurses and nursing in the ancient world

www.ingramcontent.com/pod-product-compliance
Lightning Source LLC
Chambersburg PA
CBHW021809220426
43662CB00006B/247